Problematic Relationships
IN THE Workplace

PETER LANG
New York • Washington, D.C./Baltimore • Bern
Frankfurt am Main • Berlin • Brussels • Vienna • Oxford

Problematic Relationships
IN THE Workplace

EDITED BY
Janie M. Harden Fritz & Becky L. Omdahl

PETER LANG
New York • Washington, D.C./Baltimore • Bern
Frankfurt am Main • Berlin • Brussels • Vienna • Oxford

Library of Congress Cataloging-in-Publication Data
Problematic relationships in the workplace /
edited by Janie M. Harden Fritz, Becky L. Omdahl.
p. cm.
Includes bibliographical references and indexes.
1. Conflict management. 2. Organizational behavior.
3. Interpersonal conflict. 4. Problem employees—Psychology.
5. Courtesy in the work place. I. Fritz, Janie M. Harden. II. Omdahl, Becky Lynn.
HD42.P755   658.3'145—dc22   2005027351
ISBN 978-0-8204-7400-7

Bibliographic information published by **Die Deutsche Bibliothek**.
Die Deutsche Bibliothek lists this publication in the "Deutsche
Nationalbibliografie"; detailed bibliographic data is available
on the Internet at http://dnb.ddb.de/.

Cover design by Lisa Barfield

The paper in this book meets the guidelines for permanence and durability
of the Committee on Production Guidelines for Book Longevity
of the Council of Library Resources.

© 2006, 2009 Peter Lang Publishing, Inc., New York
29 Broadway, 18th floor, New York, NY 10006
www.peterlang.com

Printed in the United States of America

Table of Contents

Preface

Marshall Scott Poole

Most of us have experienced a problematic relationship with a coworker at some time in our lives. The overly demanding boss, the team member who always seems to disrupt and derail the team, the snoop, the malicious gossip, the person out to get you at all costs—problematic coworkers come in many shapes and sizes. "Difficult people" make life difficult and sometimes miserable for their peers and subordinates. Their behavior is problematic not only because of *what* they do, but because *why* they do it is hard to fathom, because they often resist change, and because their impacts on their coworkers are often not easily remedied.

As the chapters in this book show all too clearly, problems in workplace relationships are common. Recent surveys provide some indication of their extent. In one recent survey of 800 employees, 10 percent reported witnessing incivility in their workplace daily and 20 percent said they were the target of incivility at least once a week (Pearson & Porath, 2005). A study of 600 nurses revealed that one third had experienced verbal abuse in the previous five days (Graydon, Kasta & Khan, 1994). To the best of my knowledge, no one has calculated the full economic impact of problematic relationships, but some indication of its magnitude can be gleaned by considering the case of sexual harassment. It has been estimated that sexual harassment costs the Fortune 500 companies alone $6 billion a year in absenteeism, turnover, and lost productivity, and this does not include the legal costs, the time spent managing the situation, and the tarnished reputations of the companies (Pearson & Porath, 2005). One byproduct of problematic relationships is conflict, and there are also ways of gauging its costs. It has been reported that for a typical large corporation managers may spend as much as 13% of their time managing conflicts among employees (Johnson & Indvik, 2001), a truly significant cost in economic terms, in terms of lost opportunities to improve the organization, and in terms of the emotional toll this takes on managers and other parties.

Much more research has gone into management and communication in normal, functional workplaces than into the study of problematic relationships. There has been, however, research into related phenomena, including aggression, harassment, rudeness, and verbal abuse in the workplace. These show the most dramatic face of problematic relationships. Sometimes they show up in tragic headlines.

Most problematic relationships are not so dramatic. They are more subtle than this and may take many forms, as the first section of the book illustrates. The first two chapters describe the terrain of problematic work relationships, discussing, respectively, the range of roles difficult co-workers may take and a typology of problematic others. These chapters avoid the common mistake of conceptualizing problematic others as "difficult people" whose personalities are the roots of the problem. While personality certainly contributes, as this book demonstrates, complex interaction processes are involved in the development of problematic relationships.

The study of problematic work relationships, as for other types of relationships, should include various ways they emerge. Three chapters present different ways through which problematic responses can be fostered: through particular events in which the private and emotional aspects of life intrude on the workplace, as occurs during pregnancy leaves and returning to work, more gradually, through deterioration of friendships in the workplace, or through turning points that serve to trigger problematic relationships. These chapters are groundbreaking in that they do not presume that problematic relationships occur full-blown, as do the various works dealing with "difficult people," but rather examine how they develop and change over time.

The context, types, and development of problematic relationships comprise an important element of the topic, followed by a section addressing the significance of the topic through coverage of personal and organizational outcomes of problematic relationships. The wide range of outcomes include stress, burnout, mental health effects, decreased job satisfaction, diminished commitment, and cynicism, emotion management, effect of emotion management of negative relationships on other relationships, distress, and psychosomatic responses. These chapters illustrate the profound depth and range of these impacts, continuing the emphasis of Section I on interaction processes in problematic relationships, exploring the dynamics of relational communication in problematic situations. By highlighting a variety of outcomes, new avenues for research emerge that are critical to a broader understanding of this significant problem. This section reveals the complexity of the phenomenon of problematic relationships in the workplace by highlighting the multiplicity of resulting outcomes.

Completing the first two sections' focus on definition and description, explanation, and outcomes is the final section, which addresses the critical issue of how to deal with problematic relationships. These last chapters are necessary to lend practical wisdom to those who seek to ameliorate or cope with these challenges at work. Employees are often at a loss as to how to cope with difficult others and negative relationships. Unlike sexual harassment, the types of negative behaviors and interactions that characterize most problematic relationships are not subject to legal action. The negativism and incivility in many problematic relationships tends to be difficult to detect, get acknowledgement of, and counteract. As Pearson and Porath (2005) observe:

> Although an individual may experience an uncivil comment or deed as purposefully offensive, the instigator may deny any negative intent. Instead the offender may claim that the target was simply too sensitive or that his words or behaviors were meant in jest...Some managers may ignore incivility because they do not want to get involved in messy interpersonal conflicts; some never hear about the incidents or, if they do, they discount their importance as so-called personal matters (p. 9).

Through these approaches employees may use to manage problematic relationships, hope for greater organizational health is offered. The chapters avoid simple formulas and frame dealing with problematic relationships as an ongoing process that must be pursued with some persistence. Most of these approaches accept the problem relationship and attempt to counter or minimize the damage that it does. For instance, a discussion of distancing oneself from problematic coworkers is complemented by a positive vision of professional civility offering a model for cultivation of a civil workplace. The important and uplifting topics of forgiveness and reconciliation in response to problematic relationships lead to the book's final chapter, a discussion of how to develop a healthy workplace.

This is an important book that goes beyond formulaic treatments and simplistic answers. It focuses instead on the processes that underlie problematic work relationships and on interaction strategies for responding to difficult others and for building healthy relationships. In so doing it offers authentic hope for a civil workplace. This volume will help us understand and hopefully remedy the quiet desperation so many workers experience on a day-to-day basis.

References

Graydon, J., Kasta, W., & Khan, P. (1994, November-December). Verbal and physical abuse of nurses. *Canadian Journal of Nursing administration*, 70-89.

Johnson, P. R., & Indvik, J. (2001). Rudeness at work: Impulse over restraint. *Public Personnel Management, 30*, 457-465.

Pearson, C. M. & Porath, C. L. (2005). On the nature, consequences, and remedies of workplace incivility: No time for "nice"? Think again. *Academy of Management Executive, 19*, 7-18.

Introduction

Becky L. Omdahl

Janie M. Harden Fritz

Susan checks on her employees constantly. In fact, she over monitors, constantly evaluates, and delegates few tasks. Instead of feeling respected, her employees feel on edge. They call Susan "controlling" and "demeaning" and report her behavior invites a level of anxiety which inhibits effective performance.

Bill is an employee whose life sounds like a soap opera. He obligates co-workers to listen to the ups and downs of his marriage, discipline challenges he faces with his drinking adolescent children, and his mother's recent bout with cancer. His colleagues think of him as the "drama king."

Pat throws sand in the gears of those working on projects, often failing to provide important information in a timely manner and sidetracking them with unnecessary projects. Pat's employees find it frustrating to work toward deadlines.

Having collected data from well over a thousand individuals to date, our data indicates these examples are not unique or even rare. Virtually all of the participants in our studies have been able to identify a problematic relationship within their work groups (e.g., Omdahl & Fritz, Fritz & Omdahl, this volume). While the scenarios and behaviors vary, it is apparent that there are numerous personal relationships creating pressures for workers. Undoubtedly, employees ranging from line workers to administrators feel the challenges.

Some challenges have become high profile media reports. Terms like "going postal," "school shootings," and "courthouse violence" have become common references to types of violence occurring in workplaces. The eruption of violence in the workplace elicits fears for both managers and employees on how to manage anger and rage. The on-air and on-line discussions of nationally renowned crimes have often focused on the extent to which the perpetrator felt alienated, bullied, dismissed, or powerless in situations with colleagues or supervisors. These discussions have raised concerns about the impact of relationships on thoughts, behaviors, and feelings. While this volume devotes attention to more common forms of problematic interactions and relationships, the growing concern with incivility and bullying spawned by high profile criminal cases has undoubtedly contributed to interest in and awareness of this topic.

Until about a decade ago, there was a virtual dearth of scholarly research on problematic relationships in the workplace (but cf. Hochschild, 1983; Rafaeli & Sutton, 1989). Work on "the dark side" of interpersonal communication and relationships (Spitzberg & Cupach, 1994) was emerging, and many researchers studied conflict and organization management, but few scholars had looked at the emergence of, fallout from, and remedies for working with difficult others. In the last decade, scholars and students in organizational communication, management studies, interpersonal communication, small group communication, conflict, and organizational ethics have become increasingly interested in how people navigate relationships with people they dislike or find problematic in the workplace.

Early research relevant to negative work relationships includes Holt's (1989) work on students' images of enemies and Davis & Schmidt's (1977) work on obnoxiousness. Other work emerged addressing the climate or nature of work relationships as a variable for predicting stress or work satisfaction (e.g., Chapman, 1993; Cooper & Cartwright, 1994; Repetti, 1993). Though these studies were related to rather general measures of peer or work relationship quality, they pointed to the importance of further theorizing and work exploring a topic increasing in salience and importance.

Within the last decade and a half, more specific focus on types of problematic others and problematic relationships received attention. Problematic supervisor and peer relationships and/or interactions (Karasek & Theorell, 1990; Leiter & Maslach, 1988), problematic subordinates (Monroe, Borzi, & DiSalvo, 1992), petty tyranny of bosses (Ashforth, 1994), and dysfunctional workgroups (Stohl & Schell, 1991) brought attention to specific behaviors of problematic role inhabitants in the workplace. Studies of features of problematic others from a constructivist perspective (e.g., Sypher & Zorn, 1988) identified the scope of behaviors, features, and attributes of problematic persons. Types of troublesome others at work were identified (Fritz, 2002 and this volume) on the basis of clusters of perceptions. The work of Omdahl and Fritz (this volume) moved to examine the relative effects of different relative power levels on outcomes, a focus they identified as lacking in previous research.

Another area of research advancing our knowledge has focused on the communicative accomplishment of work relationship deterioration, particularly Sias's work (see Sias, this volume, for a review of that research), highlighting processes pointing to the etiology of problematic others. Responses to hypothetical problematic others (Fritz, 1997) and responses to disliked others (Hess, 2000) provided groundwork for understanding how problematic relationships are managed.

Some research relevant to problematic work relationships does not address the topic directly, but focuses on communicative or other behavioral microprocesses that may contribute to them and offers insight into research on problematic relationships and broader organizational contexts that shape opportunities for encounters leading to problematic relational forms. Incivility, abuse, and bullying (see Metts, Cupach, & Lippert, this volume), workplace aggression (Baron & Neuman, 1998), employee emotional abuse (Lutgen-Sandvik, 2003), cynicism (Dean, Brandes, & Dharwadkar, 1998), social undermining (Gant et al., 1993), employee deviance (Robinson & Bennett, 1995), and employee misbehavior in the workplace (Vardi & Weitz, 2004) appear to be factors contributing to perceptions of unpleasant work relationships or to environments that may spawn them. This research holds promise for embedding the study of problematic relationships in larger organizational contexts, an important focus for theorizing about problematic relationships. Such work would move the focus away from "the other" and onto more general processes that shape our understanding and reaction to behavior in the workplace that could be considered problematic (e.g., Duck, Kirkpatrick & Foley, this volume).

By examining theory, research, and application, this book seeks to inform scholars and students with interests in this field as well as providing information which may be used by managers who are reading a larger array of professionally-focused books on the subject (e.g., Cava, 2004; Crowe, 1999; Gill, 1999; Jakes, 2005; Lubit, 2003; Solomon, 2002).

Overview of the Book

The chapters in this volume present a picture of the challenges of problematic relationships in the workplace. This book explores how problematic relationships are conceptualized, how they impact people, and how health and wellness can be promoted in workplace relationships.

Part I: Conceptualizations of Problematic Work Relationships. In the first section of the book the difficult images are described and attributed to an array of theoretical perspectives. Steve Duck, Megan Foley and D. Charles Kirkpatrick assert that difficulties in workplace relationships have the same characteristics of human behavior and social perception operating in a wider array of social situations. They argue that social life constructs and influences identities and that in the workplace, this construction occurs in the context of organizational role expectations. A key point in their chapter is that problematic relationships in the workplace do not necessarily mean the other is a problem, but rather that the other's identity has been constructed as problematic.

Rather than conceptualizing problematic work relationships in terms of social construction, in Chapter 2, Janie Harden Fritz explores types of problematic bosses, co-workers, and subordinates in a confirmatory factor analysis of work behaviors creating difficulty. The factor analysis confirmed most of the types identified in previous research (Fritz, 2002). Thus, the argument is made that there are kinds of bosses, coworkers, and subordinates that are stable over time and situations.

In Chapter 3, Meina Liu and Patrice Buzzanell explore the conceptualization of pregnancy in the workplace. They examine the construction of meanings around pregnancy and analyze a case study revealing both support from co-workers and challenging communication from bosses. They discuss gendered workplace processes evident in the difficulties pregnant women face in negotiating workplace relationships, especially in working-class jobs.

Another way in which some problematic workplace relationships can be conceptualized is as deteriorating friendships. Patricia Sias, in Chapter 4, explores why workplace friendships deteriorate and the consequences of deterioration, including how strategies for deterioration are selected and implemented.

The loss and change highlighted in deteriorating workplace friendships were also evident for a wider array of relationships at work experiencing turning points. In Chapter 5, Jon Hess, Becky Omdahl, and Janie Harden Fritz look at the forces of significant interactions (i.e., turning points) on the trajectories of relationships with others at work. Turning points can promote positive or negative changes in workplace relationships, but overall, the finding is that once a negative trajectory is initiated, most often, the turning points that follow lead to increasingly negative perceptions of the relationship.

Part II: Processes and Effects of Problematic Work Relationships. Regardless of whether the relationship is perceived as problematic due to social construction of the other, the type of behaviors exhibited, gender constructions during time-bound experiences such as pregnancy, deteriorating friendships, or turning points, the potential costs of problematic work relationships are daunting. In the second section of the book, the research addressing different types of costs is explored.

In Chapter 6, Becky Omdahl and Janie Harden Fritz look at the fallout problematic work relationships create in terms of stress, burnout, and impaired mental health. They report a clear relationship between problematic bosses and coworkers and all of these variables. In addition, they explore the progression of burnout and provide compelling evidence that emotional exhaustion leads people to cut down the emotional demands by depersonalizing others, and the resultant lack of genuine interactions with others fuels perceptions of reduced personal accomplishment.

Beyond these personal costs, Becky Omdahl and Janie Harden Fritz present another study in Chapter 7 outlining costs to organizations associated with problematic workplace relationships: reduced job satisfaction, diminished organizational commitment, and workplace cynicism. It is readily apparent that working with difficult others generates a ripple effect in organizations, characterized by problematic attitudes to work and companies.

In Chapter 8, Michael Kramer and Claire Tan examine the costs of emotion management. They argue that individuals manage emotion differently in workplace relationships with liked and disliked others, with greater costs arising for the latter. Their findings indicate that interactions with disliked others are more likely to result in downward spirals in which interactions create even more negativity in relation to the other. In contrast, interactions with liked others more often create upward spirals observed in interactions that elicit greater positivity toward the other. Overall, organizations in which problematic relationships abound face greater costs in the form of emotion management than organizations with fewer problematic relationships.

Terry Kinney, in Chapter 9, focuses on the costs arising in problematic relationships between graduate students and advisors. Looking at these workplace relationships, Kinney examines the self-protection motivation leading to high costs when advisors send messages to their advisees that have high self-discrepancies. Among the deleterious fallout were intrusive thinking, thoughts of revenge and escape, negative affect, social strategies designed to change the nature of the relationship, distress, and decreased well being.

Overall, the chapters in this section provide strong empirical evidence that problematic workplace relationships warrant serious concern. Potentially, they pose very high costs for both individuals and organizations.

Part III: Dealing with Problematic Work Relationships. Given the costs incurred as a result of problematic workplace relationships, what can individuals and organizations do? The final section of the book explores avenues to greater health, wellbeing, and productivity.

This section begins with a realistic look at the nature of most problematic workplace relationships. In Chapter 10, Jon Hess argues that these relationships are largely non-voluntary and the primary coping mechanism available is distancing from the problematic other. After exploring the use of distancing tactics in organizational settings, Hess argues that the underlying act of maintaining relationships is driven by the need to regulate arousal. The chapter ends with a model delineating the role of arousal regulation in maintaining relationships with disliked others.

Agreeing with Hess that workplaces are made up of people with diverse backgrounds, reasons for working, work styles, values, and goals, Ronald C. Arnett emphasizes the need for professional civility as an organizational communication ethic. In Chapter 11, Arnett argues that professional civility calls people to hold different expectations for and exhibit different behaviors in the public sphere and private sphere. Expectations for the workplace (public sphere) involve the notion of the unseen neighbor, the third. The call is to behave in a manner that makes it possible for all in the workplace to remain focused on achieving the tasks essential to fulfillment of organizational goals, seeking deeper personal fulfillment outside the workplace.

In cases where behavior violates social or personal codes, one possible response is forgiveness. Sandra Metts, Bill Cupach, and Lance Lippert discuss the scholarly research on forgiveness in Chapter 12. They present an original research study that examines the extent to which affective orientation and anger impact forgiveness and whether apologies increase the likelihood of forgiveness and reduce damage to workplace relationships.

Finally, in Chapter 13, Becky Omdahl offers an overview of ways to manage self, interactions with others, and use of third parties to promote greater wellbeing in the workplace. Throughout this chapter, she draws on research addressing emotion management and conflict.

Thanks to Non-Problematic Others

Working on this project was a wonderful experience due to the dedication, graciousness, and professionalism of our colleagues who contributed chapters and our editors at Peter Lang. In addition, all of them supported our plan to donate all proceeds from this book to graduate student awards given out by the National Communication Association.

References

Ashforth, B. (1994). Petty tyranny in organizations. *Human Relations, 47,* 755-778.

Baron, R. A., & Neuman, J. H. (1998). Workplace aggression—the iceberg beneath the tip of workplace violence: Evidence of its forms, frequency, and targets. *Public Administration Quarterly, 21,* 446-464.

Cava, R. (2004). *Dealing with difficult people: How to deal with nasty customers, demanding bosses and annoying coworkers.* Buffalo, NY: Firefly.

Chapman, J. (1993). Collegial support linked to reduction of job stress. *Nursing Management, 24*(5), 52-56.

Cooper, C. L., & Cartwright, S. (1994). Healthy mind, healthy organization—A proactive approach to occupational stress. *Human Relations, 47,* 455-470.

Crowe, S. A. (1999). *Since strangling isn't an option: Dealing with difficult people—common problems and uncommon solutions.* New York: Penguin Putnam.

Davis, M. S. & Schmidt, C. J. (1977). The obnoxious and the nice: Some sociological consequences of two psychological types. *Sociometry, 40,* 201-213.

Dean, J. W., Brandes, P., & Dharwadkar, R. (1998). Organizational cynicism. *Academy of Management Review, 23,* 341-352.

Fritz, J. M. H. (1997). Responses to unpleasant work relationships. *Communication Research Reports, 14,* 302-311.

Fritz, J. M. H. (2002). How do I dislike thee? Let me count the ways: Constructing impressions of troublesome others at work. *Management Communication Quarterly, 15,* 410-438.

Gant, L. M., Nagda, B. A., Brabson, H. V., Jayaratne, S., Chess, W. A., & Singh, A. (1993). Effects of social support and undermining on African American workers' perceptions of coworker and supervisor relationships and psychological well-being. *Social Worker, 38,* 158-164.

Gill, L. (1999). *How to work with just about anyone: A 3-step solution for getting difficult people to change.* New York: Simon & Schuster.

Hess, J. A. (2000). Maintaining nonvoluntary relationships with disliked partners: An investigation into the use of distancing behaviors. *Human Communication Research, 26,* 458-488.

Hochschild, A. R. (1983). *The Managed Heart: The commercialization of human feeling.* Berkeley, CA: University of California Press.

Holt, R. R. (1989). College students' definitions and images of enemies. *Journal of Social Issues, 45,* 33-50.

Jakes, T. D. (2005). *The ten commandments of working in a hostile environment.* New York: Penguin Group.

Karasek, R. A., & Theorell, T. (1990). *Healthy work: Stress, productivity, and the reconstruction of working life.* New York: Basic Books.

Leiter, M. P., and Maslach, C. (1988). The impact of interpersonal environment on burnout and organizational commitment. *Journal of Organizational Behavior, 9,* 297-308.

Lubit, R. H. (2003). Coping with toxic managers, subordinates ... and other difficult people: Using emotional intelligence to survive and prosper. Upper Saddle River, NJ: Financial Times/Prentice Hall.

Lutgen-Sandvik, P. (2003). The communicative cycle of employee emotional abuse. *Management Communication Quarterly, 14,* 471-501.

Monroe, C. , Borzi, M. G., & DiSalvo, V. S. (1992). Managerial strategies for dealing with difficult subordinates. *Southern Communication Journal, 58,* 247-254.

Rafaeli, A., & Sutton, R. I. (1989). The expression of emotion in organizational life. In L. L. Cummings & B. M. Staw (Eds.), *Research in organizational behavior, 11,* 1-42.

Repetti, R. L. (1993). The effects of workload and the social environment at work on health. In L. Goldberger and S. Breznitz (Eds.), *Handbook of stress: Theoretical and clinical aspects (2nd ed.,* pp. 368-385). New York: The Free Press.

Robinson, S. L., & Bennett, R. J. (1995). A typology of deviant workplace behaviors : A multidimensional scaling study. *Academy of Management Journal, 38,* 555-572.

Solomon, M. (2002). *Working with difficult people* (Rev. and exp. ed.). Upper Saddle River, NJ: Prentice Hall.

Spitzberg, B. & Cupach, W. (Eds.) (1994). *The dark side of interpersonal communication.* Hillsdale, NJ: Lawrence Erlbaum.

Stohl, C., & Schell, S. E. (1991). A communication-based model of small-group dysfunction. *Management Communication Quarterly, 5,* 90-110.

Sypher, B. D., & Zorn, T. E. (1988). Individual differences and construct system content in descriptions of liked and disliked co-workers. *International Journal of Personal Construct Psychology, 1,* 37-51.

Vardi, Y., & Weitz, E. (Eds.) (2004). *Misbehavior in organizations: Theory, research, and management.* Mahwah, NJ: Lawrence Erlbaum Associates.

Part I:
Conceptualizations of
Problematic Work Relationships

1 Uncovering the Complex Roles Behind the "Difficult" Co-worker

Steve Duck, Megan K. Foley, & D. Charles Kirkpatrick

Difficult relationships at work have a number of important features that resemble those found in other difficult relationships. Indeed, we believe that they resemble and draw from general human processes that guide both good and bad behavior, both easy and difficult relationships, both the development and decline of relationships. Because specific cases and topics of human behavior are only unwisely separated conceptually from the broader principles underlying behavior more generally (Duck, 1981), we place "difficult relationships at work" within that broader context of relational difficulty at large.

It is our case that much of the oppressiveness of difficult relationships at work is not in a simple sense interpersonal, but rather is a complex of psychological, communicative, and organizational processes that exemplify human activity more generally than solely in the work context. Accordingly, we draw from some observations of Hopper (1999) about the underlying and often ignored nature of divorce processes.

> Divorce often constitutes a dramatic transformation of a close, personal, and usually harmonious relationship into one that is deeply antagonistic and bitter. Explanations among family researchers typically focus on opposed material interests, the adversarial nature of the legal system, latent or manifest conflict in marriage, and/or psychological reactions to the pain of divorce [but] ... an important dimension [is] largely ignored by these explanations: the symbolic, or cultural. [Hopper, 1999]

Using this compelling thought about the importance of the symbolic and the cultural in divorce, Hopper (1993, 1999) notes that much of the insiders' descriptions of divorce is a rhetorical presentation of the "motives" of Self and Other. His stress on the symbolic nature of divorce, given this background, strongly latches it to questions of identity in the minds of the participants. Intricately involved in such analysis is the social representation of successful marriage and hence the symbolic meaning of the ending of a marriage. Many of the phenomena of divorce take on a different light when seen from this framework where the symbolism is given at least as much weight as the (highly contested) "realities" that are presumed and credited in other accounts of divorce.

In like manner, we suggest that difficulties in relationships more generally, including difficulties at work, have a rhetorical and symbolic function whose reckoning takes one away from a simple search for causes and toward a more sophisticated understanding of the social, identity, and symbolic issues that lie beneath any claims that one is surrounded by difficult others. Instead of seeing difficult relationships at work as founded on the practices and behaviors of other people, we will argue that difficult relationships at work are founded instead on rhetorics of motives, attributions, and accounts that have as much to do with the identity and identity management of the *reporter* as they do with the actions of other people. Although it is a convenient rhetorical device to attribute blame for "difficulty" to the inherent characteristics and styles of another person, we follow Kirkpatrick, Foley, and Duck (in press) in focusing at the dyadic and social level, emphasizing the influence of role forces, of situating social discourses and of human tendencies to self-justification. In brief, we will depict power, hierarchy and the concept of "difficulty" that results from interaction with other people as discursive resources rather than as reflections of some sort of reality.

What is a "Difficult Person"?

Suppose someone declares that a person at work is "difficult." What are they saying? Attributions of "difficulty" can be a mechanism for coping and for dealing with a troublesome and complex situation which cannot be dealt with in other ways. Indeed it is a well established psychological principle that symbolic labeling processes occur in all relational contexts and are characterized by personal rather than situational attributions (Ross, 1977). Labeling of people in this way (so as to make attributions that turn their traits into those of consistent and enduring "people" or "types") solves many issues at the superficial level without coming to grips with underlying causes and functions. In the workplace, labeling a person as difficult is a social construction leading those creating the label to believe that the difficulty is an intrinsic characteristic of the person.

"She is difficult" is a very different construction from "she's suffering some difficulty" or "this is a difficult time for her" or "that task is difficult for her." The first construction makes difficulty an immutable characteristic; the second construction makes difficulty an affliction from which she could be restored; the third and forth examples construct difficulty as extrinsic to her with an expectation that things will change when the difficult time has passed and an expectation that the person will become more proficient at the task. Unlike the last three examples, once a person is branded as difficult it becomes hard for coworkers ever to construct the person differently.

For example, one of the authors worked for a number of years with a colleague who invited co-workers to a Super Bowl party. A secretary in the office told the author that she would not attend the party because twelve years earlier she had gone to one of the colleague's parties and he had shown an adult film. She called over one of the other secretaries who was present at the party to verify the story. The colleague's "difficulty" emerged when members of the larger network maintained this characterization of him as engaging in inappropriate behavior. Twelve years later, it redeveloped as part of an identity socially constructed among network members, including ones who were not present at the party who had not known the colleague until years later—like the author. Thereafter, whenever the secretary and the author talked about their colleague this became part of the mutually constructed identity for him. In this case, the secretary constructed the colleague as difficult because of the film he showed twelve years earlier, and the colleague constructed the secretary as difficult because she brought up the story to the author. The secretary imposed an undesired social face onto the colleague that he then had to manage. This caused the colleague to confront a sense of self that he wanted to avoid. He was forced to live down the behavior yet again. Once a person is identified as difficult, any lack of cooperation is taken as evidence of difficulty while instances of supportive behavior are downplayed and forgotten. The characterization of a person as difficult leaves no rhetorical space for coworkers to modify this construction.

While a label like "difficult person" suggests that difficulty is an immutable personal characteristic, Davis and Schmidt (1977) point out that obnoxiousness is not straightforwardly a person's quality. Some characteristics of individuals are inherently social and hence transcend both the workplace and any other place, applying with equal force to any social situation or relational experience. For example, although we can describe someone as ambitious or selfish, these qualities have a social overlay to them. Ambitious people judge their performance relative to the performances of others, and selfish people are so judged because they put their own interests before others'. It is probably not possible to be selfish on a desert island where you live alone. Over and above such examples, other apparently individual characteristics are actually rather ambiguous. For instance, qualities like "lonely" are only *apparently* individual and in fact describe a social performance or a socially attuned style. In short, for this characteristic to make sense, sociality has first to be assumed. Davis and Schmidt (1977) further point out that such terms as "niceness" or "obnoxiousness" simply mean nothing outside of a social referent: they refer to how people react to an individual's behavior in relation to themselves. Finally, Davis and Schmidt (1977) offer the term "microdeviance" for those infractions of social norms that lead to a person's (for example an excessively nice or an excessively hostile person) becoming regarded as antisocial without becoming entirely outcast in the way that sexual offenders are outcasts. Microdeviants appear just not to know how to behave well, rather than knowing how to behave well but choosing not to do so.

Furthermore, behavior itself need not affect another person individually or personally for the effect to be seen as a social one. All that is necessary for behavior to be socially charged is merely that one be aware of the possible impact of a behavior upon others. Hence many concepts describing both self and other people are inherently about the possible or real effect of behavior upon the presumed presence of others (for example, describing someone as "honest" or "open" describes not just personality traits but personality styles *relative to other people)*. Taking this further, one can add that the possibility of judgment by others is all that is necessary for a behavior to be regarded as social rather than individual. If a person acts conscientiously for fear of being found out, then conscientiousness becomes not a personal but a *social* characteristic in this sense. Difficult people, whether at work or more generally in life, are therefore at least as likely to be people who infringe upon the rights of others as people who do anything inherently offensive when judged outside of the social sphere (Kirkpatrick, Foloey, & Duck, in press).

Connecting the symbolic elements of (so-called) disruptive or difficult behavior at work with the inherent sociality of these descriptors, this chapter is an analysis of the ways in which work roles, public behaviors at work, and the interaction of different elements of dyadic activity can serve to affect a person's sense of identity. From this point of view, difficult behavior at work is seen as difficult because of its effect on the identity perceptions of those who claim to be on the receiving end of its negative impact. Difficult people at work are so characterized because they impose undesired social identities on others. The engagement of those subjects with the "difficult other" therefore reinforces a negative sense of self that the subject wants to avoid and yet cannot because the difficult person persists in imposing or reifying it.

An interesting example that takes us further into our analysis is provided by Hepburn and Crepin (1984), who published one of the very few studies that appear in print about non-voluntary relationships. The study demonstrates that common fate renders people intertwined in ways they may not desire and which are not explicable in simplistic ways in terms of power structures. Hepburn and Crepin (1984) noted that prison guards augment the limitations of their formal authority over prisoners by the informal control derived from an arrangement of reciprocity with prisoners. The needs of their employment create a state of mutual interdependency that provokes a pattern of mutual accommodation between guards and prisoners. Both benefit from the maintenance of some form of order and stability within the environment where they either live or work. The prisoners benefit from predictability in the situation, can gain a relaxation of strict rules by being accommodating, and can ease their time in jail by making life more agreeable for the guards. On the other hand, the guards are quite dependent on the prisoners for many things in their work that are not immediately apparent (for example, as detailed below, personal safety and effective job performance).

The key concept here is mutual interdependence (and hence dependency) in involuntary relationships. The study makes much of the fact that even in apparently asymmetric relationships there can be a degree of dependency at the informal level of operation of the relationships. Prisoners depend on guards in obvious ways, but there are often anti-staff attitudes and the availability of an alternative "prisoner society" from which resources can be obtained. Furthermore, guards are outnumbered significantly and therefore depend on the prisoners for personal safety and successful completion of their duties (and hence for reward and acknowledgement by their superiors). For example, guards who gain a reputation with their superiors as unable to maintain order tend to be passed over for promotion. So the ability to get along with prisoners, irrespective of the apparent benefits of formal powers bestowed on the guards, can make a difference to the guards' career success.

Given strong pressures to compromise with prisoners in order to win an easier life at work, guards are likely to acquiesce to an informal corruption of formal authority. Friendships between guards and prisoners can be useful in the service of each one's goals. Such cozy but manageable relationships can become more difficult for all parties as a result of extra constraints on their activities that affect their trust and relaxation with prisoners. The increasing dependence of guards, though, increases the repression of prisoners by guards' uses of formal powers, but the more the prisoner is dependent on the guard, the more the guard's relationship with the prisoners is one of accommodation. Even in such a coercive and highly structured environment where official power is markedly scalene, it is possible to see that "difficulties" at work exist within a complex relationship between the actual social practices of organizing and the formal reified structure of organizations.

Further and perhaps more common examples, but ones that nevertheless exemplify the same principles of compromise through interdependence, are provided by Lovaglia and Lucas (in press), who note the tensions between formal power in an organization and the informal powers that stem from social status that depends on liking. Hence a liked boss can exert power without encountering the resistance that a disliked, and hence lower status but equally powerful (in the formal organizational sense), boss may be able to exert acceptably. It is all too frequently the case that many difficulties at work arise precisely from this difference between the formal powers granted by the organization and the informal status that is created by getting along with other people in the environment. It also works both ways in that there are difficulties created when status (liking) conflicts not with the powers but with the duties of formal position, as when a friend is promoted to boss and must sometimes choose between one role and the other while at other times being able to benefit from the happy conjunction of the two (Zorn, 1995).

The Process of Organizing

Putnam, Phillips, and Chapman (1999) identify three relationships that scholars have posited between communication and organization: containment, production, and equivalence. The containment metaphor conceptualizes organizations as reified, material entities in which social action occurs. The production metaphor sees organization and communication as two moments in the process of symbolic co-creation. That is, the communicative practices of members concretize patterns of the organization, which then become rules and resources for future communication. The equivalence metaphor suggests that organization *is* communication; communicative practices constitute organization.

Of the three metaphors identified by Putnam, Phillips, & Chapman (1999), the equivalence metaphor provides the most helpful conceptual framework for examining difficult work relationships. A definition of organization as a communicative process enables scholars to take a micro- rather than macro-level approach to social difficulty in organizing. While particular social problems are often generalized to overall dissatisfaction with an organization (Knight & Cunningham, 2004), organizational members generally experience social problems with specific others in specific situations. Even structural problems in the workplace are manifested through problems with particular social actors (Taylor & Van Every, 2003). The definition of organization and communication as equivalent allows scholars to look at workplace difficulty processually, as it is understood by organizational members. Although taking an equivalence perspective enables a micro-level approach, this does not come at the expense of ignoring the organization. This perspective positions organization as a significant phenomenon in itself rather than as a contextual background for social behavior. Instead of looking at difficult relationships in workplace settings, the lens focuses analysis on how the process of organizing itself may lead to social difficulties.

The equivalence perspective sees organization as an interactional process; it is more appropriate to talk about organizing rather than organizations. Taylor (2003) claims that while communication and organization exist at different levels of analysis, they are moments in the same process of double-translation. Conversation (social acts) constitutes organization (social structure); organization constrains and enables conversation. Taylor explains, "Conversation is the site of organizational emergence, text, its surface" (p. 37). For Weick (2003), enactment (i.e., conversation) bonds organization to sense-making. Through enactment, organizational members simultaneously make sense of and change their environment:

> Enactment is about knowing and learning, which means it is about issues of epistemology. But the form of knowing that is involved in enactment, active probing that both shapes and meets resistance, means that it is also about issues of ontology . . . enactment is about ontologizing one's epistemology (Weick, 2003, p. 191).

As actors organize their social world, that organization produces their identities. Kelly (1969) explains that an individual's self-becoming is characterized by this same process of environmental investigation: anticipating events in the social world, acting on the basis of those anticipations, and revising anticipations in light of the new experience. These anticipations and behaviors constitute individuals' selves: "Man was shaped by his commitments and what he did to fulfill them [*sic*]" (Kelly, 1969, p. 53). While several studies (e.g., Ashforth & Saks, 1996; Black & Ashford, 1995) have focused on how individuals' identities are assimilated into larger organizational identities, our conceptualization further suggests that the organization produces individual selves as a function of individuals' own agentive organizing actions. As Weick (2003) explains, "*People are in a complex reciprocal relationship with their environments*" (p. 186). The social actor's enactment is transactively linked to the textuality of the organization. Because the process of organizing is autopoetic, the problematic identities of organizational members can be understood as the ground for organizational difficulty.

Social Difficulty in Organizing

Difficult organizational relationships thus have a number of important features that resemble those found in other interpersonal difficulties. Another key feature of organizational relationships shared with other relationships and particularly important for the organizational context is that work involves two personae for each individual: *self as person* and *self as worker*. This necessary component of the organizational experience can involve the person in role strain between the two personae and adds a crust to the pie of other difficulties. We will comment here on the nature of difficulty as it is likely to manifest given the elements of an organizational setting. Whatever is difficult between two individuals acquires extra threat or promise as a function of workplace features that reflect these roles, the structure of the workplace itself (involving much more formal structures of power and control than the everyday world of friendship does), and the nature of work as a place where people perform tasks that may involve little inherent interest and investment of their "true selves." Conflict at the workplace persona [role] level is therefore of a somewhat different nature than conflict at the person level. One major issue for this book is precisely how and why some spillage occurs between the two spheres of life.

Everyone in the workplace takes something along into the roles that work requires, and that thing is personal style. Whereas the roles in the workplace may be defined and designated within a hierarchical structure, personal styles have no such boundaries and formats. By their very definition, personal styles permit and indeed specify individuality, idiosyncrasy, even eccentricity. Where the requirements of a role and the embodiment of a personal style collide, there is opportunity for energy to be spilled. A person may carry out the role performance in a personally designated way, such that beyond some relatively superficial descriptions of the role requirements, the actual performance is not predictable and can vary considerably between one performer and another.

In the workplace then, the person-role duality can create an interesting mix of possibilities for difficulty, including (a) *person-role incompatibility*, where the requirements of a role do not suit the person's style, (b) *person-person incompatibility*, where the personal styles of two social actors conflict, and (c) *between person role-role incompatibility*, where the organizational roles of two social actors conflict.

Person-Person Incompatibility

Person-person incompatibility is based on personal dislike. The two organizational members simply are not suited to each other as individuals, regardless of their roles. Person-person incompatibility gets in the way of their performance of the job requirements, and although the problem happens at work they are not strictly generated by the work environment or its requirements. For example, a person might interrupt another during a meeting out of personal disrespect and impede the entire work team's ability to hold discussion. Unlike role-role or person-role strain, where roles tie social actors to the organization, person-person strain is based on individual differences independent of the organization. Examination of person-person strain provokes the question: what makes person-person strain organizational?

While person-person incompatibility begins in a particular interaction, these chain out across time and space personally, interpersonally, and organizationally. Wood (1992) finds that women who are sexually harassed when starting a first job underestimate the future importance of sexually harassing behaviors and are less likely to report the behavior to superiors. While the textuality of an organization can constrain and enable social behavior, the enactment of single behaviors can also limit the field for subsequent behaviors. For the same reason, unchecked workplace conflict enters negative communication spirals in which negative behaviors are reciprocated and escalated (Andersson & Pearson, 1999). Cunningham (2004) refers to these differences as "asynchronous behaviors." He finds that interpersonal dislike in the workplace is often due to minor, irritating behaviors that build over time rather than to large-scale conflict. Interaction moments are sedimented and institutionalized: objectivized reality is the sum of recurrent patterns of meaning and interaction (Berger & Luckmann, 1966). Whether the behavior of organizational members shapes the future behavior of a particular social actor or generates a particular pattern of interpersonal interaction over time, person-person incompatibility *organizes*.

Role-Role Incompatibility Between Persons

A difficult person at work may be quite pleasant in a bridge group. However, when the only context in which coworkers see the person is at work, there is no opportunity for them to find evidence that the context, not the person, is the source of the difficulty. If coworkers all went on a fishing trip they might have the opportunity to see, "He's really a nice guy when you get him away from work." The work context may create incompatible instrumental roles for ordinary folks that lead to judgments from coworkers about the difficulty of one person or both. In many ways, these task-oriented difficulties create relational difficulties; instrumental conflict often leads to interpersonal hostility (Van Oostrum & Rabbie, 1995). Most work tasks are highly time-dependent, often leading to stress from incessant looming deadlines. In addition, new time challenges have arisen from innovative organizational principles such as mass customization and "just in time" production methods, principles born of an increasingly service-based economy. Besides the time dependency of tasks, many workers experience tasks that are highly complex, tedious, boring, repetitive, protracted, or ambiguous. All of these conditions can lead to tired and unhappy workers with diminished personal resources for effectively performing work roles, particularly as performed in concert with others. While role incompatibilities may be a result of poor organizational planning, often these situations emerge from everyday organizational life. In other words, two employees' roles may be structurally incompatible or only incompatible in practice: role-role incompatibility can exist as organizational text or conversation.

Role-role incompatibility is a classic example of job-related difficulty, existing at an institutional rather than immediately personal level. Role-role incompatibility may be based on overlapping or parallel task jurisdictions (for example, it may be unclear whether the accountant or the project manager is responsible for a project's budget) or contradicting objectives (a consultant is hired to conduct layoffs while a human relations manager is hired to raise employee morale). Both are cases of distributive conflict, where one organizational member or department's successful performance is dependent on the failure of the other (Wilmot & Hocker, 1998). The dynamics of different departments in the same organization can lead to difficulties between groups or personnel. Various departments in an organization must ultimately work together even when they have competing departmental goals. For example, a design department might create designs that are difficult for the fabrication department to build. Incompatible goals and limited departmental resources (e.g., pay raises, status, and power) are at stake, yet departments depend on one another for success (Hepburn & Crepin, 1984).

Up to this point, we primarily have been discussing horizontal role-role conflict, where the parties involved have the same formal power. Role-role incompatibility is perhaps more strikingly apparent when vertical, that is, based on a formal power disparity. Power is the real or perceived ability to get someone to do something s/he does not want to do (Lovaglia & Lucas, in press). Because power involves bending someone to one's own will, the exercise of power or even the perceived potential to exercise power leads to negativity. Status, unlike power, does not lead to difficulty. Status is conferred upon someone when the recipient is judged to be a valued member of the group (Lovaglia & Lucas, in press). Status is a way of ruling because workers confer status onto a person and are therefore willing to do what the high status person wants. Since people confer status willingly, there is presumably no conflict and no difficulty. Even though power may not be granted willingly, it cannot be exercised unilaterally, as is indicated in the earlier discussion of relationships in prisons. Power does not sit in one place or with one person; it is constructed between people. Organizational members can rely on many sources of power, including role-based authority, personal expertise, the ability to reward others, and the ability to punish others.

Because organizational members rely on informal power sources unrelated to their structural role, power is not the sole prerogative of management. Laborers can invoke power as well with unions, by working to the rules, or through individual or group efforts to change the way tasks are performed. Managers are also workers. Sometimes they may undermine the power of executives. Executives may neglect their accountability to stockholders or a board of directors. In turn, the stockholders might vote out the company leadership. No one person is a source of absolute power and since anyone can leave the company for another job, no one has power over another unless they both construct it that way. If the supervisor tells a person what to do and s/he does not want to do it, ultimately, s/he has a choice; s/he can always leave the company.

Person-Role Incompatibility

In the case of person-role strain, the stakeholder is simply not personally suited to the organizational role. Diffident people are called upon to lead, unreliable people are in positions of great responsibility, and so forth. Unlike role-role or person-person strains, which are clearly dyadic, person-role strain may appear to be an intrapersonal phenomenon unrelated to problematic relationships in the workplace. However, resistance to the organizational role requires engagement with other organizational members who hold the individual accountable for performing the problematic role. For example, flight attendants mocked pilots for a lack of self-reliance when the pilots expected flights attendants to follow airline policy and serve them beverages (Murphy, 1998). Here, a person-role problem that flight attendants have with organizational policy leads to confrontations with pilots. Uncomfortable with their confessional role in counseling, social service clients complained about and refused to attend monthly group meetings with their social worker; one even went so far as to state publicly that the social worker was "on [his] hit list" (Tretheway, 1997, p. 214). Both cases demonstrate that the problems stakeholders have with their organizational roles become manifest in interaction with other organizational members who participate in the maintenance and reification of those roles.

Conflict between individuals and their organizational roles, that is, the agency of the social actor and the organizational "text," often results in acts of appropriation that both work within the problematic role and rearticulate it. For example, office folklore both relies on tropes from dominant organizational meanings and resists them. For example, the sign, "Warning! I can go from 0 to bitch in 4.3 seconds (or less)" (Bell & Forbes, 1994, p. 192) combines masculine corporate quantification and rationalization with an emotional, even hysteric, feminine admonition. While it may seem that organizational members in less powerful roles are more likely to resist them, LaNuez and Jermier (1994) report that managers and technocrats dissatisfied with their organizational roles are increasingly likely to resist them. Although problematic roles often can be subverted, appropriation of organizational constraints as resources also helps to reify those constraints. For example, Hatcher (2000) demonstrates that women in organizations can employ gendered performances to make them more visible in organizational life; however, gendered performances at the same time mark women as managerially incompetent. De Certeau's (1994) concept of "making do" in everyday life explicates the ability of social actors to appropriate material and discursive resources through strategies, which produce and reify organizational textuality, and tactics, which manipulate and divert it.

Roles in Relational Difficulty: The Nexus of Person, Interaction, and Organization

As we have pointed out above, difficulties in workplace relationships are often experienced as the fault of a "difficult person." However, we have endeavored to complicate this attribution by tracing the ways in which others become difficult. The other is not difficult on his or her own, but only insofar as he or she brings organizational constraints to bear through interpersonal interaction. In other words, it is not enough to speak about relational difficulty in solely structural, interactional, or personal terms. Instead, relational difficulty is located at the nexus of these three strands, in the concept of *role*. While workplace relationships provide a particularly useful (and perhaps experientially resonant) site for illustrating relational difficulty, social actors negotiate multiple and conflicting roles across all relationship forms. Families, for instance, work within societal constraints manifested in particular interactions on the basis of enacted identities. For example, despite his desire to be an involved parent, a man in a traditional nuclear family may resist being a stay-at-home dad due to social pressure to act as the family's breadwinner. These constructions may contribute to his experience of relational difficulty as he interacts with his wife and children. Role, as the nexus of the personal, interactional, and structural, is the location of relational difficulty in the workplace and elsewhere.

Workplace difficulty is one special case within a multiplicity of cases that are almost limitless in examples. The general issue is to deploy understanding of relational problems at work but to find the place of work difficulties in the realm of relationship difficulties as a whole.

Conclusions

Given that many characteristics often thought to be individual are in fact social, and given that relationships at work are based on involuntary association with others who are managing competing roles, we conclude that difficulties with workplace relationships are instances of broader human social perception and behavior. In seeking to understand difficulty in relationships at work, it is important, we believe, to focus first on those principles and features of human behavior and social perception that occur in many different places and circumstances, of which the workplace is one example.

The organizing principles that create a workplace full of norms, roles, rules and hierarchy tend to be built on those principles that structure human social life in aggregate. The organization of social life constructs and influences identities, and the forces present in the workplace add an overlay of workplace identities to the mix. Where a person brings in roles from non-work contexts that are in conflict with the roles required in the workplace, that person imports difficulty. Where the person experiences strain between two requisite workplace roles, that person experiences difficulty.

By placing difficulty at work within the broader requirements of human participation, we hope to have shown that one is an extension of, rather than a replacement for, the other. Workplace difficulty is a key area for scholars to investigate given that most people spend a third of their waking life at work. The more we understand relational difficulty in general, the more we will understand difficulty at work.

References

Andersson, L. M., & Pearson, C. M. (1999). Tit-for-tat? The spiraling effect of incivility in the workplace. *Academy of Management Review, 24,* 452-471.

Ashforth, B. E., & Saks, A. M. (1996). Socialization tactics: Longitudinal effects on newcomer adjustment. *Academy of Management Journal, 39,* 149-178.

Bell, E., & Forbes, L. C. (1994). Office folklore in the academic paperwork empire: The interstitial space of gendered (con)texts. *Text and Performance Quarterly, 124,* 181-196.

Berger, P. L., & Luckmann, T. (1966). *The social construction of reality: A treatise in the sociology of knowledge.* Garden City, New York: Doubleday.

Black, J. S. & Ashford, S. J. (1995). Fitting in or making jobs fit: Factors affecting mode of adjustment for new hires. *Human Relations, 48,* 421-437.

Davis, M. S. & Schmidt, C. J. (1977). The obnoxious and the nice: Some sociological consequences of two psychological types. *Sociometry, 40,* 201-213.

de Certeau, M. (1994). The practice of everyday life. In J. Storey (Ed.), *Cultural theory and popular culture: A reader* (pp. 474-485). New York: Harvester Wheatsheaf.

Duck, S. W. (1981). Towards a research map for the study of relationship breakdown. In S. W. Duck & R. Gilmour (Eds.), *Personal relationships: Vol. 3. Personal relationships in disorder* (pp. 1-29). London: Academic Press.

Hatcher, C. (2000). Making the visible invisible: Constructing gender through organizational micropractices. *Electronic Journal of Communication, 10*(1).

Hepburn, J. R. and A. E. Crepin (1984). Relationship strategies in a coercive institution: A study of dependence among prison guards. *Journal of Social and Personal Relationships, 1,* 139-158.

Hopper, J. (1993). The rhetoric of motives in divorce. *Journal of Marriage and the Family, 55,* 801-813.

Hopper, J. (1999). The symbolic origins of conflict in divorce (Document No. 98-10). Chicago: University of Chicago, Population Research Center.

Kelly, G. A. (1969). Ontological acceleration. In B. Maher (Ed.), *Clinical psychology and personality: The collected papers of George Kelly* (pp. 7-45). New York: Wiley.

Kirkpatrick, C. D., Foley, M. K. & Duck, S. W. (in press). Some conceptual problems with "problematic relationships" and difficulties with "difficult people." In S. Duck, C. D. Kirkpatrick, & M. K. Foley (Eds.), *Difficult relationships.* Mahwah, NJ: Lawrence Erlbaum.

Knight, M. T., & Cunningham, C. M. (2004). An inside look at the structure of women in engineering programs. *Journal of Women and Minorities in Science and Engineering, 10,* 20-31.

LaNuez, D., & Jermier, J. M. (1994). Sabotage by managers and technocrats. In J. M. Jermier, D. Knights, & W. R. Nord (Eds.), *Resistance and power in organizations* (pp. 219-251). London: Routledge.

Lovaglia, M. J. & Lucas. J. W. (in press). Leadership as the management of power in organizations. In S. W. Duck, C. D. Kirkpatrick, & M. K. Foley (Eds.), *Difficult relationships.* Mahwah, NJ: Lawrence Erlbaum.

Murphy, A. G. (1998). Hidden transcripts of flight attendant resistance. *Management Communication Quarterly, 11,* 499-536.

Putnam, L., Phillips, N., & Chapman, P. (1999). Metaphors of communication and organization. In S. Clegg, C. Hardy, & Nord, W. (Eds.). *Managing Organizations: Current Issues* (pp. 125-158). London: Sage.

Ross, L. D. (1977). The intuitive psychologist and his shortcomings: Distortions in the attribution process. In L. Berkowitz (Ed.), *Advances in Experimental Social Psychology* (Vol. 10, pp. 174-214). New York: Academic Press.

Taylor, J. R. (2003). Dialogue as the search for sustainable organizational coorientation. In R. Anderson, L. A. Baxter, & K. N. Cissna (Eds.), *Dialogue: Theorizing difference in communication studies* (pp. 125-140). Thousand Oaks, CA: Sage..

Taylor, J. R., & Van Every, E. J. (2003). *The emergent organization: Communication as its site and surface.* Mahwah, NJ: Lawrence Erlbaum.

Tretheway, A. (1997). Resistance, identity, and empowerment: A postmodern feminist analysis of clients in a human service organization. *Communication Monographs, 64*, 281-301.

Van Oostrum, J., & Rabbie, J. M. (1995). Intergoup competition within autocratic and democratic management regimes. *Small Group Research, 26*, 269-296.

Weick, K. E. (2003). Enacting an environment: The infrastructure of organizing. In R. Westwood & S. Clegg (Eds.), *Debating organization: Point-counterpoint in organization studies* (pp. 184-191). Malden, MA: Blackwell.

Wilmot, W. & Hocker, J. (1998). *Interpersonal conflict* (5th ed.). Boston: McGraw-Hill.

Wood, J. T. (1992). Telling our stories: Narratives as a basis for theorizing sexual harassment. *Journal of Applied Communication Research, 20*, 349–362.

Zorn, T. (1995). Bosses and buddies: Constructing and performing simultaneously hierarchical and close friendship relationships. In J. T. Wood and S. W. Duck. (Eds.), *Understanding relationship processes: Vol. 6. Under-studied relationships: Off the beaten track* (pp. 122-147). Thousand Oaks, CA, Sage.

2 Typology of Troublesome Others at Work: A Follow-up Investigation

Janie M. Harden Fritz

Much of our time is spent at work in the company of other people, some of whom we find problematic for a variety of reasons. Some simply do work differently than we do or serve as irritants by bringing personal troubles to work; others are problematic in more egregious ways, inflicting interpersonal trauma on others through gossip, unprofessional behavior, self-promotion, and other forms of troublesome behavior (Fritz, 2002). Research on social undermining (Gant, et al., 1993), workplace aggression (Baron & Neuman, 1998; Coombs & Holladay, 2004), workplace deviance (Robinson & Bennett, 1995; Bennett & Robinson, 2000), bullying (e.g., Namie & Namie, 2000; Tehrani, 2001), employee abuse (Lutven-Sandvik, 2003), antisocial behavior (Giacalone & Greenberg, 1997), and other types of problematic work misbehavior (Vardi & Weitz, 2004) reflects growing interest in understanding and managing workplaces increasingly marked by physical and psychological violence (Vardi & Weitz, 2004).

Workplace relationships are the interactional locus of many of these undesirable workplace phenomena as well as more benign and even beneficial exchanges (e.g., Comer, 1991; Sias & Cahill, 1998). Research suggests that organizational relationships are powerful contributors to the well-being of organizational members. When work relationships are problematic, employees and organizations suffer in a variety of ways. Stress and burnout (Omdahl & Fritz, this volume), absenteeism (Kimura, 2003), turnover (Chapman, 1993), and the potential for reduced productivity (Mann, 1993; Monroe, Borzi, & DiSalvo, 1992) have been associated with reduced quality of work relationships.

Recent scholarship has advanced our knowledge of how work relationships may become problematic (e.g., through deterioration: Sias, this volume) and outcomes resulting from these relationships (Fritz & Omdahl, this volume; Omdahl & Fritz, this volume). My research on troublesome others at work identified a typology of negative or "troublesome" bosses, peers, and subordinates (Fritz, 2002) based on perceptions of the structural attributes or dimensions of problematic others at work that affect perceptions of the relationship. Differences in factor structure well as differing numbers of clusters and cluster patterns across hierarchical levels suggested that perception of troublesome others at work is affected by the organizational context within which these relationships take place, supporting Duck, Foley, and Kirkpatrick's theoretical work on the importance of contextual, structural, and role factors in our understanding of "difficult" organizational relationships (Duck, Foley, & Kirkpatrick, this volume).

This chapter reports a follow-up study of troublesome others at work designed to assess the adequacy of the original typology, including factors identified at each organizational level and the structure and nature of the clusters originally identified. The next section reviews the original Fritz (2002) typology.

Original Typology of Troublesome Others at Work

To investigate the phenomenon of troublesome work relationships, I conducted a cluster analysis based on factors identifying features of problematic others at work for three different status levels: bosses, peers (coworkers at the same status level), and subordinates. Factors similar across each status level and unique to each status level emerged. For example, sexual harassment, being distracting, an unprofessional focus of attention, being different from the respondent, and defensiveness emerged for each of the three status levels, but a factor for troublesome bosses, "lording power," constituted two separate factors labeled "self-promotion" and "controlling/bossy" for troublesome peers.

The six negative bosses constructed from the cluster analysis varied in levels and configurations of the factors that emerged for this level of relationship. These troublesome boss types are described briefly as follows: the *Defensive Tyrant* is "an incompetent, unethical petty tyrant who is fearful that others may steal his or her job" (p. 423); the *Taskmaster* is characterized by control and excessive task demands, sometimes unrelated to work, who is believed to flout workplace ethical standards; the *Different Boss* does work differently than the respondent would carry it out; *Sand in the Gears* is "an interfering, backstabbing, distracting petty tyrant who brings personal problems to work" (p. 423); the *Extreme Unprofessional* exhibits sexual harassment, distracts others with personal problems, is critical of others, fearful of losing the position, incompetent, and engages in behavior in order to "look good"; and the *Okay Boss* exhibits very low levels of negative attributes.

The eight troublesome peer types are as follows: the *Independent Other* is troublesome only in rejecting the legitimate role-based authority of coworkers and is seen as being different in work style and interaction than the respondent; the *Soap Opera Star* is distracted by and distracts others with personal problems discussed in the workplace and is seen as somewhat incompetent, self-centered, and interfering with others' business. The *Bully* insists on work being done his/her own way, gets others to do work that person should be doing, and takes credit for that work; the *Adolescent* is fearful of losing the job, someone who screams and yells, is demanding, self-promoting, distracting, and controlling; the *Self-protector* is focused on self-interest and advancement of the self; the *Mild Annoyance* is not a very problematic coworker, with low scores on all negative attribute factors; the *Rebellious Playboy or Playgirl* harasses others sexually, ignores legitimate authority of coworkers, and talks about non-work topics and personal problems; and the *Abrasive, Incompetent Harasser* fits the profile of someone who commits sexual harassment, is incompetent and unprofessional (yelling and screaming), distracting, bossy, and fears job loss.

The five clusters of troublesome subordinates included the *Intrusive Unprofessional*, who intrudes in others' matters, exhibits a poor work attitude and behaves rudely; the *Backstabbing Self-promoter*, who is critical of others and attempts self-advancement; the *Harmless Busybody*, who intrudes slightly into others' business and conversations but is an otherwise non-troublesome person; the *Incompetent Renegade*, portrayed as incompetent, resistant to orders, and distracting to others; and the *Abrasive, Incompetent Harasser*, who displays sexual harassment, fears job loss, and is rude to and critical of others.

The Second Study

The second study was designed to replicate and extend the first study. This chapter reports the replication attempt.

Method

Participants. This study's 751 participants were (1) parents of students in communication classes in a mid-sized, private, northeastern university; (2) students enrolled in courses in the same university's School of Leadership and Professional Advancement (continuing education) undergraduate and master's program and participants recruited by these students; and (3) students enrolled in graduate courses in the traditional curriculum. Students received extra credit for participation and/or for recruiting parents/co-workers as participants. See Table 1 for sample demographics. The table reflects cases included in the analyses of the three status levels where status was specified (4.9% did not specify status level); problematic others in categories other than immediate supervisor, peer, or immediate subordinate constituted 2.4 % of the sample and were not included in the analysis.

Table 1
General Characteristics of the Sample

Age	*Respondent Gender*	*Company size*		*Status of problematic person*	
M=36.38	F: 59.2%	< 100:	52.0%	Boss/supervisor:	35.7%
	M: 40.8%	100 - 1000:	30.9%	Peer/coworker:	49.6%
		>1000:	17.0%	Subordinate:	12.3%

Number of Participants/Percent of Total Sample Arrayed by Organization Type and Size

Size Type of Organization	*(<100)*	*(101-1000)*	*(> 1000)*	*Total*
Construction	8 (0 1%)	0 (0.0%)	0 (0.0%)	8 (1.1%)
Manufacturing	29 (4.0 %)	37 (5.1%)	44 (6.1%)	110 (15.3%)
Communication	5 (0.7%)	14 (1.9%)	0 (0.0%)	19 (2.6%)
Retail	43 (6.0%)	13 (1.8%)	4 (.6%)	60 (8.3%)
Finance	18 (2.1%)	10 (1.3%)	13 (1.8%)	41 (5.7%)
Service	249 (34.6%)	132 (18.3%)	46 (6.4%)	427 (59.3%)
Government	23 (3.2%)	18 (2.5%)	14 (1.9%)	55 (7.6%)
Total	375 (52.1%)	224 (31.0%)	121(16.8%)	699 (100.0%)

Measurement

Participants were asked to consider a work associate with whom they typically experienced unpleasant or negative interactions. They rated this work associate on the 54 original 7-point Likert items ranging from 1 (*not at all*) to 7 (*very much or very often*) designed in the previous study to measure attributes of work associates (see Fritz, 2002, for details of the origins of categories from which the items were derived). These items constituted the first section of the questionnaire. I generated other items representing these attributes as well, including them in a second portion of the questionnaire for future analysis. Demographic items were included in the final section of the questionnaire.

Analysis and Results

The problematic others (35.7% bosses, 49.6% peers, and 12.3% subordinates; see Table 1) targeted by respondents consisted of 45.7% men and 49.4% women, with 4.9% not identified as male or female. Following the procedure of the original study, I identified attributes to serve as classification variables for the cluster analyses by performing separate principle components factor analyses with varimax rotation on the 54 attribute items from the initial study for troublesome bosses (n = 225; first study n = 223), troublesome peers (n = 354; first study n = 328), and troublesome subordinates (n = 88; first study n = 104) (n was reduced in some cases for each status level due to missing data). As in the first study, there were fewer than the recommended number of participants for the subordinate group for a reasonable solution (Guadagnoli & Velicer, 1988), but I proceeded with the analysis anyway.

Factors. At each status level, I eliminated the same items inappropriate to that status level before the factor analysis as I did in the first study (one item for bosses, three items for subordinates). Afterwards, I eliminated items from each solution loading .4 or more on more than one factor or failing to load at least .4 on any one factor. I performed a reliability analysis for items on each factor to assess their suitability as composites for classification variables in the cluster analysis. In each case, I judged the interitem correlations and alphas values to be adequate for this replication study. In the original study, I retained one item that composed a single factor for the case of negative peers ("refuses to take orders from me though I have authority over this person"), which I did not retain in the current study since it loaded with another item ("this person yells and screams") but did not constitute a reliable factor. As in the first study,

I labeled the factors based on the gestalt impression of the factor's items. I examined the original factors as well in order to assist my interpretation and to assess the extent to which the factors constituted similar or different "gestalts" (see Table 2 for the original and second study factors and alphas for each status level; for complete details on each factor's items for the original and current study, contact the author).

Table 2
Factors and Alphas for Classification Variables for Troublesome Bosses, Troublesome Peers, and Troublesome Subordinates for Original and Second Study

Boss Factors (Original Study)	α	Boss Factors (Second Study)	α
1 Lording power	(.94)	1 Self-promoting	(.90)
2 Busybody behavior	(.93)	2 Unethical incompetence	(.85)
3 Backstabbing	(.86)	3 Interfering	(.87)
4 Different from me	(.92)	4 Lording power	(.85)
5 Sexual harassment	(.92)	5 Distractingly different	(.82)
6 Poor work ethic	(.82)	6 Unprofessional focus	
7 Unethical	(.82)	of attention	(.77)
8 Unprofessional focus		7 Sexual harassment	(.81)
of attention	(.90)	8 Obnoxiousness	(.84)
9 Distracting	(.87)	9 Social undermining	(.72)
10 Excessive demands	(.69)		
11 Defensive	(.68)		

Peer Factors (Original Study)	α	Peer Factors (Second Study)	α
1 Busybody behavior	(.93)	1 Professional incivility	(.86)
2 Controlling/bossy	(.89)	2 Irritatingly "other"	(.88)
3 Self-promotion	(.87)	3 Busybody behavior	(.89)
4 Different from me	(.87)	4 Self-promotion	(.82)
5 Unprofessional		5 Poor work ethic	(.84)
behavior	(.82)	6 Sexual harassment	(.84)
6 Incompetent	(.78)	7 Unprofessional focus	
7 Sexual harassment	(.87)	of attention	(.85)
8 Unprofessional focus		8 Defensively demanding	(.61)
of attention	(.92)	9 Performance	
9 Hustling	(.72)	misrepresentation	(.83)
10 Distracting	(.81)	10 Distracting	(.63)
11 Defensive	(.86)		
12 Rebellious (single item)			

Table 2, continued
Factors and Alphas for Classification Variables for Troublesome Bosses,
Troublesome Peers, and Troublesome Subordinates for Original and Second Study

Subordinate Factors (Original Study)	α	Subordinate Factors (Second Study)	α
1 Self-aggrandizement	(.93)	1 Bullying	(.90)
2 Busybody behavior	(.95)	2 Self-centered	(.79)
3 Backstabbing	(.81)	3 Unethical incompetence	(.85)
4 Unprofessional attitude	(.82)	4 Busybody behavior	(.91)
5 Different from me	(.86)	5 Different from me	(.82)
6 Unprofessional focus of attention	(.90)	6 Sexual harassment	(.84)
7 Sexual harassment	(.70)	7 Defensive	(.78)
8 Defensive	(.81)	8 Unprofessional focus of attention	(.89)
9 Incompetent	(.90)		
10 Distracting	(.80)		
11 Above the law	(.75)		

Clusters. Cluster analysis identifies groups with similar characteristics (in this case, troublesome persons in the work environment) on a set of variables (in this case, variables derived from the factors assessing problematic or troublesome characteristics). For this analysis, as in the original study, standard scores for the constructed variables from the factors for each status level served as classification variables for the cluster analysis at that status level. Two sets of criteria, internal and external, can be used to determine the adequacy of a cluster solution. Internal criteria refer to features of the cluster itself. One internal criterion is interpretability, or the ease with which the researcher assigns reasonable meaning to the clusters as a set; the other is heuristic value, or the extent to which the cluster solution is interesting (Shepard, 1974). External criteria refer to more objective means of determining adequacy. One external criterion is assessing cluster solution sufficiency by using the original set of clustering variables as independent variables and cluster membership as groups to which they are assigned through the procedure of discriminant analysis (Romesburg, 1984). The extent to which classification efficiency exceeds chance indicates the adequacy of the solution through corroboration by an alternative statistical procedure. Another external criterion is number of cases in a cluster. Adequate solutions should have no clusters composed of a single case.

My guide for choice of cluster solutions, as in the original study, were the subjective criteria of being interesting and interpretable and a discriminant analysis classification rate of at least 90%, along with cluster membership greater than one. A final guide was comparison with the cluster solutions at each status level from the original study, which served as a touchstone for interpretation and assisted with assigning cluster labels.

Comparison of Results from Original and Current Study

Bosses

Boss factors. The troublesome boss factors that emerged in study two were similar in some ways and different in others to the factors in the original study. Several factors in the current study shared items with factors in the first study but were assigned different labels because the presence of different items or the absence of some original items created a different overall impression of the factor in the current study. For instance, the factor labeled "Self-promoting" is composed, with the exception of one item, entirely from items from the original "lording power" factor. The original lording power factor included additional items related to controlling and/or bossing (the respondent or others). The second study's "lording power" factor, however, contains two items related to bossiness and control along with criticism and excessive work demands. "Sexual harassment" was the only factor with identical items in the original and current study. The current study generated a more parsimonious set, with 9 rather than 11 factors.

Boss clusters. As in the first study, six clusters provided the most intuitively appealing, interesting, and interpretable structure for types of troublesome bosses, with discriminant analysis classification efficiency on the original variables of 97.4% (80.73% above baseline). Of the troublesome bosses, 125 (56.1%) were men and 98 (43.9%) were women. As in the first study, clusters displayed a range of scores on the troublesome attributes. Negative boss clusters were labeled *The Different Boss* ($n = 52$; 22.4%); *The Good Old Boy/Girl* ($n = 19$; 8.2%); *The Okay Boss* ($n = 26$; 11.2%); *The Toxic Boss* ($n = 51$; 22.0%); *The Self-Centered Taskmaster* ($n = 62$; 26.7%); and *The Intrusive Harasser* ($n = 22$; 9.5%). Table 3 provides means and standard deviations for each of the factor variables along with z scores for each boss cluster.

Table 3
Troublesome Boss Cluster Labels and Z Scores on Factors[a]

Factor	M	SD	Cluster 1 The Different Boss (n = 52) z score	Cluster 2 The Good Old Boy /Girl (n = 19) z score	Cluster 3 The Okay Boss (n = 26) z score
Self-promoting	5.08	1.46	-.47	-.57	-1.68
Unethical incompetence	3.70	1.60	-.56	-.06	-1.33
Interfering	3.82	1.53	-.82	-.14	-1.20
Lording power	4.39	1.60	-.51	-.34	-1.20
Distractingly different	5.43	1.18	-.21	-1.04	-1.60
Unprofessional focus of attention	3.73	1.52	-.71	-.07	-.80
Sexual harassment	1.87	1.34	-.53	1.25	-.38
Obnoxiousness	5.25	1.55	-.46	-.50	-1.77
Social undermining	4.55	1.83	-.62	-.86	-1.09

Factor	M	SD	Cluster 4 The Toxic Boss (n = 51) z score	Cluster 5 The Self-Centered Taskmaster (n = 62) z score	Cluster 6 The Intrusive Harasser (n = 22) z score
Self-promoting	5.08	1.46	.89	.47	.20
Unethical incompetence	3.70	1.60	1.00	-.01	.63
Interfering	3.82	1.53	.97	.23	.75
Lording power	4.39	1.60	.56	.40	.34
Distractingly different	5.43	1.18	.86	.39	.06
Unprofessional focus of attention	3.73	1.52	1.12	-.21	.73
Sexual harassment	1.87	1.34	-.16	-.42	2.06
Obnoxiousness	5.25	1.55	.92	.42	.33
Social undermining	4.55	1.83	.93	32	.27

[a] 1=*not at all; 7=very much* or *to a great extent*

The troublesome boss clusters bore some resemblance to those in the original study, with two being similar enough in patterning to warrant names identical to those in the original study. Two others bore a family resemblance to two in the original study, but had attributes that shifted the gestalt enough to warrant different labels.

Similar to the cluster of the same name in the original study, the *Different Boss* cluster's highest score (though below the mean) is on the "distractingly different" factor (standard score = -.21). This cluster has lower than average scores on all dimensions (the original study's cluster scored .34 on "different from me," the factor corresponding most closely to "distractingly different" in the second study). The current analysis identified 52 (22.4%) members of the Different Boss category, but only 28 (14.4%) emerged in the original study.

The Okay Boss, in identical fashion to the cluster of the same name in the original study, scored below the mean on every attribute and manifested the lowest scores on every attribute except one (sexual harassment). A similar proportion of this troublesome boss type emerged across the two studies: 11.2 % (26) (for the current study and 10.8% (21) for the original study.

The Good Old Boy/Girl, which has no counterpart in the original study, manifests lower than average scores on all factors except "sexual harassment," but does not have the highest score for that variable of all the clusters. "Unprofessional focus of attention" and "unethical behavior" are the next highest scores, though below the mean (-.06 and -.07). This cluster's lowest score was on "distractingly different" (-1.04), with relatively low scores on "social undermining" (second lowest of all the clusters), "self-promotion," and "obnoxiousness" as well. The gestalt impression is that of a boss who, compared to other troublesome bosses, is interpersonally competent and perhaps even gracious. The sexual harassment component coupled with the score on "unethical behavior," within the context of other relatively benign attributes, puts one in mind of one who refuses to consider sexual advances toward others in the workplace problematic, but rather part of normal work life to be accepted by persons of goodwill, hence the label "Good Old Boy/Girl."

The Intrusive Harasser, similar in many ways to The Extreme Unprofessional of the original study, has scores above the mean on every factor, with the "sexual harassment" score two standard deviations above the mean, constituting this cluster's most marked (highest scoring) attribute. "Interfering" and "unprofessional focus of attention" are the next strongest attributes for this cluster, which, together with sexual harassment, generate a gestalt impression of intrusion and interference in both professional and personal life, hence the label. The original study's similar type (Extreme Unprofessional) scored the highest of all boss types on "unprofessional focus of attention," but the second study's type did not. Although the second study's type was above the mean on that factor, it was not the cluster with the highest score for "unprofessional focus of attention," so I was reluctant to use the label of "The Extreme Unprofessional." "Sexual harassment," "unprofessional focus of attention," and "backstabbing," followed by "busybody behavior" ("interfering" in the second study), were the most prominent characteristics of the boss in the first study. Except for this cluster's second-place position on "unprofessional focus of attention" rather than first place (of all the boss clusters), this cluster almost replicates the original study's Extreme Unprofessional type. The original study revealed 12.4% (24) in the Extreme Unprofessional category; the current study shows 9.5% (22) Intrusive Harassers.

The Toxic Boss scores highest of all clusters on "unprofessional focus of attention," "unethical," "interfering," "social undermining," and "obnoxiousness." This cluster's pattern resembles the description of the manager discussed in Kimura's (2003) article entitled "Overcome Toxic Management," which prompted the cluster label. "Sexual harassment" is the only factor on which this cluster showed a score lower than the mean.

The Self-centered Taskmaster has some of the attributes of The Taskmaster from the original study in that "excessive work demands" are high for this cluster (found in the "lording power" dimension of this second study, but forming a separate factor in the original study). "Unethical incompetence" and "unprofessional focus of attention" are both below average for *The Self-centered Taskmaster*, following the below average scores of original study's Taskmaster on "poor work ethic" and "unprofessional focus of attention." The *Self-centered Taskmaster's* highest score was on the factor of "self-promotion," followed by "obnoxiousness" and "lording power," which, combined with low scores related to incompetence, generated the impression of a boss focused on getting the job done in order to advance his/her own goals, without concern for others. In the current study 26.7% (62)

bosses were identified as the *Self-centered Taskmaster*, and the previous study identified 20.1% (39) bosses in the Taskmaster category.

Peers

Peer factors. The peer factors that emerged in the current study were comparable to the factors in the original study, with some reconfiguration. Three peer factors were identical to the original study: "busybody behavior," "sexual harassment," and "unprofessional focus of attention." Although the "self-promotion" factor was composed entirely of items composing the factor of the same name in the original study, some items on the factor in the original study were not included in this factor in the current study because of loadings of .4 or above on other factors (as was the case in the current study's troublesome boss analysis compared to results for the original study). With 10 rather than 12 factors, the configuration of peer factors in the current study is more parsimonious. The factor of "professional incivility" in the current study contributes to that parsimony, picking up items from "unprofessional behavior," "controlling/bossy," and "hustling" from the first study. The gestalt sense of this factor is consistent with theoretical work describing professional civility (Arnett & Fritz, 2004) and incivility (Andersson & Pearson, 1999) in work environments (contact author for complete details).

Peer clusters. As in the first study, the eight cluster solution was the most interpretable and intuitively appealing for peers and provided excellent classification efficiency through discriminant analysis of 96.6% (84.1% above baseline). One hundred thirty-three men (42.4%) and 181 women (57.6%) were identified as negative coworkers. Clusters ranged from peers perceived as having work or communication styles different from the respondent's to overbearing bullies. The clusters were labeled *The Adolescent* (n = 51, 15.8%); *The Bully* (n = 36, 11.2%); *The Mild Annoyance* (n = 36, 11.2%); *The Independent Self-promoter* (n = 9, 12.1%); *The Pushy Playboy/Playgirl* (n = 32, 9.9%); *The Independent Other* (n = 47; 14.6%); *The Soap Opera Star* (n = 58, 18%); and *The Abrasive, Incompetent Harasser* (n = 23, 7.1%). Table 4 provides means and standard deviations for each of the factor variables along with z scores for each peer cluster on each variable.

Table 4

Troublesome Peer Cluster Labels and Z Scores on Factors[a]

Factor	M	SD	Cluster 1 The Adolescent (n = 51) z score	Cluster 2 The Bully (n = 36) z score	Cluster 3 The Mild Annoyance (n = 36) z score
Professional incivility	4.26	1.41	1.00	.41	-1.52
Irritatingly "other"	5.62	1.25	.66	.77	-1.60
Busybody behavior	4.56	1.52	.69	.42	-1.30
Self-promotion	5.01	1.52	.82	.59	-1.15
Poor work ethic	3.94	1.65	.45	.84	-1.19
Sexual harassment	1.91	1.37	-.36	-.33	-.47
Unprofessional focus of attention	4.64	1.69	.88	-.40	-.94
Defensively demanding	3.17	1.49	.91	.61	-.89
Performance misrepresentation	3.33	1.83	.41	1.23	-1.00
Distracting	4.34	1.41	.56	.83	-1.27

Factor	M	SD	Cluster 4 The Independent Self-Promoter (n = 39) z score	Cluster 5 The Pushy Playboy/ girl (n = 32) z score	Cluster 6 The Independent Other (n = 47) z score
Professional incivility	4.26	1.41	.45	-.20	-.20
Irritatingly "other"	5.62	1.25	.15	-1.09	.13
Busybody behavior	4.56	1.52	.35	-.20	-.88
Self-promotion	5.01	1.52	.68	-.35	-.36
Poor work ethic	3.94	1.65	-.65	-.21	.01
Sexual harassment	1.91	1.37	-.29	1.16	-.44
Unprofessional focus of attention	4.64	1.69	.16	.05	-.89
Defensively demanding	3.17	1.49	-.13	.47	-.56
Performance misrepresentation	3.33	1.83	.55	.10	-.51
Distracting	4.34	1.41	-.63	-.20	-.47

[a] 1 = *not at all;* 7 = *very much or to a great extent*

Table 6, continued
Troublesome Peer Cluster Labels and Z Scores on Factors[a]

Factor	M	SD	Cluster 7 The Soap Opera Star (n = 58) z score	Cluster 8 The Abrasive, Incompetent Harasser (n = 23) z score
Professional incivility	4.26	1.41	-.53	.94
Irritatingly "other"	5.62	1.25	.24	.50
Busybody behavior	4.56	1.52	.32	.71
Self-promotion	5.01	1.52	-.57	.68
Poor work ethic	3.94	1.65	.12	.86
Sexual harassment	1.91	1.37	-.25	2.53
Unprofessional focus of attention	4.64	1.69	.65	.68
Defensively demanding	3.17	1.49	-.67	.93
Performance misrepresentation	3.33	1.83	-.81	.67
Distracting	4.34	1.41	.51	.82

[a] 1 = *not at all*; 7 = *very much* or *to a great extent*

The eight troublesome peer clusters in the current study formed patterns very similar to the eight troublesome peer clusters in the original study, evoking identical or similar labels, sometimes with minor variations. Although exact duplication did not emerge, the resemblance of patterns for the clusters on identical or closely corresponding factors was striking. The peer status level came the closest of the three (bosses, peers, subordinates) to replicating the original study's findings. The proportion of negative peers of each type, however, showed some variation from the original study to the current one.

The Adolescent in the current study had the same attributes as the cluster of the same name in the original study. "Professional incivility," "unprofessional focus of attention," "self-promotion," and "defensively demanding" marked this cluster. "Defensiveness," "unprofessional behavior," "controlling/bossy," and "self-promotion" most defined *The Adolescent* in the original study. For this cluster in the original and in the current study, "sexual harassment" was not a defining feature, falling below the mean. *The Adolescent* represented 15.7% (42) of troublesome peers in the original study and 15.8% (51)

in the current study.

The Independent Other in the current study was marked by its most representative dimension "irritatingly other," with a standard score slightly higher than the mean (.13), followed by a score at the mean (.006) on "poor work ethic." The original study's Independent Other's highest score was also on the dimension representing difference from the respondent ("different from me"), followed by "rebelliousness" (refusing to obey legitimate authority of a peer). For each of these variables, however, the score was below the mean. For all other variables, this peer type in both studies scored below the mean. The Independent Other represented 18.7% (50) of troublesome peers in the original study and 14.6% (47) in the current study.

The Soap Opera Star in both studies was marked most by "unprofessional focus of attention" and next by "distracting." Both had higher than average scores on "busybody behavior" and lower than average or average scores on "defensively demanding" ("hustling" and "defensive" in the original study). Both had higher than average scores on factors representing not doing the job properly ("poor work ethic" for the second study and "incompetence" in the original). This type was not as self-promoting or uncivil as the first study's type by that name. The *Soap Opera Star* cluster constituted 18% (48) of troublesome peers in the original study and 18% (58) in the current study.

The Bully of the original study emerged recognizably, though not identically, in the second study. In this study, the factors of "defensively demanding" and "performance misrepresentation" had, taken together, many items on the factor of "hustling" in the first study. Unprofessional behavior for the first study and "professional incivility" for the second study were prominent factors for each cluster. Neither was marked by unprofessional focus of attention or sexual harassment. However, the defensiveness component in "defensively demanding" did not emerge for *The Bully* in the first study, nor did the perception that the person is different from the respondent, whereas in the present study, both emerged. Nonetheless, the gestalt impression of the bully remains, as in the first study: that of a bossy, controlling person who makes demands of others, takes credit for their work and is at the same time insecure, the prototype of a schoolyard bully, hence the label. In the current study, there was an apparent decrease in the appearance of *The Bully*, with 11.2% (36) of troublesome peers falling into that category in the current study, down from 17.2% (46) in the original study.

The Mild Annoyance, as in the original study, scored far below average on every attribute and in a very similar pattern. This peer is not very problematic. The same proportion of *The Mild Annoyance* peer type emerged in the current study as *The Bully*, 11.2% (36). In the original study, The Mild Annoyance comprised 7.1% (19).

The Independent Self-promoter scored highest on the "self-promotion" factor, which was the second-highest attribute of The Self-protector in the original study, the first being "defensive." *The Independent Self-promoter* scored below average on "defensively demanding." This factor, unlike the original study's factor of "defensive," included the attribute of demanding that others do one's work. This "demanding" attribute was not part of *The Independent Self-promoter*'s pattern, nor was it part of The Self-protector's pattern (with a low score on "hustling" in the original study, the variable that tapped that attribute). "Performance misrepresentation" was a distinctive characteristic of *The Independent Self-promoter*, but not of The Self-protector. This distinction between the two clusters, coupled with the lack of defensiveness on the part of the new study's cluster, led to the shift in label. *The Independent Self-promoter* seems to be a more actively self-focused peer than The Self-protector, due to the former's tendency to take credit for other's work and the latter's fear of losing the job. Nonetheless, the attribute of self-focus is highlighted in both as a distinctive feature. The original study's peer type was defensive and self-promoting, while the second study's was self-promoting and would take credit for others' work to get ahead. *The Independent Self-Promoter* comprised 12.1% (39) of the current study's peers; The Self-protector comprised 13.1% (35) of the original study's peers.

The Pushy Playboy/Playgirl represents another type similar to one in the original study, The Rebellious Playboy/Playgirl. The cluster in this second study was marked by high scores on "sexual harassment," being defensively demanding (making unreasonable task demands, asking that tasks unrelated to work be done, being fearful for one's job) , "performance misrepresentation" (taking credit for the work of others, including that of the respondent), and "unprofessional focus of attention." The first study's cluster was marked by sexual harassment, "rebelliousness" (rejecting orders coming from a fellow peer with legitimate authority over the person), "unprofessional focus of attention," and "hustling" (making unreasonable task demands, asking that tasks unrelated to work be done, taking credit for the respondent's work, being hard to satisfy). The absence of the factor "rebellious," making this cluster different from the original study's closest similar type, coupled with the similarity in pattern of low scores on other attributes (such as "busybody behavior," "self-promotion," and being different from the respondent and/or irritating) and the high score on sexual harassment prompted this cluster's name of "Pushy Playboy/playgirl" rather than "Rebellious Playboy/playgirl." In the original study, The Rebellious Playboy/playgirl represented 7.1% (19) of troublesome peers; the current study revealed 9.9% (32) in the *Pushy Playboy/playgirl* category.

The Abrasive, Incompetent Harasser reappeared in very similar form in the second study, marked by extremely high scores on sexual harassment, the primary manifestation of this type. "Professional incivility," "incompetence," and being defensively demanding represented the next highest factor scores for the second study's type, while "incompetence," "unprofessional behavior," "defensiveness," being controlling and bossy, and "hustling" were the next highest scores for the original type. Both scored high on all other variables as well, with rather similar patterns; this type in the second study exhibited a higher "busybody" score than the first type (.71 compared to .44). As in the first study, this type was similar to a boss type exhibiting sexually harassing behavior as well as scores above the mean on all other negative attributes. There were 7.1% (23) of this type in the current study and 3.0% (8) in the original study.

Subordinates

Subordinate factors. The eight subordinate factors that emerged in the current study had five factors in common with the 11 factors in the original study (with one difference: one of the four sexual harassment items did not load appropriately in the original study, but all four did on this study). "Self-aggrandizement" in the original study decomposed into "bullying" and "self-centered," while some items from the original factors of "incompetent," "above the law," "unprofessional behavior," and "distracting" formed the new factor of "unethical incompetence."

Subordinate clusters. As in the first study, five clusters of troublesome or problematic subordinates provided the most intuitively appealing, interesting, and interpretable structure for problematic subordinates, with a discriminant analysis classification efficiency on the original variables of 91.8% (71.8% above baseline). Men accounted for 43.4 % (36) of subordinates, and women constituted the other 56.6% (47). As in the first study, clusters represented subordinates scoring below average to above average on the factor attributes, with a variety of patterns distinguishing the clusters. Problematic subordinate clusters were labeled *The Okay Subordinate* (n=3, 3.5%); *The Incompetent Renegade* (n=19, 22.4%); *The Bully* (n=21; 24.7%); *The Abrasive Harasser* (n=18, 21.2%); and *The Different Other* (n=24, 28.2%). Table 5 provides means and standard deviations for each of the factor variables along with *z* scores for each subordinate cluster on each variable. Of the five subordinate clusters in the current study, two clusters were very similar to those appearing in the original study, with a third showing family resemblance.

The Incompetent Renegade is very similar to the troublesome subordinate type of the same name in the original study. This type's highest score is "ethical incompetence," which contains items from each factor by which The Incompetent Renegade in the original study was marked: "incompetence," "above the law," and "distracting." The second highest score for the second study's Incompetent Renegade was "unprofessional focus of attention," which was the final marker of this type in the first study (though the standard score was higher in the second study). This subordinate rejects authority from bosses and the organization itself, is incompetent, and takes credit for others' work. This type is not a bully, a sexual harasser, or defensive. In the current study, 22.4% (19) of the subordinates fell into this category, and in the original, 16.8% (16) were of this type.

The Abrasive Harasser was similar on the variables that most marked the type by that name in the original study: "sexual harassment" (for the original study and the second study), "bullying," and "self-centered" (factors with items that corresponded roughly to those on "self-aggrandizement" and "unprofessional behavior" in the first study). This cluster type in the second study had a lower score on the "different from me" factor than the type in the original study. As in the original study, this sexually harassing type with scores above the mean on the other variables was also found at the other status levels. In the current study, this type comprised 21.2% (18) compared to the previous study's 7.4% (7).

Table 5

Troublesome Subordinate Cluster Labels and Z Scores on Factors[a]

Factor	M	SD	Cluster 1 The Okay Subordinate (*n* = 3) z score	Cluster 2 The Incompetent Renegade (*n* = 19) z score	Cluster 3 The Bully (*n* = 21) z score
Bullying	3.75	1.57	-.88	-.88	1.08
Self-centered	4.76	1.56	-1.48	-.00	.79
Unethical incompetence	4.16	1.43	-1.69	-.47	.52
Busybody behavior	4.21	1.73	-1.45	.01	.69
Different from me	5.74	1.18	-2.27	.07	.73
Sexual harassment	1.96	1.47	-.65	-.35	-.19
Defensive	3.92	2.04	-.67	-.83	.91
Unprofessional focus of attention	4.59	1.82	-1.21	.41	.34

Factor	M	SD	Cluster 4 The Abrasive Harasser (*n* = 18) z score	Cluster 5 The Different Other (*n* = 24) z score
Bullying	3.75	1.57	.42	-.44
Self-centered	4.76	1.56	.37	-.82
Unethical incompetence	4.16	1.43	.23	-.81
Busybody behavior	4.21	1.73	.26	-.52
Different from me	5.74	1.18	-.77	.27
Sexual harassment	1.96	1.47	1.44	-.50
Defensive	3.92	2.04	.34	-.24
Unprofessional focus of attention	4.59	1.82	.08	-.42

[a] 1 = *not at all*; 7 = *very much* or *to a great extent*

The Bully showed the highest score on "bullying," followed by "defensiveness" and "self-centered." The original study's Intrusive Unprofessional scored highest on "busybody behavior," followed by "unprofessional behavior," which includes some items on the "self-centered" dimension from the second study. Both clusters were above average on every variable for their status level except sexual harassment, in which each was below the mean; the first study's type was also below the mean on "defensive," unlike the second study's type. The defensiveness score's prominence, which follows the high score on bullying and precedes self-centeredness in rank, generates a gestalt impression of a subordinate who bosses others, usurps authority, is competitive, and is at the same time insecure. This pattern of factors and items has similarities to the Bully type found in the peer clusters as well. There was no corresponding type in the original study.

The Okay Subordinate did not emerge in the original study, bearing the closest resemblance to The Harmless Busybody. *The Okay Subordinate* scored well below the mean on every variable, whereas the Harmless busybody scored slightly above the mean on busybody behavior and unprofessional focus of attention. *The Okay Subordinate* is not problematic. There were 22.1% (21) of The Harmless Busybody type in the original study and 3.5% (3) of *The Okay Subordinate* type in the current study.

The Different Other scored below the mean on every variable except "different from me." The next highest score (-.24) was for "defensive." This subordinate was the next least problematic subordinate. *The Okay Subordinate's* lowest score was on "different from me" (-2.27), which distinguishes *The Okay Subordinate* from *The Different Other*. There was no closely corresponding type in the original study.

Discussion

This study was designed to replicate Fritz's (2002) original research identifying types of troublesome bosses, peers, and subordinates. The findings offer additional insight into perceptions of troublesome others at work, pointing to potential perceptual regularities across historical moments (the studies were conducted about five years apart) as well as persistent differences in the way organizational members perceive persons at different status levels.

Factors

The second study saw the reemergence of some factors identical (or almost so) to those in the first study across status levels, specifically those highlighting difference from oneself: "distractingly different" (bosses), "irritatingly other" (peers), and "different from me"(subordinates), intrusion of private matters into the work sphere ("unprofessional focus of attention"), sexual harassment ("sexual harassment"), and butting into others' and one's own business/conversations ("interfering" for bosses; "busybody behavior" for peers and subordinates). In both studies, these factors appeared in similar or identical form across each status level. Therein lies the consistency across time periods and status levels. Within status levels, both consistency and variation emerged on other factors. Despite some item variations, five of the 10 troublesome peer factors identified in this study were recognizable as factors in the original study, which may have helped account for the similarity in cluster configurations of the peer types. The eight factors for subordinates shared five in common with the first study's 11 factors, but there was less commonality across subordinate clusters than for the peer clusters across studies. However, the small number of subordinates in each case prevents definitive conclusions. For bosses, shifts in items and changes in cluster patterns are worth note; the relative consistency in peer clusters from study one to study two suggests that the difference is not a psychometric artifact.

In the original study, the boss factor entitled "lording power" manifested at the peer level as two factors, "self-promotion" and "controlling/bossy" (one item of which involved "giving orders without having the proper authority"). In this second study, items on the original boss factor of "lording power" composed a "self-promoting" boss factor and (one item) part of a dimension related to control (which I labeled "lording power") composed of items from different original boss factors and some that did not load on the original boss factors. This latter boss dimension was different from the original study's peer factor of "controlling/bossy" in its inclusion of two items related to task issues: making excessive work demands and being hard to satisfy. This new "lording power" factor had more of a task "flavor" to it than either the original "lording power" boss factor or the "controlling/bossy" original study peer factor. This latter "lording power" factor, with its task focus, seems to sharpen the focus on hierarchy and job related power, permitting, at least in theory, dimensions of task focus and self promotion to function independently. In the troublesome boss clusters, although these two factors shared valences (that is, a cluster below the mean on one was below the mean on the other), the cluster scores on the dimensions were not necessarily identical. For example, *The Toxic Boss* showed more self-promotion than lording power (z scores of .89 vs. .56), whereas *The Self-centered Taskmaster* showed less disparity on the two factors (z scores of .47 and .40, respectively).

"Unethical incompetence" was the label given to a factor for both bosses and subordinates in the second study. The difference between the two factors is that the item "The person's behavior distracts others from their work" did not appear on the boss factor but did appear on the subordinate factor; the item "This person takes credit for others' work" appeared for subordinates, but "This person takes credit for my work" appeared for bosses. This different configuration seems reasonable, given that a boss's concern would be for the effect of subordinate behavior on other subordinates (distracting and taking credit for others' work), and a subordinate's concern for a boss might lie with credit taken for one's own work. The shared items all reference incompetence, a poor work attitude, and failure to follow rules/regulations. Instead of the single identifiable factor of "unethical incompetence," two factors of "poor work ethic" and "performance misrepresentation" emerged for peers. This distinction points to potential differences in perception between hierarchical equals and hierarchical unequals.

Clusters

As in the first study, clusters derived their names from the two or three factors on which they scored the highest. This method worked well to permit identification of similarities and differences among types across the two studies. While very few types emerging had identical patterns on all of the variables, the resemblances on these most prominent identifying variables showed highly recognizable patterns on two of the five troublesome subordinate types, two of the troublesome boss types, and six of the eight peer types. In the case of bosses, two additional types were very similar to types in the previous study, but with a variation that propelled an alteration to the label (e.g., The Taskmaster became *The Self-Centered Taskmaster*). For the peer types, the two that varied enough to add a minor alteration to the label registered essentially the same general prototype as those of the previous study.

Implications

Together, the original study and the current study suggest insights about perception and work life. In the current study, as in the first, different overall factor structures emerged for different status levels, but a few salient "common" factors were found across levels. The evidence from the first study had suggested that variation by status level is not total, but targeted to areas where role differences lie; that the same "common" factors emerged in the second study offers further evidence for that conclusion. The emergence of two new types of bosses compared to those in the first study and the relative consistency of the peer types suggests that patterns of perception of persons at one's own status level may be a relatively enduring part of the perceptual landscape of organizational roles. Perception of bosses and subordinates do not appear to share the same degree of consistency.

Two explanations for these differences could be offered. One lies in the external organizational environment, in the prevalence of leadership books and seminars and management philosophies that shift with time. These philosophies may not alter the presence of "extreme" types (e.g., the "Okay" or "Different" boss, and the very harassing, intrusive boss), but might work in the middle, more malleable ground of those who both desire and are able to alter their behaviors and who adopt a different management style (e.g., Gardyn, 2000). Such changes over time would produce a different mix of manager/boss "types" based on employee perceptions. Even a shift in the formality of the managerial climate could trigger a difference in perception. Additionally, expectations for leaders/managers/bosses in an increasingly educated workforce with greater expectations for flexibility (Gardyn, 2000) might contribute to differences in perceptions of bosses from one time point to another. The "population" of persons in managerial positions who are consistently gracious or blatantly harassing, however, might not show much change: both the "nice" and the "nasty" may be permanent parts of organizational life. This explanation might account for change in the set of boss types over a 5-year period (about the time between data collections for these two studies) and for the relative consistency of peers. A second explanation is that heightened attention to persons in positions of legitimate power over oneself is likely to produce greater awareness of behavior, suggesting that any variation taking place over time would be perceptually highlighted or exaggerated for observations of bosses, causing variations across time. That explanation would not hold for variation in subordinates types across time, except to the extent that one is judged by the quality of work one is responsible for directing and hence understands one's fate as dependent, to some degree, upon one's direct reports. Alternatively, training in leadership might lead to new perceptual sets for managers (bosses), which might alter perceptions of subordinate features. That would account for differences in subordinate types over time, if these differences are more than artifactual.

Future Research

Future research should examine how the nature of a organization affects perception of troublesome "other" types. For instance, Coombs and Holladay's (2004) research suggests that organizations vary in their tolerance of types of aggressive behavior, such that some organizational environments curtail overt problematic behaviors. Such contexts would alter or eliminate the manifestations of behavior on which judgments of negative attributes are made, leading to less extreme constructions of troublesome others. In environments where attention is focused on task aspects of work rather than on the social environment, troublesome behaviors may be less noticed or such behaviors may be less likely to invoke negative judgments. Furthermore, as Duck, et al. (this volume) suggest and experience bears out, what is considered a troublesome attribute in one context may be a strength in another, leading to positive constructions of the person exhibiting them. For example, very directive leadership in emergency situations could be interpreted as decisiveness, but in routine situations as "lording power." Finally, in work environments where expectations for having a variety of one's needs met through work experience are relatively low and a rich private life is encouraged (that is, work is not the sole or primary location of meaning for a person; see Arnett, this volume), perceived characteristics of troublesome peer types may be perceptually attenuated.

References

Andersson, L. M., & Pearson, C. M. (1999). Tit for tat? The spiraling effect of incivility in the workplace. *Academy of Management Review, 24,* 452-471.

Arnett, R. C., & Fritz, J. M. H. (2004). Sustaining institutional ethics and integrity: Management in a postmodern moment. In Iltis, A. S. (Ed.), Institutional integrity in health care (pp. 41-71). Dordrecht: Kluwer.

Baron, R. A., & Neuman, J. H. (1998). Workplace aggression—the iceberg beneath the tip of workplace violence: Evidence of its forms frequency, and targets. *Public Administration Quarterly, 21,* 446-464.

Bennett, R. J., & Robinson, S.L. (2000). The development of a measure of workplace deviance. *Journal of Applied Psychology, 85,* 349-360.

Chapman, J. (1993). Collegial support linked to reduction of job stress. *Nursing Management, 24*(5), 52-56.

Comer, D. (1991). Organizational newcomers' acquisition of information from peers. *Management Communication Quarterly, 5,* 64-89.

Coombs, W. T. & Holladay, S. J. (2004). Understanding the aggressive workplace: Development of the workplace aggression tolerance questionnaire. *Communication Studies, 55,* 481-497.

Fritz, J. M. H. (2002). How do I dislike thee? Let me count the ways: Constructing impressions of troublesome others at work. *Management Communication Quarterly, 15,* 410-438.

Gant, L. M., Nagda, B. A., Brabson, H. V., Jayaratne, S., Chess, W. A., & Singh, A. (1993). Effects of social support and undermining on African American workers' perceptions of coworker and supervisor relationships and psychological well-being. *Social Worker, 38,* 158-164.

Gardyn, R. (2000). Who's the boss? *American Demographics, 22*(9), 52-57.

Giacalone, R. A., & Greenberg, J. (1997). *Antisocial behavior in organizations.* Thousand Oaks, CA: Sage.

Guadagnoli, E., & Velicer, W. F. (1988). Relation of sample size to the stability of component patterns. *Psychological Bulletin, 103,* 265-275.

Kimura, H. (2003). Overcome toxic management. *Nursing Management, 34,* 26-29.

Lutven-Sandvik, P. (2003). The communicative cycle of employee emotional abuse. *Management Communication Quarterly, 14,* 471-501.

Mann, R. B. (1993). *Behavior mismatch: How to manage "problem" employees whose actions don't match your expectations.* New York: AMACOM.

Monroe, C., Borzi, M. G., & DiSalvo, V. S. (1992). Managerial strategies for dealing with difficult subordinates. *Southern Communication Journal, 58,* 247-254.

Namie, G., & Namie, R. (2000). *The bully at work. What you can do to stop the hurt and reclaim your dignity on the job.* Naperville, Illinois: Sourcebooks.

Robinson, S. L., & Bennett, R. (1995). A typology of deviant workplace behaviors: A multi-dimensional scaling study. *Academy of Management Journal, 38,* 555-572.

Romesburg, H. C. (1984*). Cluster analysis for researchers.* Belmont, CA: Wadsworth.

Shepard, R. N. (1974). Representation of structure in similarity data: Problems and prospects. *Psychometricka, 39,* 373-421.

Sias, P. M., & Cahill, D. J. (1998). From coworkers to friends: The development of peer friendships in the workplace. *Western Journal of Communication, 62,* 273-299.

Tehrani, N. (Ed.) (2001), *Building a culture of respect: Managing bullying at work*. New
    York: Taylor & Francis
Vardi, Y., & Weitz, E. (Eds.) (2004). *Misbehavior in organizations: Theory, research, and
    management*. Mahwah, NJ: Lawrence Erlbaum Associates.

When Workplace Pregnancy Highlights Difference: Openings for Detrimental Gender and Supervisory Relations

3

Meina Liu & Patrice M. Buzzanell

When women are pregnant, take maternity leaves, and return to market work, they may experience changing workplace relationships. Although some changes may be positive in that employees find greater rapport with other workers who already have families (Buzzanell, 2003, 2004), many are negative in that they call into question pregnant employees' abilities to perform tasks, promotability, and organizational commitment (Halpert, Wilson, & Hickman, 1993; Hughes, 1991; Liu & Buzzanell, 2003; Swiss, 1996). Negative changes may provide the impetus for the development of problematic work relationships. Whether changes engender truly beneficial or problematic relationships, or types in between, depends on the interactants, tasks, organizational context, supportive work-family cultures, and other factors (e.g., Thompson, Beauvais, & Lyness, 1999). While researchers know that supportive cultures help lessen negative processes and outcomes for women transitioning into working motherhood (e.g., Brown, Ferrara, & Schley, 2002; Lyness, Thompson, Francesco, & Judiesch, 1999) and companies are trying to lure working mothers back to the office with benefits beyond telecommuting and flexible hours (Chaker, 1993), little is known about the ways these changes are reflected in everyday talk and actions which constitute relationships. In particular, there is a need to study the differences women notice in workplace conversations, expectations, interactions before pregnancy and after returns to paid work, and changes in relational dynamics with bosses and co-workers.

For instance, during pregnancy, some women find that the nature of conversations and relationships with bosses and coworkers change.[1] The women suggest that topics of conversation shift to health, fetus development, and child care arrangements rather than centering on work projects. Bosses may express concerns about reliability and work accomplishment. Coworkers may anticipate shouldering the burden of extra work when temporary help is not hired to cover the maternity leave taker's clients or accounts.

Moreover, taking maternity leaves poses challenging interactions as some women want, but may not know how, to negotiate leave arrangements that they feel are appropriate for their own and their families' needs (for maternity leave as role negotiation, see Miller, Jablin, Casey, Lamphear-Van Horn, & Ethington, 1996). These negotiations may not simply concern the length of time that they will be away from the office on a daily basis but also may involve the kinds of work interactions that continue throughout maternity leaves. They might find that they receive calls from their places of employment as bosses and coworkers have questions about standard operating procedures, project deadlines, clients, and other details. They may feel as though they are powerless to request additional time off or to suggest alternative work arrangements.

Finally, women's return to paid work brings with it issues that are different from concerns previously experienced during employment. Some women may undergo separation anxiety from their infants, worries about child-care arrangements, questions about breastfeeding opportunities, and challenges to their competency, reliability, and commitment. They also may find that they simply want to spend more time with their newborns than they had ever anticipated and decide not to return to work, at least not in the near future (e.g., Chaker, 2003).[2]

While laws and policies such as the Pregnancy Discrimination Act and the Family Medical Leave Act attempt to provide broad guarantees of jobs and of leaves, they do not and cannot address the micropractices of gender and supervisory relations in specific workplaces. In this essay, we use theory and research on gender and superior-subordinate relations as analytic lenses to see how different gendered and organizational associations imbued with power imbalances play off of each other within a particular workplace context. Although we focus on a single woman, Lucy (#83), our case is representative of other women who were not employed in managerial or professional occupations (e.g., they were pink collar workers, see Buzzanell, Liu, Bowers, Remke, Meisenbach, & Conn, 2003), and who engaged in discouraging workplace interactions, particularly superior-subordinate exchanges during their transitions into working motherhood (for details on this group as a whole, see Liu & Buzzanell, 2003).

Literature Review on Gender and Supervisory Relations

"Doing" Gender Relations

Feminist theories depict organizations as gendered constructions with masculine forms, values, and approaches inherent in every aspect including ways of doing work, interacting with others, and creating organizational structures (see Acker, 1990; Marshall, 1993). Masculine aspects are seen as commonsensical and natural, meaning that feminine behaviors and concerns often are trivialized, ignored, or penalized. While theorists display how masculinities are prioritized over femininities in everyday practices and organizing themes (e.g., Buzzanell, 1994, 1995), gender relations involve more complex processes in which both men and women actively participate in constructing, resisting, reproducing, and accommodating gendered meanings, values, and behaviors. Because analyses of gender relations portray subtle ways in which interactional parties routinely "do gender" (Ashcraft & Pacanowsky, 1996; West & Zimmerman, 1987), they may only take place in the situated communicative choices of interactants.

At the time of workplace pregnancy, maternity leave, and return to paid work, women are vulnerable to dominant constructions of ideal (masculine) workers, work habits, and meanings of professionalism because they (and their coworkers) may be especially aware of the extent to which they contrast with the ideal (see Fondas, 1995; Trethewey, 2000; Williams, 2000). Gender difference salience and the privileging of the masculine suggest that these women's identities may be restricted (and they may unwittingly constrict their identities) in ways that do disservice to their own best interests. Their worlds are constructed hegemonically, meaning that intersecting gender, discourse, and organizing processes are seen "as embodying simultaneously (and in a tension-filled and contradictory manner) the dynamic of power and resistance" (Mumby, 1997, p. 346). Thus, gender relations can be both empowering and disempowering as women create and find discursive openings for resistance, accommodation, and complicity with gendered norms as their different performances of femininities play off of and co-construct certain forms of masculinities.

"Doing" Supervisory Relations

Similar to the ways people do gender, employees also intersubjectively construct their workplace relationships. Workplace relationships are jointly constituted and reconstituted in everyday interactions. Of particular importance for promotability, employability, and quality of work life are superior-subordinate relations, one of the most popular areas of organizational communication research (Dansereau & Markham, 1987; Jablin, 1979, 1985). Affirmative boss-employee relationships and routine exchanges are associated with a number of positive outcomes for workers, including higher job satisfaction and reduction of work-family conflicts (e.g., Fairhurst, 2001; Frone, Russell, & Cooper, 1992; Greenhaus & Parasuraman, 1986; Kirby, 2000; Warren & Johnson, 1995). Although some studies have focused on difficult or negative relationships, such as work on downwardly spiraling boss-worker interactions, interactions with disliked others, low leader-member exchange, dysfunctional mentor-protégé relations, and abusive supervision (e.g., Bunker, Kram, & Ting, 2002; Eby, McManus, Simon, & Russell, 2000; Fairhurst, 2001; Feldman, 1999; Fritz, 2002; Manzoni & Barsoux, 1998; Solomon, 2002; Tepper, 2000), most research has focused on ways to construct and sustain productive and satisfying workplace relationships. In many cases, researchers and practitioners consider bosses accountable for effective superior-subordinate relations, but work on "managing your boss," office politics, career happiness, and the new career or social contract (including the "free agent" mentality) positions subordinates as responsible for work outcomes in general, and for their employability, workplace relationships, and careers (e.g., Arthur, Inkson, & Pringle, 1999; Gabarro & Kotter, 1993; Henderson, 2000; Hirsch, 1987; Nadesan & Trethewey, 2000).

Summary and Data Analytic Procedures

In order to focus on these micropractices that are so important and yet neglected, we locate our case analysis of one woman's transition from pregnancy through maternity leave and eventual return to paid work at the intersection of gender and supervisory relations. The meanings and conduct of both relations are socially constructed in terms of larger narratives of what should and does happen, what is considered permissible, and what is never questioned, as well as multiple participants' expectations for specific local contexts and mundane micropractices (e.g., routine conversations and enactment of standard operating procedures). We take our research participant's discourse as accurate and representative of her realities and of her relationships with others.

The main questions that we ask are whether and how pregnancy provides discursive openings for different types of positive and negative gendered workplace interactions that can have both short- and long-term consequences for both parties and for organizing processes in general. Although we focus specifically on negative boss-worker interactions, we also delve into the contrastive positive interactions Lucy experiences with her coworkers. These collegial relations provide counterpoints to her boss's contention that Lucy is unable to get along with others and to Lucy's argument that she could not do anything to convince management that they should accommodate her physical needs.

For this analysis, we utilized a grounded theory approach in which we read and reread Lucy's transcript, met repeatedly in face-to-face and computer mediated contexts, wrote memos about ideas and preliminary findings, and discussed themes or semantic patterns that occurred repeatedly within Lucy's interview (see Charmaz, 2000; Glaser & Strauss, 1967; Locke, 2001; for additional details about the interview protocol development and transcription procedures, see Buzzanell, 2003).

Synopsis of Lucy's Case

"Lucy" is a white, middle-class lab technician in a midwestern United States chemical company who was 25 years of age during her first and only pregnancy and maternity leave. She had been employed with her company for a year prior to her maternity leave, and this year was her first position in her occupation after her bachelor's degree was completed. She, like the other lab techs, was female and white while her boss was male and white.

Lucy defined maternity leave as, "It'd be, being allowed to stay home and take care of the child for a certain period of time and not losing your job. Be it paid or unpaid." She elaborated on her response by noting that some leaves should be longer than 6-8 weeks. Her company's policy was to provide 6 weeks of paid leave but "after that you can use your vacation time and then you could take unpaid leave." The maternity leave policy, along with "a whole list of their policies," was presented to all workers upon employment. Lucy said that she read through the policies before she took her job because she was planning to have children. Thus, there were no surprises when she became pregnant because policies were consistent with the handbook. When Lucy found out that she was pregnant, she went to the personnel director and "went through a briefing."

Lucy was ill at the beginning of her pregnancy and could not be on her feet for more than 8 hours at a time. When her company was unable or unwilling to accommodate her request for changes in work arrangements, Lucy's doctor put her on leave. After Lucy's morning sickness ended, she tried to return to work but still could not meet the physical demands:

> After my first three months, I felt great and things were wonderful. But I still could not be on my feet more than 8 hours which is normal for most pregnant women and the company still refused. So I stayed on maternity leave until the baby was born.

Lucy reiterated that she "would have liked to have gone back after the morning sickness was done. But they weren't willing to be flexible."

From 6 weeks of pregnancy through her maternity leave, Lucy did not engage in paid work. Toward the end of her leave, she spoke to company representatives about returning to work on a modified schedule or in a new position that was posted. Both flexibility in her current job and forwarding of her interest in the new job were denied:

> I later found out that there was a job opening coming up just after I would have gotten back, and they weren't even going to consider me for the position. When I found that out, that was also part of the reason why I didn't want to go back. Here I had an opportunity to have a regular 8-hour-a-day job and they wouldn't even think about it.

Lucy explained that she felt as though she had to leave her place of employment because there was neither work flexibility nor opportunities for promotion:

> After 4 weeks after the baby was born, I decided I was not going to go back to the company, because it would have been too hard working 12-hour shifts and working 6-on-1-off for days with the baby and trying to nurse. So I went in at 5 weeks and gave them my 2 weeks notice. Six weeks I was done and I took my 2-week vacation after that and was done being employed.

Despite these difficulties, leaving the company was not Lucy's first choice.[3] She wanted to engage in market work and still wishes that "they could have been more cooperative." During the initial months of her leave, she was "bored" ("I watched a lot of soap operas") and missed some coworkers along with the "guys that worked in the plant." She brought her son to visit when she cleared out her workspace: "I brought him in at 6 weeks when I went in to clean out my locker and everything. I brought in the baby and everyone was all excited. Yeah, 'oh what a big boy!'"

At the time of the interview, Lucy remarked that she still keeps in touch with a few of her former coworkers. In fact, she had been talking to a woman who was experiencing a high-risk pregnancy and was concerned about insurance and work options:

> In fact there's a lady who's pregnant now who's talking to me about how I did, 'cause she's on the maternity leave early, because her child's high risk, and she's thinking she might quit when she gets back. She's worried about, "Do I have to pay the money back that I got as disability?" And I said "no." I told her what I went through so she's a little bit more prepared.

Lucy was "glad" that she is engaging in paid work again. She was "self-employed now" and has been since her son was 18 months old. Lucy and her husband began talking about her starting her own business a year prior to the time she first began to take on projects. Even though she has her own business, Lucy was considering other work options: "I'm looking at going into teaching, maybe using my degree to teach...I like to work."

Case Analysis from a Gendered Supervisory Relations Lens

From the beginning, Lucy's experiences with her supervisor can be considered problematic. In contrast with her enjoyable coworker interactions, she was never able to get along with her supervisor during her two years of working in the chemical company. While she developed noticeably stronger rapport with her coworkers during her pregnancy and maternity leave, it also was a time when conflict with her supervisor escalated and eventually led to an impasse. Lucy ended up quitting her job despite the fact that she perceived herself as competent, qualified, and "would have been thrilled to go back [to work]." Analysis of Lucy's case reveals conflict escalation patterns and consequences with her supervisor that contrasted with the positive relationships she enjoyed with her coworkers and "guys at the plant."

Conflict Escalation Patterns and Consequences

According to Lucy, her unsatisfactory relationship with her supervisor was "due to a conflict of wills so to speak":

> Before [my maternity leave], my boss and I did not get along. I received, when I had my one year rating right before I got pregnant, even though I was probably considered the best lab tech, I mean, I had no problems with anyone, he told me I didn't work well with others And that kind of floored me. That I could not understand. But he and I did not get along, due to a conflict of wills, so to speak. So I don't think we got along well before. And during, I wasn't there long enough to have him get really mad. And I haven't seen him since the baby was born…I don't really want to.

Lucy offered no details about her alleged problems with others in the workplace. She might not have asked her supervisor for specifics because she was "floored" or stunned about the performance appraisal and had anticipated an evaluation of "best lab tech." Indeed, there might not have been anything explicit to coincide with the evaluation. As Manzoni and Barsoux (1998; see also Solomon, 2002) point out, difficulties with supervisors can begin for petty or irrational reasons that would be difficult to describe. These difficulties escalate if left unchecked and subordinates often become demoralized or leave the organization. Lucy attributed problems to a "conflict of wills" and not getting along.

Based on her evaluation, Lucy seemed to have anticipated further unfavorable exchanges with her supervisor. Although she "was excited" about her pregnancy, she reported, "I didn't let my supervisor know until I'd sit down and talked [with the other lab techs]." Later, Lucy "was very sick" and "needed to be off [her] feet as much as possible" according to her doctor's note, but "the company refused to follow that":

As I said, they don't, they require you to work 12 hours, we get two 15-minute breaks and a half hour lunch and that would be the only time that I could have been off my feet. Otherwise, I would be on my feet constantly and there was just no way. Plus, I worked at a chemical company, working with some pretty bad things, and I don't think the quality of the lab at work was that high and I don't think it was that safe.

Because there was no workplace accommodation, even in minimally acceptable ways, Lucy went on maternity leave as early as the first trimester. Yet her absence from the workplace did not lessen difficulties in an already strained superior-subordinate relationship.

For instance, the work-related interruptions caused by Lucy's "premature" maternity leave seemed to have upset. Lucy's supervisors: "They [her supervisors] would call and say 'Well, when are you coming back! When are you coming back!'" Lucy considered these exchanges to be "a kind of harassment of sorts." After she "kept explaining to them 'Well, if you're willing to cut my hours back, I would come' and they refused," Lucy's doctor "finally sat down and called [her] supervisor and told him to quit [calling]," which lessened the conflictual exchanges temporarily. As Lucy said, "Once the doctor explained, 'She's not coming back until after the baby's born,' then it was fine."

Just because "it was fine" did not mean the conflict between Lucy and her supervisor was resolved. Not only did her supervisor refuse to be flexible with the 12-hour working shift, but when "there was a job opening coming up just after [Lucy] would have gotten back," which was "an opportunity to have a regular 8 hour day," he "would not consider [Lucy] for the position" despite her qualifications "as the only one working at that time who had a degree." Seeing "no hope in advancing anywhere in the company," and "no way" to accept the rigid working hours, Lucy ended up quitting her job toward the end of her maternity leave. At the time of her interview, she had started up a business but was thinking about "using my degree to teach." She seemed uncertain about where her career was headed but she enjoyed the activity of work:

I want to work, I like to work. I don't need to, but I'd like to work…And I don't have a problem with leaving the child with someone, because I have some very good sitters. Very good people to take care of him. And family, so that's nice.

On the surface, Lucy's problematic relationship with her boss might simply have been a "conflict of wills" or interpersonal conflict that eventually affected resource allocation (e.g., performance evaluations, promotion opportunities, and, perhaps, work arrangement flexibility). However, there were hints that the relations were gendered in at least a couple of ways.

First, Lucy seemed to have some masculine qualities that might have bothered her supervisor: she was capable, confident, assertive, not very compliant (e.g., she stipulated that her return to work would necessitate changes in how her and when work was done), perhaps arrogant (e.g., she noted that she was the best lab tech and the only one with a degree), and interested in working and keeping busy outside the home (for masculine characteristics, see Marshall, 1993). She wanted to engage in paid work so that she had "something educational and intelligent to do." In her demeanor and actions, she may have defied gendered expectations (e.g., women who are interested in engaging in paid work for non-economic reasons are viewed negatively, see Riggs, 1997). She had checked the maternity leave policy before accepting a job at the company because she planned a pregnancy and actively sought information from others before telling her boss (actions that may have disturbed the chain of command and information flow in a bureaucratized office):

> But a couple people knew I was pregnant before, a couple of the other lab techs knew, and we had talked about it because one had gone through the maternity leave, the process of the maternity leave, before so we talked about that, but other than that, no [I didn't talk to others]. I didn't let my supervisor know until after I'd sat down and talked.

Lucy's interview did not provide evidence about the extent to which her assertive qualities might have defied her supervisor's gendered expectations and possibly engendered a problematic relationship (for ways that subordinates' behaviors might be perceived negatively, see Fritz, 2002; Solomon, 2002). In addition, the influence tactics she reported, particularly her use of persistence and repetition (e.g., "I would keep explaining to them 'well, if you're willing to cut my hours back, I would come back...'"), are considered as defiant and are rarely chosen by most subordinates (Keys & Case, 1990; see also Kipnis, Schmidt, & Wilkinson, 1980, for ways subordinates may try to influence superiors). So the ways she seemed to engage in influence attempts were neither feminine nor respectful of traditional hierarchical relations.

Second, the workplace was masculine in its establishment of rules and procedures from which there could not be deviations. Leave policies were outlined in the employee handbook and were followed "by the book." Lucy said that "the company refused to follow that [doctor's instructions] so they put me on maternity leave as of six weeks." Throughout the interview, Lucy maintained that the company was absolutely inflexible about work hours and work conditions: "they weren't willing to be flexible." When Lucy had to stay home to avoid the long work hours and detrimental work conditions that she believed would harm her health and the baby, her supervisors "were just asking 'when are you coming back,' 'when can you come back to work' is all they just kept on saying."

Companies that align with traditional themes of cause-effect linear thinking, separation and autonomy, competitive individualism, and efficiency-oriented thinking often find it difficult to deviate from these themes and locate alternative, particularly cooperative and case-by-case, ways of processing situations (Buzzanell, 1994). In this kind of thinking, if managers had accommodated Lucy, they would have had to assist others. It must have been simpler not to change procedures. Lucy kept asserting: "I really didn't have a choice…I just, it wouldn't have been my choice." But Lucy had no real choice (for lack of choice, see Williams, 2000). Her own, and presumably others', desires to combine both work and family simply were not organizational priorities.

As a result of this gendered organizing process reading, it was likely that the conflict escalation was not personal at all, certainly not a "conflict of wills," but the result of a traditionally masculine workplace. Lucy herself may have fallen into the trap of impersonality. She justified coworkers' lack of much personal talk by saying that they were always so busy. She often referred to "they" and "the company" rather than the singular form of "he" or "she." She tried to change her situation by herself and only turned to coworkers for maternity leave advice behind the scenes. She neither considered other ways of transforming the workplace nor enlarging her bargaining range (i.e., the spread between the negotiators' resistance points is incompatible, see Lewicki, Saunders, & Minton, 1999). In short, she was unwilling to change her resistance point (which would have involved feminine qualities of being compliant and docile) as was her boss. In cases such as these where there is no flexibility on either party's part, the interactions could only lead to a stalemate (i.e., when the negotiators fail to reach an agreement or resolve the conflict, see Lewicki et al., 1999).

Lucy's inability to locate the source of problematic relations with her boss at the time of her transition into working motherhood meant that she could not derive adequate solutions to remedy her difficulties. In the highly gendered workplace where occupational sex differences ("all the lab techs were female and all the superiors and that were male") and gendered thinking were commonplace, traditional patterns of male dominance and female subordination were normalized. So taken-for-granted were these gendered patterns that Lucy still could not put her finger on what went wrong almost two years after the events: "I just, I didn't know if it was the maternity leave, or just conflicts between the people. I don't know." Lucy was, nevertheless, aware of the fact that everything was done by the book, procedures were standardized, work was prioritized over everything else, and conversations were tied to "important" issues:

> Interviewer: Did your conversations change with people at work after they knew you were pregnant?
>
> Lucy: Not really, because it's a lot of, everything out there, there's so much that you have to get done. Everything is more work related than anything.

In a gendered workplace, problematic boss and pregnant worker relations may be related more to dominant masculine values that are in conflict with feminine values and needs than with individual people.[4]

Positive Coworker Relationships

Although the focus of this essay is gendered supervisory relations as micropractices leading to the perception of problematic work relationships, a brief analysis of Lucy's coworker relations provides insight into how the workplace could be organized differently. Lucy's interactions with her supervisor and company representatives were markedly different from those with her coworkers and the guys at the plant: "The guys at the plant, a majority of the workers at the company where I worked were men, and they were very sweet." In contrast with the exclusively "work-related" interactions with her superiors, Lucy seemed to engage in considerably more personal, informal, feminine communication, and detailed interactions with her peers (for feminine communication styles, see Wood, 2001). Lucy used coworker relationships as sources of information and support. Before Lucy would start conversations with her superiors regarding pregnancy and maternity leave, she first consulted other lab techs who had gone through the same process. When Lucy's superiors failed to make any effort to accommodate her requests and needs, "the guys at the plant" offered support, work accommodations, and positive responses to her news about her pregnancy:

> Lucy: Everybody was "Congratulations," "When you due?," "How are you feeling?" Everybody was very positive about it.
>
> Interviewer: How did you feel about their reactions?
>
> Lucy: I was happy that everybody was very supportive, very positive.
>
> Interviewer: Were there any other changes in others' behaviors?
>
> Lucy: The guys at the plant, a majority of the workers at the company where I worked were men, and they were very sweet. They would come move the heavy tanks, so I wouldn't have to do that. They offered a little bit more to help, so I wouldn't get hurt. So they were a little bit more protective.
>
> Interviewer: What did you think about these changes in behavior?
>
> Lucy: That was very nice of them, because it was probably best I didn't move big helium tanks like that. It was probably safer to have them do that, and it was nice that they were willing to.
>
> Interviewer: Did you have to ask, or did they just volunteer?
>
> Lucy: They volunteered. And they even went out of their way not to smoke around me and things like that. They actually made an effort.

In these passages, Lucy indicated that she did get along with her coworkers and other personnel at the plant (a counterargument to her boss's claim that she did not get along with others). She also implied that there was a supportive non-managerial community in which people engaged in caring behaviors, exhibited happiness at others' good news, and embodied positive interactions of connection and nurturance that were opposite of supervisory and managerial employees' behaviors. The distinctions were so prominent that one might assume, from Lucy's description, that there were two subgroups in this organization (see differentiation lens of culture, Martin, 1992). The coworker subgroup mitigated the rules-orientation and control values of the managerial subgroup. They resisted impersonalization and standardization of procedures by passing information from one pregnant woman to another, by organizing celebrations for personal events, and by marking significant life course events. For instance, Lucy's coworkers "sent flowers and a balloon," "a couple of presents and kept in touch," and visited her (for workplace community celebrations, see Lamphere, 1985). They carved out space to create an alternative personalized workplace within a highly bureaucratized structure. As such, these kinds of "offstage" behaviors that were unobserved by power holders could be considered resistance. Like Murphy's (1998) study on covert strategies of resistance among flight attendants, Lucy and her coworkers voiced opinions to one another (despite the heavy work load that left little time for coworker conversation), prepared themselves for confrontations, and resisted the gendered hierarchy. However, these discourses of camaraderie and resistance were private. Lucy and her coworkers (apparently) never considered developing coalitions to change their situation.

With regard to problematic interactions between supervisors and employees, the micropractices and macrostructures of the gendered workplace coalesced into taken-for-granted procedures, exchanges, and interactions that rendered pregnant women powerless in the public forum. However, they retained some power through information sharing and feminine communication patterns. Lucy herself not only resisted in ways similar to her coworkers but quit her job when the company refused to make any accommodations to her physical needs. She felt that she had exhausted every legitimate means available by requesting accommodations and by applying for a regular job.

In short, a brief analysis of Lucy's perceptions of interactions with coworkers reveals that there were workplace relations that not only contrasted with management's impersonality and inflexibility but that enabled workers to engage in covert resistance through information sharing, assistance with tasks, and celebrations of life events. Thus, workplace relations were demarcated along subgroup lines into problematic and masculine, and unproblematic and feminine. Furthermore, the boss and coworker differences discredited Lucy's words that her difficulties with her boss were due to a "conflict of wills" (interpersonal conflict and relationship) and, perhaps, not due to her pregnancy and maternity leave. There seemed to be much more going on in this case than even Lucy realized.

Discussion

Analysis of Lucy's case displays how workplace pregnancy, maternity leave, and return to paid work may exacerbate already strained relations between supervisors and pregnant workers. While one reading of the case would suggest that Lucy's difficulties were due only to interpersonal conflict, or a "conflict of wills," alternative readings show how gendered expectations of individuals, work, and organizational cultures legitimize standardization of procedures and interactions that can prove detrimental to individuals' and some group members' (e.g., female workers') needs. Accommodations to the coworker group simply did not fit dominant cultural thinking.

On a broader level, this analysis calls communication scholars to question where gender, organizing, and discourse intersect and produce situations that render some parties in problematic workplace relationships vulnerable. In their daily interactions, participants may be "doing gender" in ways that seem so normal to them that gender explanations for problematic relations become invisible. Gendered organizations influence structures, procedures, and participants' abilities to voice concerns.

While there are some promising implications of this analysis for problematic relations in general and gendered supervisory communication in particular, as noted in endnote #4, this analysis was based solely on one voice, namely, that of Lucy, and lacked details about different parties, the company, work, and other points that would have contextualized the material and our interpretations. Nevertheless, it shows how traditional assumptions about what might be happening in interpersonal conflicts could be gendered on macro and microlevels.

With regard to theoretical and pragmatic implications, it is possible that superior-subordinate difficulties arise when individuals communicating from one subgroup assume that members of the other would interact with values, approaches, and emotions similar to their own. Lucy's inability to achieve compliance with her goals despite repetition could be because claims emanating from the feminine, worker/subordinate, private subgroup simply were not admissible or legitimate in supervisors' thinking. However, Lucy also did not seem to use effective influence tactics in the masculine realm of work. Effective tactics include reasoning, friendliness, coalition building, and appealing to higher authorities (see Kipnis & Schmidt, 1982). She sought information from coworkers but did not use any of these data to engage in bargaining with her supervisors (i.e., she made some initial requests, and when frustrated, she chose to avoid her supervisor but was still indirectly confrontational through her doctor as advocate). Finally, she seemed to have coworker support but never mobilized this support to make change for herself and the other female workers in her company.

In short, labeling supervisory relations as problematic without considering the ways micropractices and macroprocesses might be gendered not only neglects an important layer of analysis but also precludes opportunities to derive implications that can handle the complexities of everyday workplace situations.

Author Notes

1. Most women in the data set of 102 interviews on maternity leave from which this single case of "Lucy" was drawn reported changes in interactions and, particularly, in conversational topics as their pregnancies and upcoming maternity leaves were foremost in coworkers' and bosses' minds. Transitions into working motherhood may also be prominent in workers' thoughts. Farley-Lucas (2000) noted that working women use a number of communicative strategies to bring motherhood issues into workplace conversations. However, Brown, Ferrara, & Schley (2002) found that the large majority of their 43 participants indicated no changes in coworkers' or supervisors' attitudes (and, presumably, behaviors) toward them after the birth of their children and no detrimental effects on evaluations of their performance capabilities.

2. According to the U.S. Census Bureau, the percentage of new mothers who work fell four percentage points in 2000 from 59% in 1998 and has not risen since (Chaker, 2003).

3. Lucy reported feelings of job dissatisfaction and discouragement about work and career opportunities on the brief survey that accompanied her interview. She also indicated that she felt secure in her job prior to her maternity leave.

4. It is important to note that this analysis is based only on Lucy's version of what happened. There is no information about what behaviors she could have enacted that might have led to her less-than-outstanding performance evaluation. There is evidence that her behaviors could be viewed as stubborn and demanding (e.g., her repeated insistence that the company accommodate her pregnancy). She may have been a difficult employee for her boss to manage. In addition, she could also have been a troublemaker from the organization's standpoint (with this organization's desire for control). At the time of the interview, she was advising a pregnant employee of the company she left:

> In fact, there's a lady who's pregnant now who's talking to me about how I did, 'cause she's on the maternity leave early, because her child's high risk. And she's thinking she might quit when she gets back. She's worried about, "Do I have to pay the money back that I got as disability?" and I said "no." I told her what I went through so she's a little bit more prepared.

In addition to lack of details about Lucy, there was little information about the boss. He may have been close to retirement or uninterested in retaining Lucy. He could have been under tremendous pressure to increase work efficiencies and regularize scheduling. With an all-female division, he may not have wanted to set maternity leave precedents by allowing flexible work arrangements, particularly part-time arrangements.

Finally, Lucy may have been fighting traditional gendered processes on two fronts, work and family. She tried to persuade her boss and other supervisors to accommodate her needs while pregnant but her requests were denied despite doctor's notes. Later, company representatives phoned her at home and wanted to know when she would return to the office. It took a doctor's call to her boss to end these phone calls.

Besides the work front, there also were traditional gender expectations in her family's desire to see her stay at home with her young child. Her father-in-law created work projects to keep her busy:

I think they're glad I have something to do. In fact, the work I'm doing is for my father-in-law, and I almost think he came up with this project to keep me from bouncing off walls, 'cause I was really getting, I need something educational and intelligent to do once in a while. But I think he came up with that. But I think they're glad I'm working part time, and they're also glad I'm at home. They'd rather me be at home.

References

Acker, J. (1990). Hierarchies, jobs, bodies: A theory of gendered organizations. *Gender & Society, 4,* 139-158.

Arthur, M. B., Inkson, K., & Pringle, J. K. (1999). *The new careers: Individual action and economic change.* London: Sage.

Ashcraft, K.L., & Pacanowsky, M. (1996). A woman's worst enemy: Reflections on a narrative of organizational life. *Journal of Applied Communication Research, 24,* 217-239.

Brown, T. J., Ferrara, K., & Schley, N. (2002). The relationship of pregnancy status to job satisfaction: An exploratory analysis. *Journal of Business and Psychology, 17,* 63-72.

Bunker, K. A., Kram, K. E., & Ting, S. (2002). The young and the clueless. *Harvard Business Review, 80* (9), 80-87.

Buzzanell, P. M. (1994). Gaining a voice: Feminist perspectives in organizational communication. *Management Communication Quarterly, 7,* 339-383.

Buzzanell, P. M. (1995). Reframing the glass ceiling as a socially constructed process: Implications for understanding and change. *Communication Monographs, 62,* 327-354.

Buzzanell, P. M. (2003). A feminist standpoint analysis of maternity and maternity leave for women with disabilities. *Women and Language, 26* (2), 53-65.

Buzzanell, P. M. (2004). *De/Reconstructing transitions into working motherhood: Productive tensions in female managers' discourses and practices.* Unpublished manuscript.

Buzzanell, P. M., Liu, M., Bowers, V. A., Remke, R., Meisenbach, R., & Conn, C. (2003, May). *Discourses of pink-collar maternity leaves: Standardization, strategic control, and disability.* Paper presented to the Organizational Communication Division of the International Communication Association conference. Held in San Diego, CA.

Chaker, A. M. (2003, December 30). Luring moms back to work. *Wall Street Journal,* p. D1.

Charmaz, K. (2000). Grounded theory: Objectivist and constructivist methods. In N. K. Denzin & Y. S. Lincoln (Eds.), *Handbook of qualitative research* (2nd ed., pp. 509-535). Thousand Oaks, CA: Sage.

Dansereau, F., & Markham, S. E. (1987). Superior-subordinate communication: Multiple levels of analysis. In F. M. Jablin, L. L. Putnam, K. H. Roberts, and L. W. Porter (Eds.), *Handbook of organizational communication* (pp. 343-388). Newbury Park, CA: Sage.

Eby, L. T., McManus, S. E., Simon, S. A., & Russell, J. (2000). The protégé's perspective regarding negative mentoring experiences: The development of a taxonomy. *Journal of Vocational Behavior, 57,* 1-21.

Fairhurst, G. T. (2001). Dualisms in leadership research. In F. M. Jablin & L. L. Putnam (Eds.), *The new handbook of organizational communication* (pp. 379-439). Thousand Oaks, CA: Sage.

Farley-Lucas, B. (2000). Communicating the (in)visibility of motherhood: Family talk and the ties to motherhood with/in the workplace. *The Electronic Journal of Communication/La Revue Electronique de Communication, 10* (3/4). Retrieved January 22, 2003, from http://www.cios.org/www/ejcrec2.htm

Feldman, D. C. (1999). Toxic mentors or toxic protégés? A critical re-examination of dysfunctional mentoring. *Human Resource Management Review, 9*, 247-278.

Fondas, N. (1995). The biological clock confronts complex organizations: Women's ambivalence about work and implications for feminist management research. *Journal of Management Inquiry, 4*, 57-65.

Fritz, J. M. H. (2002). How do I dislike thee? Let me count the ways: Constructing impressions of troublesome others at work. *Management Communication Quarterly, 15*, 410-438.

Frone, M. R., Russell, M., & Cooper, M. L. (1992). Antecedents and outcomes of work-family conflict: Testing a model of the work-family interface. *Journal of Applied Psychology, 77*, 67-78.

Gabarro, J. J., & Kotter, J. P. (1993). Managing your boss. *Harvard Business Review, 71* (3), 150-157.

Glaser, B. G., & Strauss, A. L. (1967). *The discovery of grounded theory*. Chicago: Aldine.

Greenhaus, J. H., & Parasuraman, S. (1986). A work-nonwork interactive perspective of stress and its consequences. *Journal of Organizational Behavior Management, 8* (2), 37-60.

Halpert, J. A., Wilson, M. L., & Hickman, J. L. (1993). Pregnancy as a source of bias in performance appraisals. *Journal of Organizational Behavior, 14*, 649-663.

Henderson, S. J. (2000). "Follow your bliss": A process for career happiness. *Journal of Counseling and Development, 78*, 305-315.

Hirsch, P. (1987). *Pack your own parachute: How to survive mergers, takeovers, and other corporate disasters*. Reading, MA: Addison-Wesley.

Hughes, K. A. (1991, February 6). Pregnant professionals face pressures at work as attitudes toward them shift. *Wall Street Journal*, pp. B1, B5.

Jablin, F. M. (1979). Superior-subordinate communication: The state of the art. *Psychological Bulletin, 86*, 1201-1222.

Jablin, F. M. (1985). Task/work relationships: A life-span perspective. In M. L. Knapp & G. R. Miller (Eds.), *Handbook of interpersonal communication* (pp. 615-654). Newbury Parks, CA: Sage.

Keys, B., & Case, T. (1990). How to become an influential manager. *Academy of Management Executive, 4*, 38-50.

Kipnis, D., & Schmidt, S. (1982). *Profile of organizational influence strategies*. San Diego: University Associates.

Kipnis, D., Schmidt, S, & Wilkinson, I. (1980). Intraorganizational influence tactics: Explorations in getting one's way. *Journal of Applied Psychology, 65*, 440-452.

Kirby, E. L. (2000). Should I do as you say, or do as you do?: Mixed messages about work and family. *The Electronic Journal of Communication /La Revue Electronique de Communication* 10 (3/4). Retrieved January 19, 2003, from http://www.cios.org/www/ejcrec2.htm

Lamphere, L. (1985). Bringing the family to work: Women's culture on the shop floor. *Feminist Studies, 11*, 518-540.

Lewicki, R. J., Saunders, D. M., & Minton, J. W. (1999). *Negotiation*. Boston: Irwin/McGraw-Hill.

Liu, M., & Buzzanell, P. M. (2003, November). *Workplace pregnancy and maternity leave: Supervisory abuse within unethical workplace interactions*. Paper presented to the National Communication Association conference. Held in Miami, FL.

Locke, K. (2001). *Grounded theory in management research*. London: Sage.

Lyness, K. S., Thompson, C. A., Francesco, A. M., & Judiesch, M. K. (1999). Work and pregnancy: Individual and organizational factors influencing organizational commitment, timing of maternity leave, and return to work. *Sex Roles, 41,* 485-508.

Manzoni, J. F., & Barsoux, J. L. (1998) The set-up-to-fail syndrome. *Harvard Business Review, 76* (2), 101-113.

Marshall, J. (1993). Viewing organizational communication from a feminist perspective: A critique and some offerings. In S. A. Deetz (Ed.), *Communication yearbook 16* (pp. 122-141). Newbury Park, CA: Sage.

Martin, J. (1992). *Cultures in organizations: Three perspectives.* New York: Oxford University Press.

Miller, V. D., Jablin, F. M., Casey, M. K., Lamphear-Van Horn, M., & Ethington, C. (1996). The maternity leave as a role negotiation process. *Journal of Managerial Issues, 8,* 286-309.

Mumby, D. K. (1997). The problem of hegemony: Rereading Gramsci for organizational communication studies. *Western Journal of Communication, 61,* 343-375.

Murphy, A. G. (1998). Hidden transcripts of flight attendant resistance. *Management Communication Quarterly, 11,* 499–535.

Nadesan, M. H., & Trethewey, A. (2000). Performing the enterprising subject: Gendered strategies for success. *Text & Performance Quarterly, 20,* 223-250.

Riggs, J. M. (1997). Mandates for mothers and fathers: Perceptions of breadwinners and care givers. *Sex Roles, 37,* 565-580.

Solomon, M. (2002). *Working with difficult people.* Paramus, NJ: Prentice Hall.

Swiss, D. J. (1996). *Women breaking through: Overcoming the final 10 obstacles at work.* Princeton, NJ: Peterson's/Pacesetter Books.

Tepper, B. J. (2000). Consequences of abusive supervision. *Academy of Management Journal, 43,* 178-190.

Thompson, C. A., Beauvais, L. L., & Lyness, K. S. (1999). When work-family benefits are not enough: The influence of work-family culture on benefit utilization, organizational attachment, and work-family conflict. *Journal of Vocational Behavior, 54,* 392-415.

Trethewey, A. (2000). Revisioning control: A feminist critique of disciplined bodies. In P. M. Buzzanell (Ed.), *Rethinking organizational and managerial communication from feminist perspectives* (pp. 107-127). Thousand Oaks, CA: Sage.

Warren, J. A., & Johnson, P. J. (1995). The impact of workplace support on work-family role strain. *Family Relations, 44,* 163-169.

West, C., & Zimmerman, D. H. (1987). Doing gender. *Gender & Society, 1,* 125-151.

Williams, J. (2000). *Unbending gender: Why family and work conflict and what to do about it.* New York: Oxford University Press.

Wood, J. T. (2001). *Gendered lives: Communication, gender, and culture* (4th ed.). Belmont, CA: Wadsworth.

4 | Workplace Friendship Deterioration

Patricia M. Sias

"O my friends, there is no friend." This famed statement, attributed to Aristotle, provides the central focus of Derrida's (1997) examination of the politics of friendship. The statement, and Derrida's treatise, suggests that the inherent political nature of interpersonal relationships renders true friendship an impossible ideal. In the work context, rife with political dynamics and implications, such politics are only exacerbated. As a consequence, friendships among work colleagues are particularly difficult to develop and maintain. This chapter addresses the failure of coworkers to maintain their workplace friendships. Toward this end, this chapter summarizes research on workplace friendship deterioration to date and provides several directions for future research in this area.

Summary of Existing Literature

Workplace Friendships

The term *workplace relationship* refers to any relationship one has with someone with whom they work, such as supervisor-subordinate, peer, and mentoring relationships (Sias, Krone, & Jablin, 2002). These relationships often develop into affiliative bonds known as *"friendships."* Friendships are unique workplace relationships in two primary ways: (1) friendships are *voluntary*— although individuals do not typically choose with whom they work, they do choose which of those individuals to befriend; and (2) friendships have a *personalistic focus* in which individuals come to know and treat each other as whole persons, rather than simply workplace role occupants (Wright, 1984). Thus, employees choose to spend time with their friends, both at and away from the workplace, and they elect to spend time together beyond that required by their organizational roles (Sias & Cahill, 1998).

Because of their central role in the organizing process, workplace friendships have a variety of consequences for both organizations and individual employees. Effective workplace friendships contribute to the work experience of individual employees by providing sources of emotional and instrumental social support (Kram & Isabella, 1985) and enjoyment (Fine, 1986). In addition, as Rawlins (1992) notes, "friends help in finding jobs and opportunities for promotions, provide support and third party influence on important decisions, and convey warnings about policy changes and 'rumblings upstairs'" (Rawlins, 1992, p. 165-166). Workplace friendships can also enhance individual creativity (Yager, 1997) and contribute to an employee's career development and advancement (Kram & Isabella, 1985; Rawlins, 1992). From the organization's perspective, healthy workplace friendships can enhance employee commitment to the organization (Rawlins, 1992), increase morale, and reduce turnover (Kram & Isabella, 1985).

Although extant literature tends to highlight positive aspects of workplace friendships, these relationships can also have a "dark side." Fine (1986) points out, for example, that close workplace friendships provide organizations with an unobtrusive form of control over employees by "providing a personal motivation to accept the world as it is, rather than disassociate oneself through alienation" (p. 201). Similarly, Sias and Cahill (1998) found that very close friendships between coworkers often keep employees "chained" to unhealthy and dysfunctional work environments, preventing individuals from leaving such environments because they do not want to leave their friend. Bridge and Baxter (1992) revealed a number of tensions inherent in close workplace friendships that, if not appropriately managed, can destroy those relationships. Thus, maintaining functional workplace friendships is a constant challenge and struggle for the relationship partners, a struggle failed by many.

A small, but growing, body of literature addresses such failures, primarily focusing on why and how workplace friendships deteriorate, and the consequences of such deterioration both for the relationship partners and for the organizations in which they work. The importance of such a focus is indicated by recognition of relationships as central to the organizing process: Deterioration of relationships means deterioration of organizational functioning.

Bridge and Baxter (1992) were the first scholars to specifically examine workplace friendships, what they termed "blended relationships." Using a dialectic framework, they examined the tensions that arise from combining the expectations of the friend role with those of the coworker role. These dialectics derive from the politics inherent to the blending of these roles; individuals in any organization constantly negotiate their own goals and interests and the goals and interests of their workgroup and the larger organization as they go about their work. To the extent that these goals and interests conflict, the resulting tensions challenge the relationship and, if not effectively managed, can destroy it.

Bridge and Baxter (1992) identified five primary dialectical tensions individuals experience in their workplace friendships. The *equality-inequality* tension refers to tensions between the friendship norms of equality and workplace constraints and expectations that constitute inequality (e.g., rank and hierarchy). The *impartiality and favoritism* tension refers to organizational norms of impartial and objective treatment of employees and friendship expectations of unconditional support. *Openness and closedness* refers to expectations of openness and honesty among friends on the one hand, and organizational expectations of confidentiality and caution about information-sharing on the other. *Autonomy and connection* refers to the benefits of contact for friends and the possibility that ongoing and daily contact among coworkers may provide little autonomy for the relationship partners, "jeopardizing their friendship through excessive connection" (Bridge & Baxter, 1992, p. 204). The *judgment and acceptance* tension refers to expectations of mutual affirmation and acceptance among friends, and organizational requirements of critical evaluation.

With a variety of colleagues, I have pursued a line of research focused on examining those relationships that do not survive these dialectical tensions and other challenges. These projects center on three primary issues: (1) why workplace friendships deteriorate, (2) how individuals disengage from workplace friendships, and (3) the consequences of workplace friendship deterioration.

Why Workplace Friendships Deteriorate

In the first study to examine workplace friendship deterioration, Sias, Heath, Perry, Silva and Fix (2004) examined employees' narrative accounts of their deterioration experiences. Our analysis identified five primary causes of workplace friendship deterioration. *Problem personality* refers to events in which individuals found they could no longer bear an annoying personality trait exhibited by their relationship partners. Interestingly, often this personality trait was what attracted the individual to that particular coworker in the first place.

Distracting life events are incidents in which the excessive intrusion of a coworker's personal problems (e.g., marital problems, health issues) into the workplace precipitated the deterioration of a workplace friendship. These narratives are related to the "problem personality" narratives in that both respondents perceived the inability to separate work and personal lives as rooted in a personality defect. However, in these situations it was the fact that the events were distracting from the coworker's work performance, not the personality defect, that was viewed as the cause of the deterioration.

Conflicting expectations refer to events in which coworkers find their expectations regarding appropriate behavior to conflict with one another. For example, in the study of interest, such situations included not supporting a friend's opinion in a meeting or receiving a surprisingly negative annual evaluation from a supervisor/friend.

Promotion refers to events in which one of the partners is promoted to a position of authority over the other. In these instances, respondents decrease the closeness of their relationships with coworkers because they fear others will perceive favoritism.

Finally, *betrayal* refers to situations in which one of the partners feels their coworkers have betrayed their trust, typically by sharing with others information a partner has shared in confidence. Although some of the reasons for deterioration described above can apply to any interpersonal relationship (e.g., problem personality, betrayal), the others are unique to workplace friendships.

As seen above, workplace friendships deteriorate for a variety of reasons. Personality and distracting life events are actually the reverse of factors Sias and Cahill (1998) identified impacting workplace friendship *development*. In fact, our research suggests that in many cases, the same personality traits and life events that bring friends together may eventually cause the friendship to fall apart.

Certainly, an important factor in workplace friendship deterioration has to do with the inability of the relationship partners to manage dialectical tensions inherent to these types of "blended" relationships (Bridge & Baxter, 1992). Promotion, for example, introduces the "impartiality-favoritism" and "equality-inequality" dialectics into the friendship at the moment one partner is given formal authority over the other, exacerbating concerns the employees may have about appearances of favoritism. The "impartiality-favoritism" dialectic is also present in situations involving conflicting expectations (e.g., when one employee expects the favoritism presumed of friends but receives the impartiality expected from coworkers). These situations also involve the "judgment-acceptance" dialectic in which friends expect unconditional support from each other, while coworkers are required to critically evaluate each other.

While inherent to workplace friendships, dialectical tensions do not necessarily lead to relational deterioration. Indeed, many such relationships survive because the partners are able to manage the tensions (Bridge & Baxter, 1992). However, many do not, and another focus of my research program examines the disengagement process for those workplace friendships that do not survive. The following section describes the ways in which employees accomplish relational disengagement in the workplace.

Disengaging from Workplace Friendships

In addition to examining why workplace friendships deteriorate, my research program also focuses on *how* workplace friendships deteriorate, a necessarily communicative process. Consistent with other communication scholars (e.g., Duck & Pittman, 1994; Sigman, 1995), I conceptualize relationships as categories of meaning constituted in interaction. Relationships are communicative entities that depend on interaction for their existence and form (Duck & Pittman, 1994). Because communication constitutes and gives relationships their essences, relational transformation is a communicative process. Accordingly, studies of relational disengagement necessarily focus on how relationship transformation communicatively transpires.

Our work is grounded in existing research in the area of interpersonal relationships. This research suggests a variety of communication strategies that individuals use to disengage from interpersonal relationships. These strategies have two basic dimensions: directness and other-orientation (Baxter, 1985). The *directness* dimension refers to the extent to which individuals directly and explicitly discuss the transformation of the relationship. Direct strategies include *fait accompli* (explicit unilateral declaration to the partner that the relationship is over), *negotiated farewell* (explicit bilateral discussion between the partners that formally transforms the relationship), *state-of-the-relationship talk* (explicit discussion of problems and desire to transform the relationship) and *attributional conflict* (hostile discussion in which partners attribute blame to one another for the relationship problems). Indirect strategies are those by which an individual tries to terminate or degrade a relationship without directly talking about it such as *withdrawal* (reduction in intimacy and frequency of contact), *pseudo-de-escalation* (false declaration to the partner that one wants to change the nature of the relationship when, in fact, s/he really wishes to terminate the relationship), and *cost escalation* (negative behavior toward the partner that increases the relational costs). The *other-orientation* dimension refers to the extent to which an individual "attempts to avoid hurting the other party" (Baxter, 1985, p. 247). For example, direct strategies can exhibit concern for a partner's feelings, such as in the case of the negotiated farewell which lacks hostility; or they can exhibit a lack of concern about hurting the partner, as in cost escalation whereby partners force relational transformation by making the current state of the relationship too unpleasant and burdensome to maintain (Baxter, 1985).

The above strategies, however, were identified in studies of *non-work* relationships. One important way in which workplace relationships are distinct from non-work interpersonal relationships is that partners typically must continue to work together after their relationships have deteriorated. The deterioration process may be particularly difficult to negotiate in workplace relationships in which continued, frequent contact is required (e.g., complete exclusion or avoidance would be difficult, if not impossible).

Sias et al. (2004) found that respondents relied primarily on indirect and other-oriented forms of communication to disengage from workplace relationships. Among these options, people avoided talking about topics unrelated to work, and they stopped socializing outside of work (e.g., lunch, drinks after work). They also used nonverbal cues such as rudeness and a "snappy" tone of voice. Only rarely did individuals disengage from relationships via explicit and direct discussion.

A follow-up study (Sias & Perry, 2004) refined these categories. This study used a hypothetical scenario method asking respondents to indicate the likelihood of individuals using various communication tactics to disengage from a workplace friendship. The disengagement tactic items were gleaned from the interviews that formed the basis of the initial study (Sias et al., 2004). A principal components analysis of these items revealed that the items comprise three primary dimensions. *Cost escalation* refers to tactics in which an individual behaves in an intentionally negative way toward the partner. These would include, for example, expressing contempt by using a snide, snappy, or condescending tone of voice, interrupting or insulting the partner, talking about the coworker negatively behind his/her back, and the like.

Depersonalization refers to behavior by which individuals avoid interaction regarding personal issues with a coworker and avoid socializing with the coworker outside work, thus communicatively drawing a clear boundary between the work and personal spheres. Individuals, for example, will intentionally limit interaction to work-related issues only and cease extra-organizational activities such as lunching together or going out after work.

Finally, *state-of-the-relationship talk* involves direct and explicit discussion of the relationship transformation. This is accomplished via a conversation during which the partners agree to terminate the friendship aspect of their relationship to preserve the coworker relationship at a functional level.

Results of the Sias and Perry (2004) study revealed that, in general, respondents showed a clear preference for the depersonalization strategy. This strategy may be particularly effective for workplace relationship deterioration because it serves to remove the "personalistic focus" that tends to characterize close workplace friendships, while maintaining the relationship at a functional level. Sias and Cahill (1998) note that as workplace relationships become closer, partners begin to perceive and communicate with one another as whole persons and unique individuals, not merely role occupants (e.g., discussing topics unrelated to work, socializing outside the workplace, etc.). Such behavior expresses a recognition and appreciation of the partner as an individual. Communicatively constructing a boundary between work and personal spheres accomplishes the reverse; communicating only about, and only at, work removes the personal and individualistic focus and returns the partner's status to work role occupant only. At the same time, it is less face-threatening than cost escalation. Accordingly, this strategy enables the partners to both disengage from the relationships *and* fulfill their task requirements by allowing them to continue to communicate about work-related issues.

In contrast, Sias and Perry (2004) found that cost escalation was perceived as the strategy least likely to be used by individuals to disengage from a coworker relationship. Brown and Levinson's (1987) Politeness Theory provides insights into this finding. Politeness Theory encompasses the notion of *face* as introduced by Goffman (1967), which refers to an individual's public self-image. According to Goffman (1967), face is a fluid, rather than stable, phenomenon and must be continually attended to as interactants seek to achieve their message goals (Brown & Levinson, 1987). Concerns for face are reflected in communication that considers the other's feelings and desires. Threats to face are reflected in communication that shows little or no concern for the feelings of the hearer or that communicates dislike or disapproval. Other-oriented strategies, such as state-of-the-relationship talk, reflect a concern for the face of both the speaker and the hearer. Strategies that do not reflect an other-orientation (such as cost escalation) show little concern for face. Requirements to continue interaction after relational deterioration may make individuals hesitant to use any strategy that does not reflect an other orientation, regardless of the hierarchical status of the target, because to do so could impair their ability to perform their jobs effectively. Thus, the general avoidance of the cost escalation strategy is consistent with the notion that people who are required to continue interaction with those they dislike are careful not to destroy the relationship entirely by attending to the face concerns of the relationship partner. Such efforts are likely to prevent the relational deterioration from unduly impairing the partners' abilities to carry out their work.

Despite these efforts, however, the deterioration of workplace friendships results in a variety of negative consequences for the individuals involved and the organizations in which the relationships exist. The following section details these consequences.

Consequences of Workplace Friendship Deterioration

As many scholars note, relationships play an important and constitutive role in organizational processes. These scholars conceptualize organizations as systems of relationships, identifying relationships as the locus of organizing (e.g., Contractor & Grant,

1996; Wheatley, 1994). Thus, the deterioration of workplace relationships is of great consequence for both the individuals involved in the relationships and the organizations in which the relationships exist.

Our research has revealed a variety of consequences of workplace friendship deterioration. The deterioration of a workplace friendship always results in *emotional stress* for the individuals involved. These emotions are particularly difficult to manage because often the individuals' ex-friends were a primary source of emotional support. Among the emotional consequences identified by Sias et al. (2004) were feelings of isolation, frustration, anger, disappointment, and unhappiness.

Friendship deterioration can also *hinder employee job performance*. This typically results from the ways in which such deterioration harms the quality and quantity of communication between the coworkers. Our studies revealed that many individuals found it difficult to accomplish their formal tasks after friendship deterioration because that deterioration resulted in less frequent, and lower quality, communication with the former friend.

These problems can eventually become unbearable. As a consequence workplace friendship deterioration can lead to *turnover*. Sias et al., (2004) found that some individuals eventually left their jobs because the deterioration made working with their coworker unbearable.

Individuals also appear to learn general *relationship lessons* from their deterioration experiences. Sias et al. (2004), for example, found that the interpretation of deterioration as inevitable when one friend is promoted to a position of authority over the other taught respondents that promotion necessarily results in friendship deterioration. For others, the pain of friendship deterioration teaches them to be more cautious about befriending coworkers in the future.

Disengagement Strategy Choice

Our research has also examined the extent to which situational factors may influence disengagement strategy choice. In particular, Sias and Perry (2004) posited that strategy choice would be associated with both the relative hierarchical status of the partners and the cause of the deterioration.

The hierarchical status hypothesis was grounded in politeness theory, which as mentioned earlier, incorporates the notion of "face" (Brown & Levinson, 1987). The likelihood that an individual will communicate in ways that preserve face depends, however, on the amount of threat to face the person perceives in the first place. Such perceptions are highly contextualized and depend on the social context of the interaction. One contextual factor that can influence an individual's perceptions of threat is the perceived power of the other party (Baxter, 1985). Supervisors hold a position of formal authority and power (i.e., in the form of control of resources) over those they supervise. These subordinates will be motivated to reduce threat to the supervisor's esteem because of the supervisor's greater power. Thus, we reasoned that individuals may be more likely to use other-oriented strategies, such as state-of-the-relationship talk, when communicating a desire for decreased closeness to supervisors than they would when communicating the same to a peer or subordinate employee. In contrast, because cost shows contempt, not concern, for the other party, we expected employees to be less likely to use that tactic to disengage from a relationship with a supervisor than with a subordinate or peer employee.

Contrary to expectations, we found no relationship between relative hierarchical status and strategy choice. Respondents perceived individuals would rely primarily on depersonalization to disengage from relationships with their supervisors, their subordinate employees, and their peer coworkers. These results indicate that individuals are hesitant to use any strategy that does not reflect an other orientation, regardless of the hierarchical status of the target.

We have also examined the extent to which the reason for the deterioration (e.g., conflicting expectations, betrayal, etc.) is associated with the ways in which individuals choose to disengage from the friendship. Along these lines, Sias et al. (2004) found that deterioration related to promotion appeared to engender less negative emotions than deterioration caused by other factors, which appeared to make individuals less likely to use face-threatening disengagement strategies such as cost escalation. Similarly, Sias and Perry (2004) found that individuals would be more likely to use cost escalation in conflicting expectations and problem personality situations than in promotion or distracting life event situations. We also found that depersonalization was similarly associated with the reason for the deterioration. In particular, depersonalization was more likely to be used in betrayal, conflicting expectations, and problem personality situations than in promotion situations.

Shaver's (1985) model of attributing responsibility provides insights into these findings. This model suggests that an individual's response to a situation is associated with the extent to which one perceives an actor to have acted with intention and volition. Specifically, the more one perceives an actor to have committed an offensive act on his/her own volition, the more likely the observer will be to react negatively and punitively. An employee who chooses to behave in a manner that conflicts with his/her coworker's expectations (e.g., not supporting the coworker in a meeting) is likely to be perceived as responsible for that action. Similarly, in problem personality situations, individuals attribute a coworker's annoying behavior to that coworker's personality, rather than to an extenuating circumstance. This attribution of responsibility may prompt a negative or punitive response, such as cost escalation, from the relationship partner. Promotion, on the other hand, is an act officially carried out by the organization (management), rather than the promoted employee him/herself. Thus, responsibility for the event may not rest solely on the coworker. Similarly, individuals may feel some sympathy for coworkers involved in troublesome life events, particularly if the events are presumably not a result of the coworker's behavior. This attenuation of coworker responsibility may be less likely to elicit a punitive response from a relationship partner.

It is important to note, however, that although the Sias and Perry (2004) analysis indicated a statistically significant relationship between reason for deterioration and deterioration strategy, this variable accounted for little variance in strategy scores. Thus, the reason for deterioration may have minimal practical impact on strategy choice. This, along with the finding that hierarchical level was not associated with strategy selection, suggests individuals may disengage from workplace relationships in fairly consistent ways across situations. Thus, disengagement strategy use may be more likely to vary across individuals than across situations.

In sum, existing research in workplace friendship deterioration has addressed the causes of friendship deterioration, the ways in which individuals disengage from workplace friendship, and the consequences of workplace friendship deterioration. As the preceding summary indicates, however, work in the area of workplace friendship deterioration is in an early stage. There is much we still need to learn about this important organizational phenomenon. Toward this end, the following section outlines directions for future work in this area.

Future Directions

A review of existing scholarship in workplace friendship deterioration suggests several avenues for future work. Two areas, in particular, need further research development: disengagement tactic choice and deterioration consequences.

Disengagement Strategy Choice

Much work is needed toward understanding the disengagement process, and, in particular, how and why individuals use particular communication tactics to disengage from a workplace friendship.

As noted above, current literature suggests that individuals enact friendship disengagement in relatively consistent ways across various situations. Future work, therefore, should examine the role of individual differences, such as personality and dispositions, in friendship disengagement processes. The work of Infante and colleagues, for example, indicates individuals differ from one another in the extent to which they are verbally aggressive or argumentative. Verbal aggression refers to messages that attack another's self-concept and that are done with intent to make the other feel bad (Infante & Wigley, 1986). Argumentativeness, in contrast, is conceptualized as a subset of assertiveness and extroversion, and is manifested in behaviors such as negotiation, argument, and persuasion (Infante & Rancer, 1982). Much empirical work indicates the trait-like nature of verbal aggressiveness and argumentativeness (e.g., Clark & Watson, 1999; Infante & Rancer, 1996). Verbally aggressive and argumentative personality traits (e.g., Infante & Rancer, 1982) may be predictive of disengagement behavior. For example, a verbally aggressive individual may be more likely to use cost escalation, in which the intent is to treat the coworker negatively and inflict harm. In contrast, an argumentative individual may prefer to initiate a state-of-the-relationship talk, a more other-oriented strategy which requires discussion, negotiation, and, to some extent, extroversion.

Communication apprehension may also play a role in disengagement tactic choice. Communication Apprehension (CA) refers to "an individual's level of fear or anxiety associated with either real or anticipated communication with another person or persons" (McCroskey, 1997, p. 78). High levels of CA are characterized by a low level of communicative/verbal output (McCroskey and Richmond, 1979). According to McCroskey (1997), many individuals suffer from trait-like CA, "a relatively enduring, personality-type orientation toward a given mode of communication across a wide variety of contexts" (McCroskey, 1997, p. 84). Trait CA may impact individuals' disengagement tactic choice. Specifically, the hallmark of depersonalization is avoidance of interaction related to non-work issues. This avoidance, and the accompanying attempts to minimize work-related discussion, requires an overall decrease in communication. In contrast, state of the relationship talk is characterized by direct, candid, and rather brave discussion. Individuals with high levels of communication apprehension would probably prefer depersonalization, which would decrease, rather than increase, their communication anxiety. On the other hand, those with low levels of this trait would be comparatively less averse to engaging in state-of-the relationship talk.

While I encourage researchers to examine individual differences in disengagement tactic use, scholars should also examine other situational factors in future research. In particular, Weick's (1995) notion of tight and loose coupling could provide important insights. As mentioned in the literature summary above, individuals appear to have a strong preference for "face-saving" disengagement tactics such as depersonalization and an aversion to the use of the more offensive cost escalation tactics. An important aspect of depersonalization is that, while the coworkers cease extra-organizational conversation and socializing, they continue to communicate (at least, minimally) regarding work-related issues. Thus, this tactic enables both disengagement from the friendship and a continued, albeit superficial, work relationship. As Weick (1995) and others (e.g., Beekun & Glick, 2001) note, coworkers' tasks vary in the extent to which they are tightly coupled (i.e., one's ability to complete his/her task effectively is highly dependent on the other's task performance) or loosely coupled (i.e., one's ability to effectively perform his/her task relies very little on the other). Coworkers with tightly-coupled tasks may worry more about maintaining a civil working relationship after their friendship deteriorates than those with loosely-coupled tasks. Thus, individuals whose tasks are tightly coupled with their friend/coworker may be more likely to rely on depersonalization than those whose tasks are loosely coupled. Those with loosely-coupled tasks, on the other hand, may be less concerned with maintaining the coworker relationship and, therefore, less averse to using cost-escalation tactics. Future research should examine the extent to which this contextual factor influences disengagement tactic use.

Friendship Deterioration Consequences

The deterioration of friendships in the workplace presents four different types of consequences: relationship lessons; emotion and stress; impacts on other organizational members; and the benefit of learning how to better manage workplace relationships.

As noted earlier, individuals tend to learn "lessons" about workplace relationships from their deterioration experiences. Future research should examine these lessons more directly. For example, workplace friendship deterioration is likely to impact the willingness of individuals to befriend coworkers in the future. They may be more cautious and, therefore, either avoid such relationships in the future, or develop workplace friendships with a different progression pattern (e.g., more slowly) than they did previously. Future research in this area might be grounded in structuration theory (Banks & Riley, 1991; Giddens, 1984), which emphasizes the ways in which lived experience is both constrained by structures (e.g., rules and resources that are instantiated in action) and serves to transform those structures. In other words, one's development of a workplace friendship occurs within the constraints of the structure of that relationship and others. As that relationship deteriorates, the structure is transformed and serves to constrain that individual's workplace relationships in the future. Such research would make important contributions to our understanding of deterioration processes and to our understanding of individuals' perceptions of the role of friendships in organizational processes.

As noted in the preceding review, workplace friendship deterioration is an emotional and stressful experience. Although current research indicates how the deterioration causes negative emotions and stress for the partners, we know nothing about how emotion and stress might impact the deterioration process. Given the affective nature of friendships, emotions are likely to guide much of the disengagement process. Planalp (2003) recently called for researchers to incorporate emotion into theory and research on close interpersonal relationships more fully, beyond simply noting that individuals experience emotions in relational contexts. Along these lines, future research could examine the ways emotion guides decision making as coworkers disengage from their relationships. Such research might focus on the strength of emotions (e.g., the stronger the negative emotions, the more likely one might be to resort to cost escalation). Scholars also could examine the ways in which the quality of emotions influences the disengagement process. For example, an angry individual may be more likely to resort to cost escalation tactics than a sad individual who may tend toward withdrawal or depersonalization. In the same vein, an individual experiencing frustration may be more prone to try to "fix" the problem and, therefore, engage in direct discussion. Of course, an individual probably experiences multiple emotions during such an event, each of which will impact the disengagement process in different ways at different points. The point is that disengagement tactics are presented in current literature as *strategically* chosen. Conceptualizing disengagement as an emotional, rather than strategic, process would provide a more full and complex understanding of workplace friendship deteriorationdisengagement.

The above suggestions all focus research on the individuals involved in the deteriorating dyad. Workplace friendship deterioration, however, is likely to affect others in the immediate work environment. Sias, Krone and Jablin (2002) recently summarized existing research on workplace relationships and highlighted several areas that need research attention. One such area had to do with the ways in which one relationship impacts other relationships in the workplace (in the words of the authors, a "mesosystem" concern). Along these lines, the deterioration of a workplace friendship is likely to impact other organizational members not directly participating in that relationship. Interpersonal research demonstrates, for example, that when married couples divorce, their friends are often forced to "take sides" and terminate (or, at least, withdraw from) the relationship with one of the individuals in that couple (DeShane & Brown-Wilson, 1981; Udry, 1971). It seems reasonable to assume that similar dynamics occur with the deterioration of workplace relationships. Acknowledging the interdependent nature of organizational systems, one might expect a type of "snowball" effect where the deterioration of a single workplace friendship leads to the deterioration of other workplace friendships. Research in this area would provide valuable insights into friendship deterioration dynamics as embedded in the larger organizational context.

Finally, a benefit of gaining a better understanding of workplace friendship deterioration is that such understanding can help employees to maintain, rather than disengage from, such relationships. Increased understanding of dialectics in workplace friendships would make contributions along these lines. For example, Bridge and Baxter (1992) found that when faced with dialectical tensions in workplace friendships, employees respond in one of three ways. They either "separate" the roles, behaving as coworkers while at work and as friends outside the workplace, "select" one relationship over the other (for example, choosing to "break" organizational rules in favor of the friendship), or "integrate" the relationships by being flexible about their expectations of both the workplace and friend roles. The program of research described in this chapter depicts the difficulties of enacting these strategies and suggests that *consensus* is important for the successful management of dialectical tensions; if both parties do not agree on how to manage the dialectical tensions, such strategies are doomed to fail, resulting in the termination of the friendship, the work relationship, or both. One study found several cases in which one partner in a workplace friendship attempted to keep the friend and workplace roles separate, while the other partner selected the workplace relationship over the friendship (Sias et al., 2004). Future research would profit from examination of the ways individuals successfully negotiate consensus regarding management of dialectical tensions.

Conclusion

There are probably very few individuals who have not experienced the rather painful process of workplace friendship deterioration, either as active participant or as observer. We are just beginning to build a scholarly body of knowledge regarding this process. The goal of this chapter was to examine the existing body of work and develop recommendations for future research that will contribute to our understanding of workplace friendship deterioration. Such an understanding may help scholars and practitioners learn to negotiate problems in workplace friendships, making the deterioration of such relationships less traumatic and damaging. Such understanding may also provide insights into how to preserve, rather than disengage from, workplace friendships as they inevitably encounter problems and threats to their viability. These insights may render workplace friendships not, as Derrida (1997) suggest, an "impossible ideal," but a rewarding phenomenon for both individual employees and the organizations in which they work.

References

Banks, S. P., & Riley, P. (1991). Structuration theory as an ontology for communication research. *Communication Yearbook, 16,* 167-196.

Baxter, L. A. (1985). Accomplishing relationship deterioration. In S. Duck & D. Perlman (Eds.), *Understanding personal relationships* (pp. 243-265). London: Sage.

Beekun, R. I., & Glick, W. H. (2001). Organization structure from a loose coupling perspective: A multidimensional approach. *Decision Sciences, 32,* 227-251.

Bridge, K., & Baxter, L. A. (1992). Blended relationships: Friends as work associates. *Western Journal of Communication, 56,* 200-225.

Brown, P., & Levinson, S. (1987). *Politeness: Some universals in language use.* Cambridge, England: Cambridge University Press.

Clark, L. A., & Watson, D. (1999). Temperament: A new paradigm for trait psychology. In L. A. Pervin, & O. P. John (Eds.), *Handbook of personality: Theory and research* (2nd ed., pp. 399-423). New York: Guilford.

Contractor, N. S. & Grant, S. (1996). The emergence of shared interpretations in organizations: A self-organizing systems perspective. In J. Watt & A. VanLear (Eds.), *Cycles and dynamic processes in communication processes* (pp. 216-230). Thousand Oaks, CA: Sage

Derrida, J. (1997). Politics of friendship. (G. Collins, Trans.). London: Verso.

DeShane, M. R., & Brown-Wilson, K. (1981). Divorce in late-life: A call for research. *Journal of Divorce, 4,* 81-93.

Duck, S., & Pittman, G. (1994). Social and personal relationships. In M. L. Knapp & G. R. Miller (Eds.), *Handbook of interpersonal communication* (2nd ed., pp. 676-695). Thousand Oaks, CA: Sage.

Fine, G. A. (1986). Friendships in the work place. In V. J. Derlega & B. A. Winstead (Eds.), *Friendship and social interaction* (pp. 185-206). New York: Springer-Verlag.

Giddens, A. (1984). *The constitution of society: Outline of the theory of structuration.* Berkeley: University of California Press.

Goffman, E. (1967). *Interaction ritual.* Garden City, NY: Doubleday.

Infante, D. A., & Rancer, A. S. (1982). A conceptualization and measure of argumentativeness. *Journal of Personality Assessment, 46,* 72-80.

Infante, D. A., & Rancer, A. S. (1996). Argumentativeness and verbal aggressiveness: A review of recent theory and research. *Communication Yearbook, 19,* 319-351.

Infante, D. A., & Wigley, C. J. (1986). Verbal aggressiveness: An interpersonal model and measure. *Communication Monographs, 53,* 61-69.

Kram, K. E, & Isabella, L. A. (1985). Mentoring alternatives: The role of peer relationships in career development. *Academy of Management Journal, 28,* 110-132.

McCroskey, J. C. (1997). Willingness to Communicate, Communication Apprehension, and Self-Perceived Communication Competence: Conceptualizations and Perspectives. In Daly, J. A., McCroskey, J. C., Ayres, J., Hopf, T., and Ayres, D. M. (Eds.), *Avoiding Communication: Shyness, Reticence, and Communication Apprehension* (2nd ed., pp. 75- 108). Cresskill, NJ: Hampton Press.

McCroskey, J. C., and Richmond, V. P. (1979). The impact of communication apprehension on individuals in organizations. *Communication Quarterly, 27,* 55-61.

Planalp, S. (2003). The unacknowledged role of emotion in theories of close relationships: How do theories feel? *Communication Theory, 13,* 78.

Rawlins, W. K. (1992). *Friendship matters: Communication, dialectics, and the life course.* New York: Aldine de Gruyter.

Shaver, K G. (1985). *The attribution of blame: Causality, responsibility, and blameworthiness.* New York: Springer-Verlag.

Sias, P. M., & Cahill, D. J. (1998). From coworkers to friends: The development of peer friendships in the workplace. *Western Journal of Communication, 62,* 273-299.

Sias, P. M., & Perry, T. (2004). Disengaging from workplace relationships: A research note. *Human Communication Research, 30,* 589-602.

Sias, P. M., Heath, R. G., Perry, T., Silva, D, & Fix, B. (2004). Narratives of workplace friendship deterioration. *Journal of Social and Personal Relationships, 21,* 321-340.

Sias, P. M., Krone, K. K., & Jablin, F. M. (2002). An ecological systems perspective on workplace relationships. In J. Daly & M. L. Knapp (Eds.), *Handbook of interpersonal communication* (3rd ed., pp. 615-642). Newbury Park, CA: Sage.

Sigman, S. J. (1995). Order and continuity in human relationships: A social communication approach to defining "relationship." In W. Leeds-Hurwitz (Ed.), *Social approaches to communication* (pp. 188-200). New York: Guilford Press.

Udry, J. R. (1971). *The social context of marriage.* Philadelphia: J.B. Lippincott.

Weick, K. E. (1995). *Sensemaking in organizations.* Thousand Oaks, CA: Sage.

Wheatley, M. J. (1994). *Leadership and the new science: Learning about organization from an orderly universe.* San Francisco: Berrett-Koehler Publishing.

Wright, P. H. (1984). Self-reference motivation and the intrinsic quality of friendship. *Journal of Social and Personal Relationships, 1,* 115-130.

Yager, J. (1997). *Friendshifts: The power of friendship and how it shapes our lives.* Stamford, CT: Hannacroix Creek Books.

5 | Turning Points in Relationships with Disliked Co-workers

Jon A. Hess

Becky L. Omdahl

Janie M. Harden Fritz

Although most people begin their employment with the education and on-the-job training to handle the *tasks* their job entails, few long-term employees boast that they feel competent in dealing with all the difficult *people* they encounter in the workplace. These unpleasant coworkers range from annoying nuisances to major sources of job frustration and career roadblocks. Given that periodic preoccupation with unlovable coworkers is nearly a universal feature of organizational life, it is not surprising that such relationships are given due attention in the media and popular press (e.g., Bramson, 1989; Topchik, 2000). What is surprising is how little scholarly attention has been given to such interactions. Scholars have extensively examined the outcomes of positive work relationships, such as social support and friendship through coworker relationships and guidance through mentoring (e.g., Bridge & Baxter, 1992; Kram & Isabella, 1985). However, only recently has scholarly attention been focused on identifying troublesome coworkers and documenting outcomes of unpleasant work relationships such as cynicism, and reduced job satisfaction and organizational commitment (e.g., Fritz, 2002; Omdahl & Fritz, 2000). This neglect of unpleasant or difficult relationships in the workplace mirrors the more general literature on interpersonal communication. For decades the focus has been on the development and maintenance of effective relationships, and only recently has research on the "dark side" of personal relationships gained attention (Duck, 1994).

This examination of negative relationships in general and with negative coworkers in particular is long overdue. People spend considerable time and energy navigating difficult relationships, and many working hours are spent in the company of others whom we do not voluntarily seek out and may actively dislike (Hess, 2000). These relationships have many negative effects on employees and organizations. For instance, research has shown that negative relationships detract from a person's occupational experience through increased stress, workplace cynicism, and organizational turnover, and decreased job satisfaction, organizational commitment, and task effectiveness (e.g., Cooper & Cartwright, 1994; Fritz & Omdahl, 1998). Research that increases scholars' understanding of the causes, nature, and processes of such relationships can offer insight for communication theory and practice.

Review of Literature

Although "negative relationships" could be construed in many ways, this study focuses on relationships with disliked coworkers that have an affectively negative tone. The requirements of organizational involvement prohibit most employees from avoiding or exiting such relationships with coworkers, customers, or clients who they dislike. Given the non-voluntary status of these relationships, workers continue them in spite of their unpleasant natures.

Research on negative workplace relationships is sparse, but recent studies have begun to examine some important aspects of these relationships. For instance, researchers have identified features of disliked others at work (Sypher & Zorn, 1988), outcomes of negative workplace relationships (Omdahl & Fritz, 2000), and types of negative coworkers (Fritz, 2002). Furthermore, Fritz (1997) and Omdahl, Fritz, and Hess (2004) investigated the likelihood of exit, voice, loyalty and neglect responses to hypothetical situations with bosses, peers, and subordinates, and Monroe, Borzi, and DiSalvo (1992) looked at managerial strategies for dealing with difficult subordinates.

To date, however, researchers have not examined the processes in these relationships—how they begin or turn affectively negative, what cognitive processes are important in these relationships, and what happens throughout the course of these relationships that makes them such a negative experience (but see Sias, Perry, Fix, & Silva, 2000, for an investigation of work relationship deterioration). At present, our understanding of key events in these relationships and how people deal with the challenges they pose is limited.

Turning Points

One approach to the study of personal relationships that has much to offer our understanding of relationships with disliked coworkers is the turning points approach. A turning point is an "event or occurrence that is associated with a change in a relationship" (Baxter & Bullis, 1986, p. 288). The process of relationship development and deterioration can be conceived as a series of turning points. These events provide insight into the forces that impact relational trajectories, that is, they reveal the causes of relational changes. By studying turning points in relationships with disliked coworkers, we can learn about what forces or events prompt relationships to become more negative or more positive.

The examination of turning points has resulted in productive research about many types of personal relationships: courtship (Bolton, 1961); romantic (e.g., Baxter & Bullis, 1986); grandmother-granddaughter (Holladay, et al., 1998); mentoring (Bullis & Bach, 1989); chair-faculty (Barge & Musambira, 1992); post-divorce (Graham, 1997); and individuals-institutions during the organizational socialization process (Bullis & Bach, 1989). Transitions in relationships at work in a positive direction have been examined through methods much akin to turning point analysis (Sias & Cahill, 1998), and Sias et al. (2000) have looked at events that resulted in work friendship deterioration. However, this review of literature resulted in no research on turning points in negative work relationships that permitted examination of both positively- and negatively-valenced turning points. This lack is unfortunate, because the identification of turning points seems important for understanding organizational relational trajectories. Furthermore, it seems important to identify not only turning points that send a relationship into a negative trajectory, but turning points that send negative relationships onto a more positive direction as well. Research on both types of turning points would be useful for both development of theory and intervention.

A significant question that turning points can illuminate is whether negative relationships are good relationships that went awry or relationships that, from the beginning, were characterized by "bad chemistry." That is, are these relationships more commonly positive relationships that turned negative, or were they "bad" from the start? Research has demonstrated that the presence of certain qualities such as physical beauty or attitudinal similarity is one factor that makes a person attractive or unattractive to someone else (e.g., Berscheid &

Walster, 1974; Byrne, 1971). If liking or disliking results from qualities a person perceives in another, then it is reasonable to assume that disliking could be present from two persons' first meeting. On the other hand, Levitt, Silver, and Franco's (1996) research suggested that many troublesome relationships were more positive initially than they were later. Given both options seem possible, is one more common than the other?

The turning points approach to negative work relationships suggests research questions worth investigating:

RQ1: What turning points do people report in negative coworker relationships?

RQ2: Do relationships more commonly start positive and deteriorate, are they more commonly bad from the start, or is either situation equally common?

Method

Participants

The seventy-seven participants were recruited from three universities. Participants were (1) adult students in a baccalaureate program within the division of continuing education in a mid-sized, private, eastern university and coworkers they recruited (n = 30); (2) adult students in a baccalaureate program in a mid-sized, mid-western public university (n = 25); and (3) family or friends of students in a large, public, mid-western university (n = 22). Students received extra credit for participation or for recruiting a participant.

The participants ranged in age from 20 to 57, with a mean age of 39. Thirty-five percent were male, and 65% were female. They reported their race as Caucasian (85%), African-American (8%), Asian (3%), and others, including Hispanic, Arab, and mixed-race (4%). At the time they filled out the survey, 73% of the respondents indicated they were working full-time (40 or more hours a week), 21% indicated they worked between 24 and 38 hours a week, and 6% reported working 20 or fewer hours a week. The participants held a diverse array of occupations and worked for a wide variety of organizations. The most common occupations included manager (20%); doctor or nurse (16%); trainer or teacher (9%); and accountant or purchaser, administrative assistant, and salesperson or loan officer (7% each). The most common types of industries in which these people worked were health care (31%), manufacturing (19%), education (14%), financial services or insurance (10%), and non-profit or religious organizations (7%).

Instrument

At the outset of the questionnaire, participants were instructed to think of someone at work, either current or past, whom they liked the least. It was specified that the person could be a supervisor/manager, a coworker, or a subordinate. If choosing from multiple disliked others, they were to choose the relationship they could most accurately recall and that was most important to them. Participants were then asked to identify turning points in the relationship, with turning point defined as "an event that led to significant changes in the relationship." They were instructed to draw a timeline beginning with the approximate date the participant first met the person and ending when they no longer interacted with the other or the present date (if the participant still had a relationship with that person). Along this timeline they were told to mark X's at the point at which they recalled turning points. In addition, participants were instructed to indicate the valence (positivity or negativity) of the relationship across the timeline. Participants were to use a vertical axis ranging from +10 (very positive) through 0 (neutral) to -10 (very negative). Thus, the resulting timeline presented a topographical image of the perceived affective tone of the relationship that they subjectively experienced. To facilitate their understanding of this task, a sample timeline was included marked with dates, X's for turning points, and topographical lines. A written explanation followed the sample diagram to make certain that participants could learn how the different markings reflected the subjective experience of the hypothetical relationship.

Participants were then instructed to answer questions about each turning point. For each turning point event, participants were asked to describe the turning point in detail. Specifically, they were told, "Describe the event that you regard to be a turning point (i.e., a significant change in the relationship). Please be as specific as possible in describing the words, actions, and situation involved in the turning point." Next, participants were asked to "Describe the effect the event had. Specifically, how did it change your feelings and thoughts about the other, yourself, and the working relationship?" In order to make certain that participants offered a clear reason as part of their description they were asked to summarize "What specifically brought about the change in your perception?" Finally, they were asked, "How did you deal with or manage the event?"

With each turning point description, participants were asked to report the degree of distancing they engaged in at that point of the relationship. This was done using an eight-item distance index. Unpublished data (author citation) showed that this index had good reliability (alpha = .78), exhibited stable and meaningful factor structure, and performed well in tests of validity and temporal stability.

The final section consisted of Rubin's nine-item liking scale (Rubin, 1970) and a variety of demographic questions about the participant and the participant's chosen person. These additional questions (other than demographics) were included for an additional study beyond the research questions investigated here.

Procedure

Students were read an announcement in class inviting them either to participate in the study (at two universities) or to recruit someone who could do the survey (at the other university). Participants were given information about the study (which included a consent form at one university that required consent forms, even for "exempt" studies). Each participant was given a copy of the questionnaire. Upon completion, the questionnaire was returned to a member of the research team.

Results

Research Question 1

The first research question asked what types of incidents people saw as turning points in affectively negative workplace relationships. Because participants graphed the turning points, these incidents could be classified as positive or negative turning points. The following sections address each type of turning point: (1) turning points that were identical in nature, whether negative or positive; (2)

negative turning points; and (3) positive turning points.

Table 1
Equivalency Chart

NEGATIVE TURNING POINTS   POSITIVE TURNING POINTS

1. Beginning or End of Relationship
First met/started job   First met/started job
Left the job/got fired   Left the job/got fired

2. Self (Respondent) or Third Party Was the Cause of the Turning Point
Structural change   Structural change
(no match)   Third party intervention
Respondent did something   Respondent did something
other didn't like   to improve the situation
Heard a rumor   (no match)
(no match)   Sympathy/forgiveness

3. Other Was the Cause of the Turning Point
  3-A Task Issues
  Job ineptitude   Job competence
  Threats/unreasonable demands (no match)

  3-B Social/Interpersonal Issues
  Other exhibited bad traits, but not for the purpose of making an attack
  Negative vibes   Positivity/friendliness
  Other made an attack on someone
  Face threat   Positivity/friendliness
  Malicious treatment   Positivity/friendliness
  Mistreated a third party   Treated others well

  3-C Combination of Task and Social/Interpersonal Issues
  Conflict   Cooperation/constructive conflict
  Closed-minded   Cooperation/constructive conflict
  Obstructive/unsupportive   Goal/career support
  Poor moral judgment   (no match)

Negative or positive turning points. As Table 1 reveals, turning points fell within three overall categories: beginnings or endings of relationships; self or third party was cause; or other was cause. Within each of the categories, there were specific elicitors. Some of these elicitors appeared in both negative and positive turning point descriptions, while others typified turning points in one direction only. For example, meeting and parting are necessary turning points in any relationship, and it is not surprising that these events elicited both negative and positive shifts, whereas poor moral judgment was only identified as an other cause of negative turning points.

Negative turning points. Twelve categories of negative turning points were identified. In the vast majority of cases of negative turning points, the respondent saw the turning point as being the result of the other person's behavior. In a few cases, however, the respondent admitted that her or his *own behavior caused the change*. Examples of this type of negative turning point included a person's publishing a coworker's age as part of a trivia contest, and a person's failure to attend a mandatory training session. In both cases, the respondent took responsibility for causing the turning point, rather than attributing it to the other person's reaction. Also, in a few cases, a third party was responsible for the turning point. In these situations, the person reported that they *heard a rumor* about the other, and that led to a negative turn in relations. For instance, when one respondent took a new position, her boss told her that a particular person was difficult and stubborn. For all other types of turning points, however, the respondent identified the source of the downturn as being in the other person's behavior.

Many of the turning points were related solely to the other person's performance of job duties (e.g., task issues). Chief among these was *job ineptitude*, that is, the other person's failure to discharge job duties in the manner in which the respondent felt they should have been done led to a loss of respect for that other person or to unpleasant interactions. One woman asked her boss to protect her from indecent exposure by another coworker, but felt the boss did little to intervene. In another case, an engineer became critical of a new hire who changed a ceramic formula, resulting in poorer performance of the product. *Threats or unreasonable demands* by coworkers also resulted in relations with the respondent taking a turn for the worse. For example, one supervisor asked the respondent to violate company and government regulations; a different supervisor continuously asked his subordinate to do jobs in unreasonably short time periods.

Other turning points were much more personal; in fact, task duties were incidental if even relevant at all (social/interpersonal issues). The least offensive of these was giving off *negative vibes*. In this case, the disliked person exhibited excessive negativity, arrogance, selfishness, abrasive personality characteristics, or untrustworthiness. Typical examples included a coworker who became extremely negative toward everyone else at work after going through a difficult divorce, or a coworker who was strongly overbearing. While negative vibes were not directed at anyone as an attack, other types of behaviors were. One, identified as *face threat*, happened when the other person made the respondent look bad in front of others. An incidence of face threat happened when a person reprimanded the respondent (who was not the person's subordinate) in a board meeting. A more vicious type of attack was identified as *malicious behavior*. People who acted in this manner made (unprovoked) job or personal attacks, snubbed the respondent, or showed disrespect to the respondent. For instance, one person refused to show sympathy to the respondent after a death in the family, and another person called the respondent a "bitch" in front of customers. In some cases, the disliked person's malice was not directed at the respondent. Instead, these people *mistreated others*. One grocery cashier lost respect for another after she was rude to a customer on welfare, and, after the customer left, made fun of her.

Finally, some turning points involved a mix of task and social issues. *Conflict* was the most common of these turning points. This happened when the two people disagreed or experienced a conflict over some issue, for example, a disagreement over a person's negative review of the respondent or the other's work. In some cases, it was not the conflict but the fact that the other was *closed-minded* and unresponsive to communication that led to the downturn. One respondent said that it was not the disagreement but the fact that the other was not open for discussion that angered her. *Obstructiveness or unsupportiveness* was another common turning point. This happened when the other person was obstructive or unsupportive of the respondent's goals; manipulated others for selfish reasons; exerted inappropriate influence; meddled; or made the person feel left out. For example, one person began to notice that she was being left out of decisions directly related to her job. In another case, a person found it hard to access files on a coworker's computer because the coworker kept protecting them with passwords the respondent did not know. Finally, some people were turned off when the other person exhibited *poor moral judgment*. People who acted in this manner made false accusations, abused privileges or benefits, lied, demonstrated bad values, betrayed confidence (especially by gossiping), or devalued friendship. For instance, one respondent felt betrayed when a

coworker leaked personal information to others. In another case, an
employee brought charges against management of their ignoring her
being "attacked" after she bumped into another employee at the
copier. Then said she hurt her back picking up a paper clip, and took
extended sick leave. The respondent found this employee's behavior
morally problematic.

Positive turning points. Even in such negative relationships,
respondents noted plenty of incidents that sent the relationship back
on a more positive trajectory. Seven categories of positive turning
points were identified. As with the negative turning points, respondents saw most of these as resulting from the other person's
behaviors, but did suggest that their own behavior was the cause of a
few turning points. In some cases, they noted that through their own
behavior, they did *something to improve the situation.* An example of
this was a nurse who took the initiative and spoke with a disliked
colleague about the problem she (the other) was having with her feet.
Some respondents also suggested that their *sympathy or forgiveness* of
the other was a turning point in their relationship. Several
respondents simply decided to forgive the other, and many others
reported that their sympathy for the other's difficulties led to
improved relations. Likewise, *third party interventions* often improved
relations. One employer reported a disliked peer's harassment to her
boss, who took action to eliminate it. For all other turning points, the
respondent saw the other's behavior as being the cause of the change.

As with the negative turning points, the positive ones were
sometimes work-related, sometimes social, and sometimes a
combination of both. The work related ones all boiled down to *job
competence,* in which an act of job excellence or mere improvement
enhanced relations between the two. In one case a nurse gave a
detailed account to the respondent of a difficult time she had with a
family and patient, thus making the shift transition easier.

The social incidents that caused turning points were twofold.
First, showing *positivity or friendliness* often improved matters. One
person reported that when she was going through a personal crisis, a
previously disliked coworker was very supportive, which improved
relations between them considerably. Another person noted that
when a colleague gave her a gift, their relationship got better. Seeing
the coworker *treat others well* was the other social event that led to
improved relations. A nurse who was compassionate to patients
earned back lost respect in the eyes of others (including the

respondent).

The turning points that blended both task and social elements included *cooperation and constructive conflict*. This happened when the other was cooperative or engaged in constructive conflict, was responsive to feedback, or requested reconciliation in some way. For example, one respondent reported that he and a disliked coworker had a brief talk about work, and the conversation was conducted in a civil manner. Another respondent reported that the other person requested that they "bury the hatchet." A second type of turning point that blended task and social elements was *goal or career support*. In this case, the other person did something that was supportive of the respondent's goals or career development, or gave the respondent some positive task feedback or reward. Typical examples included one person who helped the respondent at work, and a boss who gave the respondent an excellent job review.

Research Question Two

The second research question asked whether negative relationships more commonly started good and then went bad, or whether they more commonly were bad from the start. Of the 77 relationships reported, 61 (79%) started positively and went bad, whereas 16 (21%) were bad from the start. Thus, it was much more common in this data set for relationships to go sour over time than to start off on the wrong foot. Interestingly, though, 18 (23%) made positive turns and were considered positive relationships by the time the respondent reported on the relationship (either at the time of completion of the questionnaire or at the time the relationship ended).

Discussion

This study investigated turning points in negative work relationships, with the goal of contributing to a small but emerging literature on the nature and outcomes of negative work relationships. Two research questions guided this study: what types of turning points exist in negative relationships, and what is the nature of the trajectory of such relationships: bad from the outset, or good relationships gone bad? The results of this study offer insights into the nature of turning points in negative relationships and the etiology of such relationships and holds implications for future study of this important topic.

Turning Points in Negative Relationships

The types of turning points reported here contribute to knowledge of similarities and differences between work relationships and those in other contexts. For instance, features of the work context that appear to influence both positive and negative turning points in relationships include structural changes (e.g., being promoted, different job duties) and job skills (ineptitude or competence). The majority of turning points seemed likely to occur in non-work contexts as well as in work contexts (e.g., malicious treatment, conflict). These findings are helpful for theory development in relationship processes, since the extent to which contexts provide unique interactional constraints and resources bounds the applicability of research about relationships across contexts.

Almost four-fifths (79%) of the relationships reported here were positive relationships that turned bad. That so many relationships were not initially negative is a hopeful sign for the possibility of preventive intervention in these cases. It would be important to determine the degree to which various negative turning point events are perceived as preventable. Furthermore, since in most cases the perceived agency for negative turning points was the other party, it seems likely that interventions involving conflict and attribution biases might help parties to negative relationships reframe events in ways that would permit interpersonal "grace" to operate in cases where a coworker is at risk of being "constructed" as a negative or problematic person.

If one arranges the turning point categories in a table, interesting parallelism is apparent (see Table 1). Many of the positive and negative turning points are the mirror image of each other – for instance, the negative turning point of "job ineptitute" has a positive turning point counterpart of "job competence"; the negative category of "obstructive/unsupportve" has a positive counterpart of "goal/career support." The table shows negative and positive instantiations of what are essentially identical categories, but are simply reversed. Only a few categories have no counterpart on the opposite valence. In most of these "unmatched" cases, it is possible to imagine a type of turning point on the other valence that would parallel the identified category, though such instances did not appear in these data. For instance, "immorality" on the negative side might have "exceeding beneficence" on the other side – that is, someone might exhibit a remarkably ethical and "good Samaritan-" or "Mother

Theresa-like" behavior that strikes the respondent as exceptionally laudable or praiseworthy, which might propel the relationship in a positive direction. "Sympathy/forgiveness" might be paralleled by "envy/jealousy," and "threats/unreasonable demands" could be paralleled with "unusual fairness" or "taking on the respondent's/another's burdens." In a larger sample, these proposed parallel categories might surface. The significance of such parallelism lies in its suggestion of underlying structural dimensions along which others at work may be perceived, extending Fritz's (2002) research by suggesting an opposing pole of dimensions for constructing "positive" others (or "nontroublesome" or "beneficent" others) at work. This finding holds implications for the literature on person perception and perception in general, as well. If a limited set of contextually-relevant (or "behavior-in-context-"relevant) dimen-sions of perception can be identified that persons in various contexts are attuned to, then interventions can be strategically targeted toward those contextual/behavioral areas.

Contributions to Current Research

This research speaks to the growing literature on negative work relationships and work relationship deterioration. The turning points identified in this study have some parallels with the work of Fritz (2002) and Sias (2000) (reported in Sias, et. al., 2000). Fritz's typology identified dimensions along which negative others were perceived for bosses, peers, and subordinates. Although not all of the categories in this study may be appropriately compared, since the Fritz study examined perceptions of others and this study examined turning points, some of the turning points identified as events characterized by the appearance or manifestation of a trait or characteristic of the other seem fruitful for comparison.

Fritz's boss factors of "poor work ethic" and "excessive demands," peer factors of "incompetence" and "hustling" (getting others to do one's work, making unreasonable work demands), and subordinate factor of "incompetence" appear similar to the task-related negative turning point categories of "job ineptitude" and "threats/unreasonable demands" identified in the current study. One of this study's combination categories (task/social) labeled "obstructive/unsupportive" appears to be a stronger and more deliberate version of Fritz's "distracting" and "busybody behavior" factor found across all three status levels in her research (which addresses meddling and distracting others from work, which could translate to blocking another's goals).

Sias's (2000) research focused on deterioration of work friendships: that is, good relationships that turned bad. She found that events categorized as personality (similar to "negative vibes" here), distracting life events, conflicting expectations ("conflict" here), promotion ("structural change"), and betrayal ("immorality") led to work relationship deterioration. This turning point research confirms and complements Sias's research on work relationship deterioration. The turning points identified here are similar in some ways to the deterioration events she identified and offer the potential clarification of task, social, and mixed categories to that line of research.

Future Research

The results of this research suggest that there are multiple concerns inherent in working relationships, any of which may be a breeding ground for negative relationships. Not only interpersonal or social concerns, but task concerns, too, can result in unpleasant relationships in the work setting. This finding interfaces with research on affect- and cognition-based trust in organizational settings (McAllister, 1995). Cognition-based trust derives from beliefs about peer reliability and dependability. Affect-based trust derives from reciprocated care and concern.

Some of the categories in this turning points research reflect these different aspects of trust. For instance, "job ineptitude" seems to address the issue of cognition based trust: that is, the person is perceived as not doing the job properly. Affect-based trust is addressed in some of these categories – "face attack," "malicious treatment," "immorality," and "negative vibes" – in which a lack of care and concern surfaces. Both cognitive- and affect-based trust may be implicated in the combination categories of "conflict," "closed-minded," and obstructive/unsupportive. The extent to which turning points are characterized as task or social (or a combination) could be explored for their connection to cognition- or affect-based trust and then linked to outcomes such as job satisfaction or individual emotional reactions to work, including cognitive appraisals.

Future research could be conducted on organizational climate, (including communication climate), which is related to organizational commitment (Guzley, 1992). One aspect of organizational climate is motivational practices, the extent to which work conditions and relationships are conducive to accomplishing tasks (Taylor & Bowers, 1972, cited in Guzley, 1992); communication climate includes the quality of superior-subordinate communication (O'Connell, 1979, cited in Guzley, 1992). Future research should examine the extent to which discourse processes in negative relationships shape perceptions of organizational climate and communication climate and how organizational climate may contribute to the likelihood of different types of turning points in negative relationships.

Future research should identify behaviors used to cope with the appearance of, particularly, negative turning points in work relationships and outcomes associated with negative relationships with different trajectories (i.e., bad from the beginning, good turned bad), and means of creating opportunities for positive turning points in negative relationships. Growing interest in professional civility (Arnett & Fritz, 2001) and incivility in organizational life (Andersson & Pearson, 1999) suggests other avenues for research. For example, the extent to which a focus of attention redirected from self and other and onto a common tasks, permitting space for a wounded relationship to heal, may be efficacious would be one area to explore. Hess's (2000) work on distancing behaviors in relationships with disliked others would be useful as a starting point for such an investigation. Finally, the extent to which interventions such as training in cognitive reframing (for those experiencing negative relationships), conflict management (for both parties), or training in social skills and anger management (for "negative others") may send negative relationships into a positive trajectory again would be a useful area to explore.

Limitations

This turning point study employed a different methodology from that used in previous turning point studies. Instead of face-to-face structured interviews, this study adopted a paper-and-pencil measure accompanied by extensive instructions to respondents. Limitations of a purely paper-and-pencil instrument must be weighed against the time saved from more labor-and time-intensive methods. For exploratory purposes, this truncated method provided a useful initial picture of the process of change in a negative relationship over time, buying efficiency at the price of enhanced richness and specificity of data available through verbal probes and clarifications.

This study of turning points in negative work relationships provides further evidence for a growing body of literature on unpleasant work relationships, the "dark side" of organizational life. Continued attention to this area offers hope for increased employee and organizational health. In an era of increasing stress and strain, it is heartening to know that organizational communication scholars can engage organizational experience to make institutions more inviting spaces for human thriving.

References

Andersson, L. M., & Pearson, C. M. (1999). Tit for tat? The spiraling effect of incivility in the workplace. *Academy of Management Review, 24,* 452-471.

Arnett, R. C., & Fritz, J. M. H. (2001). Communication and professional civility as a basic service course: Dialogic praxis between departments and situated in an academic home. *Basic Communication Course Annual, 13,* 174-206.

Barge, J. K., & Musambira, G. W. (1992). Turning points in chair-faculty relationships. *Journal of Applied Communication Research, 20,* 54-77.

Baxter, L. A., & Bullis, C. (1986). Turning points in developing romantic relationships. *Human Communication Research, 12*(4), 469-493.

Berscheid, E., & Walster, E. (1974). A litle bit about love. In T. Huston (Ed.), *Foundations of interpersonal attraction* (pp. 355-381). New York: Academic Press.

Bolton, C. D. (1961). Mate selection as the development of a relationship. *Marriage and Family Living, 23,* 234-240.

Bramson, R. M. (1989). *Coping with difficult people.* New York: Doubleday.

Bridge, K., & Baxter, L. A. (1992). Blended relationships: Friends as work associates. *Western Journal of Communication, 56,* 200-225.

Bullis, C., & Bach, B. W. (1989). Socialization turning points: An examination of change in organizational identification. *Western Journal of Speech Communication, 53,* 273-293.

Byrne, D. (1971). *The attraction paradigm.* New York: Academic Press.

Cooper, C. L., & Cartwright, S. (1994). Healthy mind; healthy organization—A proactive approach to occupational stress. *Human Relations, 47,* 455-470.

Duck, S. (1994). Stratagems, spoils and a serpent's tooth: On the delights and dilemmas of personal relationships. In W. R. Cupach & B. H. Spitzberg (Eds.), *The dark side of interpersonal communication* (pp. 3-24). Hillsdale, NJ: Lawrence Erlbaum.

Fritz, J. M. H. (1997). Responses to unpleasant work relationships. *Communication Research Reports, 14,* 302-311

Fritz, J. M. H. (2002). How do I dislike thee? Let me count the ways: Constructing impressions of troublesome others at work. *Management Communication Quarterly, 15,* 410-438.

Fritz, J. M. H., & Omdahl, B. L. (1998, November). *Effects of negative peer interactions on organizational members' outcomes.* Paper presented at the National Communication Association Annual Convention, New York.

Graham, E. E. (1997). Turning points and commitment in post-divorce relationships. *Communication Monographs, 64,* 350-368.

Guzley, R. M. (1992). Organizational climate and communication climate: Predicators of commitment to the organization. *Management Communication Quarterly, 5,* 379-402.

Hess, J. A. (2000). Maintaining nonvoluntary relationships with disliked partners: An investigation into the use of distancing behaviors. *Human Communication Research, 26,* 458-488.

Holladay, S., Lackovich, R., Lee, M., Coleman, M., Harding, D., Denton, D. (1998). (Re)constructing relationships with grandparents: A turning point analysis of granddaughters' relational development with maternal grandmothers. *International Journal of Aging and Human Development, 46,* 287-303.

Kram, K., & Isabella, L. (1985). Mentoring alternatives: The role of peer relationships in career development. *Academy of Management Journal, 28,* 110-132.

Levitt, M. J., Silver, M. E., & Franco, N. (1996). Troublesome relationships: A part of human experience. *Journal of Social and Personal Relationships, 13,* 523-536.

McAllister, D. J. (1995). Affect- and cognition-based trust as foundations for interpersonal cooperation in organizations. *Academy of Management Journal, 38,* 24-59.

Monroe, C., Borzi, M. G., & DiSalvo, V. S. (1992). Managerial strategies for dealing with difficult subordinates. *Southern Communication Journal, 58,* 247-254.

Omdahl, B. L., & Fritz, J. M. H. (November, 2000). *A longitudinal exploration of emotional experience, burnout, and coping strategies in response to problematic interpersonal relationships at work.* Paper presented at the National Communication Association Convention, Seattle.

Omdahl, B. L., Fritz, J. M. H., & Hess, J. (2004). Problematic relationships in the workplace: An exploration of Rusbult's exit-voice-neglect-loyalty model. Paper presented at the annual convention of the International Association for Relational Research, Madison, Wisconsin.

Rubin, Z. (1970). Measurement of romantic love. *Journal of Personality and Social Psychology, 16,* 265-273.

Sias, P. M., & Cahill, D. J. (1998). From coworkers to friends: The development of peer friendships in the workplace. *Western Journal of Communication, 62,* 273-299.

Sias, P. M., Perry, T., Fix, B., & Silva, D. (2000). *The communicative accomplishment of workplace relationship deterioration.* Paper presented at the National Communication Association Annual Convention, Seattle.

Sypher, B. D., & Zorn, T. E. (1988). Individual differences and construct system content in descriptions of liked and disliked co-workers. *International Journal of Personal Construct Psychology, 1,* 37-51.

Topchik, G. S. (2000). *Managing workplace negativity.* New York: AMACOM.

Part II:
Processes and Effects of
Problematic Work Relationships

6 | Stress, Burnout, and Impaired Mental Health: Consequences of Problematic Work Relationships

Becky L. Omdahl

Janie M. Harden Fritz

The deleterious consequences of burnout are well documented. Burned-out individuals have increased rates of physical illnesses ranging from colds to ulcers to chronic heart disease and a host of other psychological and physiological strains such as insomnia, inflexibility, irritation, anger, depression, anxiety, paranoia, and drug and alcohol abuse (Freudenberger, 1975; Holland, 1982; House, McMichael, Wells, Kaplan, & Landerman, 1979; Pelfrene et al., 2001; Steffy & Laker, 1991; see Holt, 1993 for a review). These individual costs translate into increased organizational costs: high absenteeism; labor turnover; industrial relations difficulties; and poor productivity (Cooper & Marshall, 1976; Maslach, 1979, 1982).

In an effort to reduce these costs, contemporary stress research focuses on identifying specific contributing factors, moderating variables, and intervention programs (Repetti, 1993; Shinn, 1982). Research has identified numerous factors including both objective (e.g., physical properties and hazards, time variables, amount of work, pacing, changes in jobs/ assignments) and subjective factors (e.g., role ambiguity, role conflict, control, complexity, person-job fit, and off-job stress) (see Holt, 1993, for a review).

Numerous moderating variables have been identified such as marital status, age, and length of time in the position (see Repetti, 1993 for a review). Recommended interventions focus on a wide range of behavioral (e.g., exercise, sleep, diet, support-seeking, meditation) and cognitive (e.g., reframing) changes (van Dierendonck, Schaufeli, & Buunk, 1998). Cognitive research recommends problem solving as opposed to emotion focused coping (Lazarus & Folkman, 1984; Bhagat, Allie, & Ford, 1991).

One under-explored and seemingly important factor contributing to burnout is the quality of relationships with people at work (supervisors, peers, and subordinates). Although studies have identified specific types of negative relationships with people at work as stressors (e.g., relationship with supervisor and peers, Karasek & Theorell, 1990; inadequate support from supervisor and subordinates, Pearse, 1977; unpleasant interactions with supervisors and coworkers, Leiter & Maslach, 1988), to date individual studies have not assessed the full range of power levels (i.e., supervisor, peer, and subordinates).

In addition, the only study addressing two of the three different power levels focused only on employees in human service professions (Leiter & Maslach, 1988). Since human service professions are known to present more inequitable emotional demands from the clients/patients (van Dierendonck, Schaufeli, & Buunk, 1998), it is important to explore whether negative interactions with co-workers and supervisors pose the same harmful consequences in other types of organizations.

Therefore, the purpose of this study is to evaluate the impact of negative work relationships of different levels of power on burnout and stress symptoms in employees in a wide range of types of organizations. In providing the rationale for this study, we present: 1. an overview of stress and burnout; 2. the reasons for believing that problematic work relationships are a significant contributor to burnout; and 3. predictions for the study.

Stress and Burnout

The concept of stress was initiated by Hans Selye (1974). Selye noticed that organisms facing a variety of threats (e.g., extreme temperatures, viral and bacterial agents, demands for over-exertion of muscle groups) responded with a common sequence of bodily changes. He called the sequence the "general adaptation syndrome" and identified the stages as: 1. an alarm reaction which engenders a mobilization of the body's defenses; 2. resistance marked by the stimulation of tissue defenses and maximum adaptation to the stressor; and 3. exhaustion during which the adaptive mechanisms collapse.

Since the inception of this construct, numerous psychological theories have addressed the interface between external stimuli and the bodily changes associated with the general adaptation syndrome (e.g., Cox, 1978; Folkman & Lazarus, 1980; Lazarus, 1991; Pearlin, Menaghan, Lieberman, & Mullen, 1981; Pelfrene et al., 2001). These approaches typically define (negative) stress as an imbalance between the perceived external demands on a person and his or her abilities to cope through the employment of cognitive, behavioral, and physiological adaptation (e.g., Cox, 1978; LaRocco, House, & French, 1980).

Research suggests that a perpetuation of significant levels of psychological imbalance culminates in burnout (Maslach, 1979; Maslach & Jackson, 1981; Schaufeli, Maslach, & Marek, 1993). While numerous definitions of burnout have been proposed, Maslach's (1982) widely accepted conceptualization proposes that it is a negative psychological experience characterized by three components: 1. emotional exhaustion is evident when caretakers feel fatigued, worn out, and generally unable to summon sufficient energy to adequately perform their jobs; 2. depersonalization is exemplified by perceiving care recipients as objects, or difficult, disliked people; and 3. reduced personal accomplishment exists when the caretaker perceives that self is a failure in some or all phases of work largely due to ineffective patterns of interaction.

Maslach and Jackson (1982) proposed that these components emerge in sequential phases. Emotional exhaustion is the first phase. In attempting to cope with emotional exhaustion, people reduce the demands by depersonalizing others. As others are depersonalized, effectiveness in interacting with others is reduced and culminates in perceptions of reduced personal accomplishment. Golembiewski, Munzenrider, & Stevenson (1986) have argued for a different sequencing (depersonalization, then reduced personal accomplishment, and finally emotional exhaustion) and both sequences have empirical support (Leiter & Maslach, 1988; Golembiewski and Munzenrider, 1984). Since further research is needed to clarify the sequencing of these stages, we propose competing hypotheses:

H1a: The stages of burnout progress from emotional exhaustion to depersonalization to reduced personal accomplishment.

H1b: The stages of burnout progress from depersonalization to reduced personal accomplishment to emotional exhaustion.

Problematic Relationships at Work and Burnout

Upon reflection of our own experiences, most of us recognize that interactions with people we find difficult require more resources (e.g., cognitive energy, management of emotions) than people we find encouraging and productive. Most of us also recognize that when demands are high, supportive relationships often provide the motivation and energy to cope with demands. Research has documented that both of these relationships are significant: Problematic relationships with supervisors and co-workers are significantly associated with higher levels of both physical and psychological maladies that are symptomatic of burnout, and supportive relationships with supervisors and co-workers are associated with lower levels of burnout symptoms (see Repetti, 1993 for a review).

Unfortunately research has failed to look at all levels of work relationships (supervisors, peers, and subordinates). A comprehensive look at the impact of people at work in all of the these different power levels will provide greater clarity about the types of problematic relationships at work that warrant relative levels of concern in reducing organizational stress.

Clearly people at all of these levels can make life more pleasant or difficult. As research by Fiebig and Kramer (1998) points out, employees identify positive and negative experiences arising from supervisors, coworkers, and subordinates. Interactions with people at all of these power levels can synergistically increase energy or they can drain energy. Bosses, peers, and subordinates who praise talents and contributions, provide useful information, and behave with such social skill in front of important audiences that we are proud of our organization's image are likely to increase energy. In contrast, people at all of these levels who point out shortcomings in unsupportive ways, withhold important information, and engage in embarrassing behaviors in front of important audiences drain energy. Since burnout results when demand continues to significantly exceed resources, the interpersonal behavior of people at all levels may impact burnout.

However, the roles of supervisor, peers, and subordinates reflect relative decrements in the power of people to reward and punish work performance as well as to provide or withhold resources essential to task efficiency, completion and effectiveness. Specifically, problematic relationships with supervisors are likely to be perceived as posing a greater threat than peer relationships to a wide array of employee objectives (i.e., receiving desirable tasks, rewards for contributions, esteem in front of colleagues, access to machines, information, and time affecting effectiveness, etc.). In turn, problematic peer relationships are likely to jeopardize trust in rewards and resources more than are problematic subordinate relationships. Since subordinates generally control fewer resources and are not in positions of formally evaluating the work done by those holding more power, negative relationships with subordinates are less likely to be perceived as threatening than relationships with supervisors or peers.

Consistent with these arguments, research to date clearly indicates that problematic interactions and relationships with supervisors negatively impact both the mental and physical well-being of employees to a greater extent than do problematic peer relationships. Although the rare study fails to find the expected negative relationship between supervisor support and mental health problems (e.g., Jayaratne & Chess, 1984), the vast majority of studies obtain significant findings in the expected direction for both depression and anxiety (e.g., LaRocco, House & French, 1980; Repetti, 1987; Winnubst, Marcelissen & Kleber, 1982) even when covariates are taken into account (see Repetti, 1993).

Research reveals studies addressing problematic relationships with coworkers consistently find relationships with anxiety (LaRocco et. al., 1980; Repetti, 1987; Winnubst, Marcelissen & Kleber, 1982). However, mixed findings have been found for the impact of negative co-worker relationships on depression. Some studies have obtained a significant relationship (Karasek, Triantis & Chaudhry, 1982, LaRocco et al., 1980; Revicki & May, 1985; Winnubst et. al., 1982) and other have not (Golding, 1989; Jayaratne & Chess, 1984; Repetti, 1987). Thus, it appears that relationships with co-workers are important, but their impact is not as great at that of supervisors.

Research to date has not included subordinates. However, we rest on our earlier arguments that while they hold the potential to contribute to burnout, this contribution will be more limited than that of supervisors and coworkers due to their more limited power to formally evaluate and control resources.

Previous research has addressed the complexity in options for conceptualizing and operationalizing relationships in the workplace. Repetti (1987) addressed both the common social environment as well as the individual social environment. The results revealed that while the aggregated ratings of the social environment did significantly correlate with individual depression and anxiety, the individual's perception was the more powerful and mediating predictor. Thus, for this research, we will focus on individual perceptions of supervisors, peers, and subordinates.

As alluded to earlier, another complexity in conceptualizing and operationizing relationships at work relates to the abstraction or specificity of the dimensions used to reflect the relationship. The majority of prior research has explored the perceived supportiveness or unsupportiveness of supervisors and/or coworkers (see Repetti, 1993 for a review). Although in many work environments the supervisor is a single individual, people usually have multiple co-workers. Typically (see Repetti, 1987 as an example), coworkers are rated as a group rather than individually. Thus it is possible that outliers (unusually horrible or saintly co-workers) could swing the positive or negative perception of the group. Thus it seems useful to explore the complex configuration of how employees rate individual colleagues (see Leiter and Maslach, 1988, as an example). Within this approach, the proportion of negative or positive people in each group (supervisors, co-workers, and subordinates) as well as the sum of the negativity-positivity ratings can be assessed for impact on burnout variables.

Using these conceptualizations, as well as the arguments presented above, we propose:

H2: The proportion of negative supervisors will be positively correlated with the burnout dimensions (i.e., emotional exhaustion, depersonalization, reduced personal accomplishment) and stress symptoms (depression, anxiety, bodily pains, negative thoughts, inability to concentrate).

H3: The proportion of negative co-workers will be positively correlated with the burnout dimensions and stress symptoms.

H4: The proportion of negative subordinates will be positively correlated with the burnout dimensions and stress symptoms.

However, we also expect:

H5: The impact on the burnout dimensions and symptoms will be greatest for the proportion of negative supervisors and least for the proportion of negative subordinates.

Method

Participants

One hundred twenty-six participants were recruited from two universities. Approximately half the sample (n = 53) was from a large, land-grant mid-western university and the other half (n = 73) were from a medium, private eastern university. We intentionally recruited communication classes that included large numbers of older-than-average students so that the findings would generalize to working populations. We permitted students to recruit others to complete questionnaires as well. The participants ranged in age from 18 to 53 (mean = 29.7 years). Sixty-one were male, fifty-eight were female, and seven did not specify their sex.

The participants reported a wide range of employment experiences. The range of time with current employer ranged from 1 month to 40 years and 5 months (mean = 7 years and 10 months). The number of prior jobs ranged from none to 5 (mean = 2.7).

Also represented in this sample was a wide range of employment contexts. Number of employees at the site of employment ranged from 3 to 5,000 (mean = 858). The participants also worked for a wide range of types of companies (see Table 1) and in the full range of positions from administrators through employees (see Table 2).

Table 1
Occupations and Positions of Participants

Type of Occupation	Number of Participants	Percentage
Service	47	37.3%
High Tech	4	3.2%
Entertainment	2	1.6%
Medical	13	10.3%
Education	15	11.9%
Manufacturing	15	11.9%
Utilities	2	1.6%
Communication	5	4.0%
Government	12	9.5%
Other/Missing	11	8.7%

Table 2
Positions Held by Participants

Type of Position	Number of Participants	Percentage
Administrators	7	5.6%
Managers/Supervisors	17	13.5%
Professionals	32	25.4%
Support Staff	16	12.7%
Direct Service	40	31.7%
Missing	14	11.1%

Questionnaire

The questionnaire consisted of four major sections: 1) items addressing employment outcome variables; 2) valence ratings of other employees; 3) description and rating of experience with one problematic co-worker; and 4) demographic information. Parts of the questionnaire were designed for this study while other sections were intended for use in other articles.

Employee outcome and stress variables. The first section of the questionnaire included indexes for eight employee outcome variables: 1) the burnout variables of depersonalization, reduced personal accomplishment, and emotional exhaustion; 2) items addressing task overload; 3) physical and mental indicators of stress; 4) job satisfaction; 5) job commitment; 6) organizational commitment; 7) occupational commitment; 8) cynicism; and 9) perceived productivity. Items addressing all of these constructs except physical and mental indicators of stress and perceived productivity were measured using Likert items for which the response scales ranged from 1 (strongly disagree) to 7 (strongly agree). Since questions for 4-9 above were developed for a second study, they will not be described in detail here (see Fritz and Omdahl, this volume). All of the items used in this study appear in Appendix A.

Maslach's three components of burnout are depersonalization, reduced personal accomplishment, and emotional exhaustion. The construct of depersonalization refers to the tendency of burned-out people to regard other people as objects. It was measured through a series of four items such as, "I feel I treat people as if they were impersonal objects." Reduced personal accomplishment (i.e., the tendency of burned-out people to feel ineffective in their interactions with others) was addressed through five items. For example, one (reverse scored) item reads, "I feel I'm personally influencing other people's lives through my work." Seven items addressed emotional exhaustion. These items (e.g., "I feel like I'm at the end of my rope.") address the extent to which people feel "used-up" and drained by their jobs. The items for these three dimensions of burnout have been used widely in other research studies (see Barker, Demerouti & Schaufeli, 2002; Maslach & Jackson, 1981) and consistently yield high reliabilities (see Miller, Stiff & Ellis, 1988; Omdahl & O'Donnell, 1999). As noted above, all of these Likert items had 7 point response scales.

Task overload at work was assessed by obtaining responses to three items: "In general, I feel that more is demanded of me at work than I can deal with," "I feel that the demands far exceed my time and energy resources," and "I come to work expecting that I will feel even further behind at the end of the day." These items also used 7 point response scales ranging from 1 (strongly disagree) to 7 (strongly agree).

Physical and mental maladies associated with stress were measured using five items responded to on scales ranging from 1(never) to 9 (alot). The five items addressed the extent to which the person experienced: body aches and pains; anxiety; depression; trouble concentrating; and negative thoughts.

Valence ratings of other employees. The second section of the questionnaire asked for a listing of those people who directly supervise/manage the participant, the people who are directly supervised/managed by the participant, and other people whom the person interacts with for important job duties or for daily unimportant job duties. It should be noted that we allowed people to list multiple supervisors as well as multiple subordinates and co-workers. We did this since many employees are supervised by multiple individuals (e.g., working in a restaurant, store, or hospital where an employee may work for a variety of managers). The questionnaire asked the participant to specify the relationship of the person to him/herself and then to rate the person from -3 (negative) to +3 (positive) with a neutral midpoint of 0. They were instructed to use this valence scale to indicate how they typically felt about the person.

Description and rating of experience with one problematic co-worker. In the third section of the questionnaire, participants were asked to identify the person at work that they find to be the most problematic and describe one specific interaction with that person. This description, ratings of the emotional reactions and appraisals they had during the interaction, as well as a series of items addressing how they respond to that person were designed for another study.

Demographics. In the final section of the questionnaire, participants provided basic demographic information. This information was requested in response to open ended questions addressing nature of the work of their employer, how long they have worked for the organization, position held, how many people at the site, state of the site, sex, age, number of prior organizations they have worked for. The demographic information was collected primarily to assess the extent to which the participants formed a diverse pool of employees and offer findings which could be generalized.

Procedure

Consent forms and questionnaires were distributed to participants at a research session. After questions were answered, the participants completed the questionnaires. Before leaving, they were debriefed and thanked for their participation.

Data Analysis

Reliabilities of all indexes were assessed by computing Cronbach's alphas. We regarded alphas greater than .65 to be acceptable.

In order to determine the sequencing of stages (Hypotheses 1A and IB), least squares path analyses was conducted using Hunter and Hamilton's (1992) program. The goodness of fit between the data and each model was assessed using three chi square tests. First a chi square was computed for the model of independent/uncorrelated variables. The independent model was tested because, especially in small samples, it is likely to fit as well as the theoretical model (Bentler, 1989). In the event that this first Chi square does not indicate that the data significantly deviates from the model of independent/uncorrelated variables fits, then the effectiveness of the hypothesized theoretical model is doubtful (Bentler, 1989). The second Chi square tested the fit between the model proposed by Maslach and Jackson (1982) and the data. The third Chi square tested the fit between the model proposed by Golembiewski et al. (1986) and the data. In addition to examining whether the data deviated significantly from these theoretical models (indicating poor fit), other links (where no causal relationships were expected) were examined to see if they represented significant relationships.

To examine Hypotheses 2 through 4, Pearson correlations between proportions of negative supervisors, co-workers, subordinates, and total employees, and the employee burnout, and stress variables were computed. In addition, we used path analysis to test the model, adding stressors, for the stage sequence identified as best fitting model (if any) in the test for the first hypothesis. Once again, Chi squares for both the independent/uncorrelated variables and for the hypothesized model were computed.

In order to determine whether the power levels of the negative others differentially impacted burnout and stress (Hypothesis 5), we followed Ferguson's (1959) procedure for calculating t-tests for difference between correlations from non-independent samples. This procedure is used instead of the more-commonly-used Fisher's test when the data for both correlations come from the same group of participants. For correlations and the correlation-comparison tests, significance was set at alpha less than or equal to .05.

Results

Index Reliabilities

Cronbach's alphas were computed for each of the indexes. All of the alphas were acceptable: emotional exhaustion .87; depersonalization .80; reduced personal accomplishment .72; and, task overload .92.

Path Analysis for Sequencing of Burnout Stages

The correlations used in the path analysis were as follows: emotional exhaustion with depersonalization r=.72; emotional exhaustion with reduced personal accomplishment r=.40; and, depersonalization with reduced personal accomplishment r=.34.

The first analysis addressed the extent to which the data fit a model in which no significant correlations were expected (independence model). The overall Chi square for this model was 9.99 (df = 2, p = .007). The chi square reveals that the data deviated significantly from the independence model.

The second and third path analyses revealed support for the model proposed by Maslach and Jackson (1982), but no support was found for the model proposed by Golembiewski et al. (1986). For the model proposed by Maslach and Jackson (1982), the overall Chi square was .67 (df=1, p = .75), and the resulting path coefficients were as follows:

Emotional   Reduced
Exhaustion   .72   Depersonalization .34   Personal
————————▶   ————————▶ Accomplishment

The chi square reflected a very good fit between the model and the data. The indirect link between emotional exhaustion and reduced personal accomplishment (not expected to be significant) had an insignificant difference score of .16 (z=.82, alpha =.29). Thus, the model proposed by Maslach and Jackson (1982) is an excellent fit with the data.

For the model proposed by Golembiewski et al., (1986), the overall chi square was 9.99 (df=1, p = .001), and the path coefficients were:

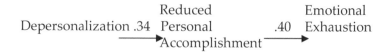

Reduced   Emotional
Depersonalization .34 Personal   .40   Exhaustion
——————▶Accomplishment——————▶

In this case the difference score for the indirect link from depersonalization to emotional exhaustion was significant (z=3.16, alpha=.0013). Thus, the data deviated significantly from the model proposed by Golembiewski et al. (1986) which argues that depersonalization begins the burnout process.

Relationships between Negative Peers and Stress

The findings reveal significant correlations between negative peers and several burnout and stress indicators. As Table 3 reveals, the proportions of negative supervisors and coworkers are significantly correlated with several indicators of burnout and stress. Specifically, the proportions of negative supervisors and co-workers were significantly correlated with all three dimensions of burnout. However the proportion of negative subordinates did not correlate significantly with any of the burnout variables.

Table 3
Correlations between Problematic Relationships and Dependent Variables

	Supervisors	Coworkers	Subordinates	Total
Depersonalize	.25**b	.47***a	-.11c	.41***
Reduced Pers. Accomp.	.41***a	.21*b	.10b	.30**
Emot. Exhaust.	.35***b	.43***a	.02c	.42***
Body Aches	.13a	.05a	-.03a	.11
Anxiety	.19*a	.20*a	.14a	.28**
Depression	.30**a	.21*b	.09b	.28**
Lack of Concen.	.04a	.14a	.10a	.13
Negative Thought	.22*b	.44***a	.11b	.45***

*p≤.05
**p≤.01
***p≤.001

Note: In each row, correlations which do not share letters in common are significantly different from each other (alpha ≤.05).

With the exception of body aches and lack of concentration, the same pattern held for stress symptoms. Specifically, both proportions of negative supervisors and coworkers correlated significantly with anxiety, depression, and negative thoughts. However, consistent with our predictions about the relative power of the negative peers, negative subordinates had no significant effect on any measured physical or mental symptom of stress.

Path analysis was used to examine an overall model proposing that negative relationships at work lead to emotional exhaustion which leads to depersonalization which leads to reduced personal accomplishment (i.e., stressors leading to the stage sequence proposed by Maslach and Jackson, 1982). The path analysis for the following model yielded an overall chi square of 5.78 (df=9 p=.22). The path coefficients were:

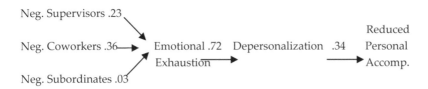

Neg. Supervisors .23

Neg. Coworkers .36⟶ Emotional .72 Depersonalization .34 Reduced Personal Accomp.
Exhaustion⟶

Neg. Subordinates .03

None of the difference scores for unpredicted links revealed significant z scores. Therefore, this model appears to be a good fit with the data. (In contrast, the test of the independence model (i.e., proposing no links between variables) resulted in a chi square of 48.86 (p=.005).)

The t-tests for differences between correlations revealed several findings consistent with the predictions and some findings contrary to predictions. The exact findings are indicated on the preceding table through the use of letters following each of the correlations. Overall, the majority of the t-tests revealed that negative relationships with supervisors and coworker are significantly more highly correlated with burnout and stress variables than are negative relationships with subordinates. However, there are twists in the data.

Looking first at the burnout variables, for both depersonalization and emotional exhaustion, the table reveals that, counter to expectations, the correlation for negative coworkers was significantly greater than for negative supervisors. However, consistent with predictions, both these correlations were greater than those for subordinates. The correlations for reduced personal accomplishment were closer to the predicted pattern. In this case, the correlation for supervisors was significantly greater than for those of either co-workers or subordinates. However, there was no significant difference expected between the correlation for co-workers and subordinates.

Turning to the stress symptoms, several notable differences emerged. First of all, the correlation between negative supervisors and depression was significantly greater than the correlation between negative subordinates and depression. In addition, negative co-workers induced a significantly higher correlation with negative thoughts than did subordinates. The other correlations revealed no significant differences across the power levels of negatively perceived workers.

Although the findings across the two studies clearly point to the deleterious impact of negative peers, we were concerned that something akin to a negative halo effect could be occurring. Specifically, it seemed likely that unhappy employees may respond negatively on all scales without carefully differentiating among the items. We included a task overload measure which should impact people independently of proportion of negative peers. Even people who have positive peers can be in work situations where they are overwhelmed by the work load. As expected, task overload was *not* significantly correlated with proportion of negative peers (supervisors -.10, co-workers -.12, subordinates -.09, total -.09). In fact, there were negative correlations (although insignificant) between all levels of negative peers and task overload. This suggests that negative employees were differentiating among the items and that the outcomes are not negative halo effects.

Discussion

Summary of Findings

The results revealed moderate support for the burnout stage sequence proposed by Maslach and Jackson (1982) (i.e., emotional exhaustion followed by depersonalization and then reduced personal accomplishment)(Hypothesis 1A). The data failed to support the sequence proposed by Golembiewski, et al. (1986) (i.e., depersonalization then reduced personal accomplishment and then emotional exhaustion) (Hypothesis 1B).

The correlations between the proportions of negative supervisors (Hypothesis 2), co-workers (Hypothesis 3), and subordinates (Hypothesis 4) and the dependent variables revealed a very clear pattern. Specifically, the proportions of negative supervisors and coworkers were significantly correlated with all three burnout variables and three (i.e., anxiety, depression, and negative thoughts) of five stress symptoms. In contrast, the proportion of negative subordinates did not correlate significantly with any of the burnout variables or symptoms. Thus, there is strong general support for Hypotheses 2 and 3, but no support for Hypothesis 4.

The data continued to support Maslach and Jackson's (1982) stage sequence model when the stressors (negative bosses, coworkers, and subordinates) were added in the path analysis. No links other than those entered into the model were significant.

Analysis of the differences between correlations (Hypothesis 5) revealed that for two of the three burnout variables (i.e., depersonalization and emotional exhaustion) and one of the stress symptoms (negative thoughts), coworkers created significantly greater correlations than did supervisors. Only for reduced personal accomplishment was the correlation for negative supervisors greater than the correlation for negative coworkers.

More consistent with predictions, differences between correlations for negative supervisors and subordinates emerged for all of the burnout variables (i.e., depersonalization, reduced personal accomplishment, and emotional exhaustion) and depression. However, expected differences were not apparent for other stress symptoms (i.e., body aches, anxiety, lack of concentration, and negative thoughts).

The differences between correlations for coworkers and subordinates were significant for depersonalization, emotional exhaustion and negative thoughts, but not for reduced personal accomplishment, body aches, anxiety, depression, and lack of concentration.

In sum the results are mixed for Hypothesis 5, but there are clear indications that for several variables the relative power of the people with whom one has negative work relationships does matter. Placed in context, the significant correlations between both the proportions of negative supervisors and coworkers (but not subordinates) and six key dependent variables leave no doubt that negative relationships at work create personal costs for employees.

Theoretical Implications and Future Research

The support for the sequence of burnout stages proposed by Maslach and Jackson's (1982) contributes to the evidence on how burnout progresses in individuals. The results of this study are consistent with the argument that when faced with stress people first feel emotionally overextended and drained. In that state, they begin to think of others as objects in order to reduce the demands upon them, and this culminates in feeling that self is accomplishing less.

However, given that Golembiewski et al., (1986) proposed sequence of burnout stages has been confirmed in at least one study (Golembiewski & Munzenrider, 1988), the remaining question is whether different groups of people produce different models or whether accumulating evidence will favor one model over the other. It may be the case that organizational cultures and/or individual variables affect the emergence of the stages.

The numerous significant correlations between negative supervisors and coworkers and burnout and stress variables is consistent with research that has identified problematic psychosocial climate as a determinant of burnout (e.g., Golembiewski & Munzenrider, 1988). The data from this study supports the importance of work relationships in a wider range of work settings and greater range of relative levels of power. The failure to find significant relationships between subordinates and burnout is very important given the limited prior research on this variable.

The findings that for some variables negative relationships with coworkers were more important than negative relationships with supervisors/managers was intriguing. One possible explanation is that people in the study had only one, two or three supervisors (most had one), but they typically had multiple co-workers. Thus, a high proportion of negative supervisors/ managers in all cases meant working with a very small number of people regarded as difficult. However, for co-workers a high proportion of negative relationships typically meant working with a large number of difficult others. It seems logical that the sheer amount of time and energy it takes to deal with more difficult people may overwhelm the impact of a single difficult boss.

The fact that subordinates had practically no impact on burnout variables and stress symptoms is an important contribution to the literature. Virtually all studies looking at the impact of people at work on stress have only measured the impact of supervisors/managers and coworkers. Thus, our insignificant findings for subordinates provide a needed piece of information in the literature.

Within the umbrella of psychosocial climate, it may be important to examine how the deleterious effects of negative relationships at work are offset by more positive relationships. Research has demonstrated that support from supervisors and coworkers increases resistance to occupational stressors. Emotional, instrumental, informational, and/or appraisal support reduce the likelihood of stress and burnout (Albrecht, 1982; Caplan, Cobb, French, Harrison, & Pinneau, 1975; House, 1981). It may be the case that people with negative relationships with some people at work who also have very positive relationships with other people may fair far better than those reporting only negative or negative and neutral relationships. Clearly organizations are emotional, conflictual spheres in which needs created by certain individuals may be offset by others (Fineman, 1993).

References

Albrecht, T. (1982) Coping with occupational stress; Relational and individual strategies of nurses in acute health care settings. In M. Burgoon (Ed.), *Communicaton yearbook 6* (pp. 832-849). Newbury Park, CA: Sage.

Bakker, A. B., Demerouti, E., & Schaufeli, W. (2002). Validation of the Maslach Burnout Inventory — General Survey: An internet study. *Anxiety, Stress and Coping, 15*, 245-260.

Bentler, P. M. (1989). *EQS: Stuctural Equations Program Manual.* Los Angelas, CA: BMDP Statistical Software, Inc.

Bhagat, R. S., Allie, S. M., & Ford, D. L. Jr. (1991). Organizational stress, personal life stress and symptoms of life strains: An inquiry into the moderating role of styles of coping. In P. L. Perrewe (Ed.), *Handbook of job stress (Special Issue). Journal of Social Behavior and Personality, 6*, 163-184.

Caplan, R. D., Cobb, S., French, J. R. P., Jr., Harrison, R. V., & Pinneau, S. R., Jr. (1975). *Job demands and worker health: Main effects and occupational differences.* DHEW (NIOSH) publication no. 75-160. Washington, D.C.: U.S. Government Printing Office.

Cooper, C. L., & Marshall, J. (1976). Occupational sources of stress: A review of the literature relating to coronary heart disease and mental ill health. *Journal of Occupational Psychology, 49*, 11-28.

Cox, T. (1978). *Stress.* Hong Kong: The MacMillan Press Ltd.

Ferguson, G. A. (1959). *Statistical analysis in psychology and education.* New York: McGraw Hill.

Fiebig, G. V., & Kramer, M. (1998). A framework for the study of emotions in organizational contexts. *Management Communication Quarterly, 11*, 536-572.

Fineman, S. (1993). Organizations as emotional arenas. In S. Fineman (Ed.), *Emotion in organizations* (pp. 9-35). Newbury Park, CA: Sage.

Folkman, S., & Lazarus, R. S. (1980). An analysis of coping in a middle-aged community sample. *Journal of Health and Social Behavior, 21*, 219-239.

Freudenberger, H. J. (1975). The staff burnout syndrome in alternative institutions. *Psychotherapy: Theory Research and Practice, 12 (1)*, 73-82.

Golding, J. M. (1989). Role occupancy and role-specific stress and social support as predictors of depression. *Basic and Applied Social Psychology, 10*, 173-195.

Golembiewski, R. T., & Munzenrider, R. F. (1984). Phases of psychological burnout and organizational covariates: A replication from a large population, *Journal of Health and Human Resources Administration, 6*, 290-323.

Golembiewski, R. T., & Munzenrider, R. F. (1988). *Phases of burnout.* New York: Praeger.

Golembiewski, R. T., Munzenrider, R. F., & Stevenson, J. G. (1986). *Stress in organizations: Toward a phase model of burnout.* New York: Praeger.

Holland, R. P. (1982). Special educator burnout. *Educational Horizon, 60(2)*, 58-64.

Holt, R. R. (1993). Occupational stress. In L. Goldberger and S. Breznitz (Eds.), *Handbook of stress: Theoretical and clinical aspects (2nd ed., pp. 342-367).* New York: Free Press.

House, J. S. (1981). *Work stress and social support.* Reading MA: Addison Wesley.

House, J. S., McMichael, A. J., Wells, J. A., Kaplan, B. H., Landerman, L. R. (1979). Occupational stress and health among factory workers, *Journal of Health and Social Behavior, 20*, 139-160.

Hunter, J. E., & Hamilton, M. A. (1992). *Path: A Program in Basica.* Department of Psychology, Michigan State University, April 4, 1992.

Jayaratne, S., & Chess, W. A. (1984). The effects of emotional support on perceived job stress and strain. *The Journal of Applied Behavioral Science, 20,* 141-153.

Karasek, R. A., & Theorell, T. (1990). *Healthy work: Stress, productivity, and the reconsruction of working life.* New York: Basic Books.

Karasek, R. A., Triantis, K. P., & Chaudhry, S. S. (1982). Coworker and supervisor support as moderators of association between task characteristics and mental strain. *Journal of Occupational Behavior, 3,* 181-200.

LaRocco, J. M., House, J. S., French, J. R. P. (1980). Social support, occupational stress, and health. *Journal of Health and Social Behavior, 21,* 202-218.

Lazarus, R. S. (1991). Psychological Stress in the Workplace. *Journal of Social Behavior and Personality, 6,* 1-14.

Lazarus, R. S., and Folkman, S. (1984). *Stress, appraisal and coping.* New York: Springer

Leiter, M. P., and Maslach, C. (1988). The impact of interpersonal environment on burnout and organizational commitment. *Journal of Organizational Behavior, 9* (4), 297-308.

Maslach, C. (1979). The burn-out syndrome and patient care. In C. Garfield (Ed.), *Stress and survival* (pp. 111-120). St. Louis: Mosby.

Maslach, C. (1982). *Burnout: The cost of caring.* Englewood Cliffs, NJ: Prentice Hall.

Maslach, C. & Jackson, S. E. (1981). The measurement of experienced burnout. *Journal of Occupational Behavior, 2,* 99-113.

Maslach, C., & Jackson, S. E. (1982). Burnout in health professions: A social psychological analysis. In G. Sanders and J. Suls (Eds.), *Social psychology of health and illness* (pp. 227-251). Hillsdale, NJ: Erlbaum.

Miller, K., Stiff, J., & Ellis, B.H. (1988). Communication and empathy as precursors to burnout among human service workers. *Communication Monographs, 55,* 250-265.

Omdahl, B. L., & O'Donnell, C. (1999). Emotional contagion, empathic concern, and communicative responsiveness as variables affecting nurses' stress and occupational commitment. *Journal of Advanced Nursing, 29,* 1351-1359.

Pearse, R. (1977). *What managers think about their managerial careers.* New York: American Management Association, 1977.

Pelfrene, E., Vlerick, P., Mak, R. P., DeSmets, P., Kornitzers, M., & DeBacker, G. (2001). Scale reliability and validity of the Karasek 'Job Demand Control Support' model in the Bestress study. *Work & Stress, 15,* 297-313.

Perlin, L. I., Menaghan, E. G., Lieberman, M. A., & Mullan, J. T. (1981). The stress process. *Journal of Health and Social Behavior, 22,* 337-356.

Repetti, R. L. (1987). Individual and common components of the social environment at work and psychological well-being. *Journal of Personality and Social Psychology, 52,* 710-720.

Repetti, R. L. (1993). The effects of workload and the social environment at work on health. In L. Goldberger and S. Breznitz (Eds.), *Handbook of stress: Theoretical and clinical aspects (2nd ed., pp. 368-385).* New York: The Free Press.

Revicki, D. A., & May, H. J. (1985). Occupational stress, social support and depression. *Health Psychology, 4,* 61-77.

Schaufeli, W. B., Maslach, C., & Marek, R. (1993). (Eds.). *Professional burnout: Recent develop-ments in theory and research.* Washington, D.C.: Taylor & Francis.

Selye, H. (1974). *Stress without distress.* New York: The New American Library.

Shinn, M. (1982). Methodological issues: Evaluating and using information. In W. S. Paine (Ed.), *Job stress and burnout: Research, theory and intervention perspectives* (pp. 61-79). Newbury Park, CA: Sage.

Steffy, B. D., & Laker, D. R. (1991). Workplace and personal stresses antecedent to employees' alcohol use. In P. L. Perrewe (Ed.), *Handbook on job stress (Special Issue). Journal of Social Behavior and Personality, 6,* 115-126,

van Dierendonck, D., Schaufeli, W. B., & Buunk, B. P. (1998). The evaluation of an individual burnout intervention program: The role of inequity and social support. *Journal of Applied Psychology, 83,* 392-407.

Winnubst, J. A. M., Marcelissen, F. H. G., & Kleber, R. J. (1982). Effects of social support in the stressor-strain relationship: A Dutch sample. *Social Science Medicine, 16,* 475-482.

Appendix A
Indices

Emotional Exhaustion (Alpha = .87)
1. I feel used up at the end of a workday.
2. Working with people all day is a real strain on me.
3. I feel frustrated by my job.
4. I feel fatigued when I get up in the morning and have to face another day on the job.
5. I feel I'm working too hard on my job.
6. I feel like I'm at the end of my rope.
7. I feel burned out from my work.

Depersonalization (Alpha = .80)
1. I worry that this job is hardening me emotionally.
2. I really don't care what happens to some people.
3. I've become more callous toward people since I took this job.
4. I feel I treat some people as if they were impersonal "objects."

Reduced Personal Accomplishment (Alpha = .72)
1. I deal very effectively with the problems of people. (R)
2. I feel I'm personally influencing other people's lives through my work. (R)
3. I can create a relaxed atmosphere with people. (R)
4. I feel exhilarated after working with people. (R)
5. In my work, I deal with emotional problems calmly. (R)

Task Overload (alpha = .92)
1. In general, I feel that more is demanded of me at work than I can deal with.
2. I feel that the demands far exceed my time and energy resources.
3. I come to work expecting that I will feel even further behind at the end of the day.

Appendix B
T-tests for Differences between Correlations for Non-independent Groups

Comparison of Correlations between:

	Supervisors and Coworkers	Supervisors and Subordinate	Coworkers and Subordinates
Depersonalization	t=10.04*	t=3.10*	t=3.94*
Reduced Pers. Acc.	t=3.90*	t=3.03*	t=.92
Emotional Exhaustion	t=5.75*	t=2.82*	t=3.88*
Body Aches	t=.85	t=1.25	t=.57
Anxiety	t=.14	t=.42	t=1.02
Depression	t=1.58*	t=1.83*	t=.97
Lack of Concentration	t=1.06	t=.43	t=.32
Negative Thoughts	t=15.60*	t=.81	t=3.92*

*p ≤ .05

NOTE: All t-test values are based on a comparison between the Pearson correlations presented in the Results section.

7 Reduced Job Satisfaction, Diminished Commitment, and Workplace Cynicism as Outcomes of Negative Work Relationships

Janie M. Harden Fritz

Becky L. Omdahl

Relationships with others at work form the matrix within which work life is conducted (Stohl, 1995) and through which individual and organizational outcomes are mediated, constructing the nature and quality of organizational life (e.g., Sias, 1996). The quality of work relationships, therefore, should texture organizational outcomes connected to perceptions and interpretation of experiences of work life. Research suggests that work relationships are not uniformly beneficent; coworkers are not only sources of social support (Schuler, 1982; Ratsoy, Sarros, & Aidoo-Taylor, 1986), but of stress as well (Beach, Martin, Blum, & Roman, 1993; Bridge & Baxter, 1992; Cooper & Cartwright, 1994; Jenner, 1986; Jorde-Bloom, 1988). In the past several years, research attention given to supportive work relationships such as friendships, peers, and mentor relationships (e.g. Bridge & Baxter, 1992; Fritz, 1997a; Kram & Isabella, 1985; Odden & Sias, 1997; Sias & Cahill, 1998) is increasingly balanced by research focused on the nature and causes of unpleasant work relationships and on work relationship deterioration (e.g., Fritz, 1997b, 2002; Hess, Omdahl, & Fritz, this volume; Sias, this volume; Sias, Heath, Perry, Silva, & Fix, 2004; Sias & Perry, 2004). Research on specific outcomes, such as stress and burnout effects, of problematic relationships has begun (Omdahl & Fritz, this volume), complementing these more general findings. This research also explores different status relationships.

Research needs to continue in this vein, identifying the nature and extent of effects of negative relationships on other relevant organizational and individual variables. Therefore, we proposed to verify relationships between negative work relationships and employee outcomes across a wide range of organizational types: reduced job and coworker satisfaction, declining organizational commitment, and high workplace cynicism. Our perspective rests in a social information processing/social constructionist model suggesting that communicative processes exert a powerful impact on perceptions of organizational life (e.g., Salancik & Pfeffer, 1978; Sias, 1996; Thomas & Griffin, 1989).

Rationale for Study 1

Research on several facets of organizational life suggests that unpleasant work relationships may affect both employees and organizations adversely through stress (Beach, et al., 1993; Cooper & Cartwright, 1994; Gant, et al., 1993; Gettman & Pena, 1986; Jenner, 1986; Scherer, Owen, Petrick, Brodzinski & Goyer, 1991; Schuler, 1982), inability to coordinate tasks (Morrill, 1989), and organizational turnover (Chapman, 1993). Beyond the time and effort individuals expend to manage such interactions, the cumulative influence of communicating in problematic work relationships may have serious implications for corporate culture.

Schneider (1987), taking an interactionist perspective, argues that the people within the organization come to define its look and feel. If people in an organization behave in ways such that conflictual relationships are common, the climate would be experienced as unpleasant and stressful. Because types of conversational resources perceived as available for use would be shaped by behaviors enacted regularly (Giddens, 1984), such an atmosphere would reproduce itself, creating the conditions for further problematic interaction. For example, constant complaint may stimulate others to perceive the organization and/or its members negatively, consistent with the complaints, similar to perceptions of equity and inequity generated by coworker conversations (Sias, 1996). Thus members of an organization may come to develop and use certain social cognitive schemata as a result of interaction at work (Louis, 1980). Rules governing communication expectations, such as what type of assertive communication should be used at work (Bryan & Gallois, 1992), could shift, altering message strategy selection.

Although an array of research provides reason to believe that unpleasant work relationships create direct and indirect damage to persons and organizations, no studies have focused specifically on the impact of unpleasant work relationships across a wide range of organizational types (but see Omdahl & Fritz, this volume). Research on interpersonal environments has focused primarily on the stressful effects of negative environments, with less focus on other organizational and interpersonal outcomes. Focus on other organizational outcomes will allow a more complete picture of the role of unpleasant work relationships. Studies have explored stress in human services organizations resulting from coworker interaction (e.g., Chapman, 1993; Gant, et al., 1993; Leiter, 1988; Leiter & Meechan, 1986). Expanding the range of organizational types affords better generalizability of findings.

From an applied perspective, research on negative relationships and their effects on outcomes such as job and coworker satisfaction, organizational commitment, and cynicism would advance understanding of interpersonal aspects of the workplace and offer insights into making organizational life healthier and organizations more productive. From a theoretical perspective, studies on unpleasant work relationships would advance a more complete picture of the domain of interpersonal life in organizations, balancing current attention given to other relationships (e.g., mentoring, superior-subordinate relationships). Such research would extend recent findings on the role of work relationships in the social construction of work life (Sias, 1996). The following section, therefore, proposes hypotheses and research questions related to negative peer relationships.

Hypotheses

Job satisfaction. The extent to which persons are satisfied with their jobs is important for quality of work life. The necessity of work is often made bearable by the joy we receive from doing productive work. Clearly, the quality of one's social relations at work affects one's experience of work, creating both gratification and distress (Crosby, 1982). Several social factors affect job satisfaction. As perceptions of group cohesion and support from others in the work environment increase, job satisfaction increases (Repetti & Cosmas, 1991). Coworkers appear to influence job satisfaction (Solly & Hohenshil, 1986). The social climate, consisting of the quality of formal and informal social interaction, has been found to be related to job satisfaction among health care providers (Repetti & Cosmas, 1991). Not surprisingly, unpleasant work interaction, specifically conflict with coworkers, is related to low job satisfaction (Argyle & Furnham, 1983).

Negative relationships with others would contribute to decreased job satisfaction in a variety of ways. The greater the frequency of unpleasant, conflictual interaction, the more likely it is to engulf one's perceptual field, distract and occupy one's mind, and contribute to a greater relative proportion of negative affect associated with work. For example, Tina has arguments over work policy with Alan, who consistently comes in late after lunch. When Tina thinks about work, these arguments come to mind. When coworkers ask her how work is going, her memory of these conversations influences her judgment and she responds with less enthusiasm than she would have had these arguments not taken place. Conversations in unpleasant relationships marked by complaint about one's boss, putting others down, and bad-mouthing the organization are likely to shape or frame the organization in negative ways, leading to less satisfaction with work, much as social and information cues about job characteristics appear to be predictors of job enrichment and job satisfaction (e.g., White & Mitchell, 1979) and perceptions of fairness of subordinate treatment by supervisors (Sias & Jablin, 1995).

Work often involves interaction with multiple people. If one has negative relationships with 3 persons but works with a total of 15 persons, that person should experience relatively fewer negative effects than a person whose total role set includes only 3 unpleasant relationships. The extent to which negative relationships occupy a significant proportion of total relationships, then, should predict deleterious effects. Therefore, we framed the following hypothesis:

> *H1:* The proportion of unpleasant work relationships will correlate negatively with job satisfaction.

Satisfaction with co-workers. One specific measure of satisfaction with work is satisfaction with one's work relationships (Hackman & Oldham, 1980). It is reasonable to suppose that unpleasant work relationships have an impact on satisfaction with work relationships as well as on job satisfaction in general through mechanisms similar to those introduced regarding job satisfaction. The more saturated one's work environment with negative peer relationships, the less satisfied one should be with one's work relationships. As for the first hypothesis, it is the relative proportion of negative relationships that we expect to generate negative effects. Therefore, we proposed the following hypothesis:

> *H2:* The proportion of unpleasant work relationships will correlate negatively with co-worker satisfaction.

Organizational commitment. Organizational commitment, defined as strength of involvement in and identification with an organization (Mowday, Steers, and Porter, 1979), is predicted by a variety of individual and organizational factors (Morris & Steers, 1980; Steers, 1977). When employees are committed to their organizations, they are willing to expend energy to make it better and are less likely to leave it. Stable organizations provide some degree of predictability to their various publics, including employees and the communities in which they reside. Therefore, factors influencing commitment warrant examination.

Leiter and Maslach (1988) found unpleasant supervisor contacts to decrease organizational commitment, as well as burnout; unpleasant coworker interactions were not examined as a direct contributor to commitment. Chapman's (1993) study, however, found that the quality of one's work relationships was related to turnover. Working from a social exchange perspective, Whitener and Walz (1993) found that rewards, which included a measure of ease of working cooperatively with others at work, and side bets, which included loss of friendships at work as one measure, were both predictors of commitment. It is reasonable, then, to propose that a workplace rife with unpleasant relationships would decrease the perception of rewards and side bets, thereby lessening commitment. Likewise, negative interactions may shape or frame perceptions of the organization as an unwelcoming place or uninviting community, lessening one's intention to invest. For example, if Roger's boss criticizes him in front of others rather than in private, Roger may make a self-attribution that he is not welcome in the organization. He is likely to seek out others who have experienced similar behaviors and their shared stories will construct an image of the organization as a hostile, uninviting place.

We expect that the greater the proportion of unpleasant work relationships, the greater would be these effects. Therefore, we predict:

H3: The proportion of unpleasant work relationships will correlate negatively with organizational commitment.

Workplace cynicism. One area that may be especially affected by the distress of unpleasant work relationships is employees' cynicism about work. In the last fifteen years, scholars have begun to address what is perceived as a trend toward cynicism about life in general as well as toward organizations and about work (Dean, Brandes, &

Dharwakdar, 1998; Kanter & Mervis, 1989). These scholars express concern about growing perceptions of meaninglessness in life and hopelessness about public life. Research connecting workplace cynicism to work relationships would increase understanding of how confidence in an organizational "home" can be encouraged appropriately.

Theoretical work on the psychological contract workers develop with their organizations upon entry (Nelson, Quick, & Joplin, 1991) provides a foundation for explaining how unmet expectations may lead to negative attitudes such as disappointment and cynicism toward the organization. For example, if one expects the organization to be a source of communal, or private sphere, friendships at work, which apparently about half the working population does (Marks, 1994), and those expectations are shattered when faced with unpleasant work relationships, one would expect a jaded view of the organization to result from these unmet high expectations.

Someone who does not expect intimacy needs to be met at work may still be affected by negative peer relationships. Lack of professional civility or organizational citizenship behaviors (Organ 1988) at work place may create discrepancy from psychological expectations for professional behavior from co-workers. Furthermore, since others are a strong source of the constructed reality of the social environment (Berger & Luckmann, 1967), then negative relationships with others may contribute to a sense of negativity about the organization, or changed perceptions of the organizational climate (Odden & Sias, 1997).

Thomas and Griffin's (1989) review of social information in the workplace suggests several areas influenced by communication from others. Therefore, negative work relationships may directly influence perceptions at work through negative communication or may be an indirect source of negative ambience by their very existence. Work by Sias (1996) and Sias and Jablin (1995) on discourse construction of fairness and unfairness of subordinates' differential treatment by their supervisors gives strong support for this perspective. For example, Tom's coworker, Sally, complains daily about how product quality has decreased. Tom begins to believe that product quality has decreased based on constant reception of these messages. His focus of attention begins to center on other ambient messages that could be construed as related to negative product quality. Over time, his image of the organization is shaped by attributions of substandard product quality.

The proportion of negative relationships relative to the total should predict the degree of social influence exerted by negative messages:

H4: The proportion of unpleasant work relationships will correlate negatively with workplace cynicism.

Method for First Study

Participants

One hundred fifteen participants participated in the study. Approximately half the sample (n=59) was from a large, land-grant midwestern university and the other half (n=56) were from a medium-sized, private eastern university. The participants in the first study ranged in age from 18 to 66 (mean = 30 years). Forty-seven were male, 63 were female, and 5 did not specify their sex. Participants received extra credit in the communication classes for which they were registered. The selected classes for recruitment included large numbers of older-than-average students who were currently working. These classes were chosen to increase the generalizability of the findings to working populations. Students were permitted to have coworkers fill out the questionnaire anonymously as well.

Employment experiences varied within the sample. The range of time with current employer ranged from one month to 35 years (mean = 5 years, 10 months). The number of prior jobs ranged from none to fifteen (mean = 4.1, mode = 3). Number of employees at the site of employment ranged from three to 10,000 (mean = 2,959, median = 100). Table 1 indicates the participants' company types and positions.

Table 1
Organization Types and Respondent Positions for Study 1

Type	Number	Percentage
Service	47	40.9%
High Tech	3	2.6%
Entertainment	6	5.2%
Medical	16	13.9%
Education	11	9.6%
Manufacturing	15	13.0%
Utilities	1	0.9%
Communication	8	5.2%
Government	3	2.6%
Other/Missing	8	7.0%

Table 1, continued
Organization Types and Respondent Positions for Study 1

Position	Number	Percentage
Administrators	11	9.6%
Managers	20	18.3%
Professionals	20	17.4%
Support Staff	19	16.5%
Direct Service	36	31.3%
Missing	8	7.0%

Questionnaire

The questionnaire consisted of four major sections, three of which were employed in this study (contact lead author for information about the other section): ratings of employee outcome variables and individual difference variables, ratings of peers, and demographic information.

Employee outcome and individual differences. The first section of the questionnaire addressed the following variables: 1) job satisfaction; 2) organizational commitment; 3) satisfaction with coworkers; and 4) workplace cynicism. Items addressing all of these constructs except satisfaction with coworkers were measured using Likert items for which the responses ranged from 1 (strongly disagree) to 7 (strongly agree).

The job satisfaction (5 items) and satisfaction with coworkers (3 items) items were measured using Hackman & Oldham's (1980) indices. Job satisfaction addresses satisfaction with the position the person currently holds. For example, one of the items reads, "I am generally satisfied with the kind of work I do on my job." Satisfaction with coworkers was measured through three Likert items for which the responses ranged from 1 (extremely dissatisfied) to 7 (extremely satisfied) (e.g., "The extent to which I get to help other people while at work"; "The people I talk to and work with on my job").

Organizational commitment, the degree to which a person reports loyalty to and pride in his/her organization, was also measured using 7 Likert items from Mowday, et al.'s (1979) Organizational Commitment Scale. For example, one item states, "I am proud to tell others that I am part of this organization." Although the original measure of organizational commitment has been refined and developed further, this scale remains in use and has desirable psychometric properties (Meyer & Allen, 1997).

Cynicism in the interpersonal realm refers to lack of trust in others, belief in others' manipulative intent, and the view that others are out for themselves (O'Hair & Cody, 1987). Dean et al. (1998) have proposed organizational cynicism as an important concept for the organizational context. Elaborating on their work (see Fritz, Williams, & Arnett, 2004), we propose that cynicism about work, or workplace cynicism, measures the extent to which employees have negative perceptions of the organization's relationship to employees, disappointment or unmet expectations about the organization's attributes, negative perceptions of coworkers, and disillusionment about the organization's product. Workplace cynicism was measured using 18 Likert items designed for this study.

Valence ratings of other employees. The second section of the questionnaire asked for a listing of up to ten people with whom the participant interacted regularly with at work. This measure was designed to focus participants on the most important work associates in their role set. Our thinking was that having negative relationships with people seen infrequently or for only unimportant tasks would not matter as much as negative relationships with people frequently interacted with or involved in important tasks. We were concerned about respondent fatigue and thought rating 10 would not be onerous. The questionnaire asked participants to specify the relationship of the person to him/herself and then to rate how the respondent typically felt about the person from 1 (negative) to 7 (positive).

Demographics. The demographics section of the questionnaire asked participants to provide answers to several open-ended questions: name of the employing organization they worked for, length employment with that organization, position, type of organization, number of people employed at the site, state of the site, sex, age, and number of organization worked for prior to the current organization.

Procedure

At a research session, consent forms and questionnaires were distributed. Participant questions were answered, and upon completion of the questionnaires, participants were debriefed and thanked for their participation. Participants at students' workplaces filled out questionnaires on their own time and returned them in a sealed envelope to the student.

Results for Study 1

Index Reliabilities

Reliabilities for each of the indexes were assessed by computing Cronbach's alpha. Reliabilities greater than .65 were accepted. The alpha for the co-worker satisfaction index fell below this threshold. As a result, this index was dropped from further analyses. The alphas for all of the other indexes exceeded .65, and those scales were retained for use in the study. Table 2 presents the alphas.

Table 2
Index Reliabilities for Study 1

Index	Alpha
Job Satisfaction	.85
Coworker Satisfaction	.60
Organizational Commitment	.88
Workplace Cynicism	.93

Relationship between Proportion of Negative Peers and Employee Outcome Variables

Proportion of negative relationships was calculated based on the ratings of people listed with whom participants interacted regularly at work. Specifically, the number of relationships perceived negatively by each participant (rated on the negative side of neutral) was divided by the total number of peers listed as people the participant regularly interacts with at work. Pearson correlation coefficients were computed between proportion of negative relationships and the employee outcome variables. Correlations with significance levels below or equal to .05 were considered to be significant.

As predicted, significant negative correlations emerged between proportion of negative relationships and job satisfaction ($r=-.39$, $p<.01$) and between proportion of negative relationships and organizational commitment ($r=-.24$, $p<.05$). Also as expected, a significant positive correlation was found between proportion of negative peers and workplace cynicism ($r=.39$, $p<.01$).

Rationale for Study 2

Negative Bosses, Co-workers, and Subordinates

The results from the first study revealed that negative work relationships have a significant influence on all three of the employee outcome variables tested. However, our concern with respondent fatigue prevented us from asking respondents to generate a comprehensive list of people in the work environment. One implication of this restriction to 10 people at work was the inability to create meaningful proportions of negative and positive coworkers at different levels (e.g. boss, subordinate, person of equal rank). That is, accurate proportional representation of the levels of negative relationships could not be guaranteed. Subsequent feedback assured us that more work relationships could be listed and rated, thereby removing that limitation.

Relative status of a negative relationship partner should be an important factor in assessing that relationship's influence (e.g., Ashforth, 1994; Kanter, 1977). Whether a person has more, the same, or less power than ourselves influences the nature and effects of interactions. For example, Argyle and Furnham (1983) found that work associates differed from work supervisors in persons' perceptions of conflict behaviors and that the relative amount of conflict was greater in involuntary relationships and in those in which one has lower power. Gant, et al. (1993) report that social workers perceive their supervisors as a greater source of social support than peers, but that supervisors may exhibit both supportive and nonsupportive behaviors. Supervisors who exhibit social undermining may lead workers to feel anxiety, depression, and irritability. Balshem (1988) reports that clerical workers' bosses are a major source of job stress. Jorde-Bloom (1988) reports that whereas coworker relationships are source of both satisfaction and frustration, supervisors are more likely to be a source of dissatisfaction than satisfaction.

Subordinates may attain the status of a negative other for supervisors when they are consistently problematic in their behavior (Monroe, Borzi, & DiSalvo, 1992; Morrill, 1989). Although not much research exists on the negative subordinate (Monroe, et al., 1992), it seems logical that the effect of unpleasant subordinate relationships would be substantial. Effective management depends on trust (McAllister, 1995). If managers have to monitor dysfunctional subordinates, they will use excessive amounts of finite managerial resources of time and energy (McAllister, 1995). If employees are engaged in conflictual interaction, valuable work time must be spent in intervention, another drain on managerial resources. The manager's job of constructing or renovating an effective organizational home (Arnett, 1999) depends on organizational members who are civil to one another despite their differences or dislike for one another.

Finally, in addition to job and coworker satisfaction, workplace cynicism, and organizational commitment, it seems reasonable to assume, given the previous reasoning and review of literature, to consider that one's perceived productivity might be influenced similarly. Given this rationale, we posed the following hypothesis:

> *H:* As the power of the other increases, the deleterious effects of the proportion of negative relationships on employee outcome variables (i.e., job satisfaction, organizational commitment, workplace cynicism, and perceived productivity) will increase.

Methods for the Second Study

Participants

One hundred twenty-six participants were recruited from two universities. Approximately half the sample (n = 53) was from a large, land-grant midwestern university and the other half (n = 73) from a medium-sized, private eastern university. As was true in the first study, we intentionally recruited in communication classes that included large numbers of older-than-average students so that the findings would generalize to working populations. Students were invited to recruit others from their workplace to fill out a questionnaires as well. The participants in the second study ranged in age from 18 to 53 (mean = 29.7 years). Sixty-one were male, 58 were female, and 7 did not specify their sex.

As was the case in the first study, the participants reported a wide range of employment experiences and contexts. Time with current employer ranged from one month to 40 years 9 months (mean = 7 years 10 months), number of prior jobs ranged from none to five (mean = 2.7), number of employees at the site of employment ranged from three to 5,000 (mean = 1,229), and participants worked for a wide range of organization types and held a wide range of positions (see Table 3).

Table 3

Organization Types and Respondent Positions for Study 2

Type	Number	Percentage
Service	47	37.3%
High Tech	4	3.2%
Entertainment	2	1.6%
Medical	13	10.3%
Education	15	11.9%
Manufacturing	15	11.9%
Utilities	2	1.6%
Communicatio	5	4.0%
Government	12	9.5%
Other/Missing	11	8.7%

Position	Number	Percentage
Administrators	7	5.6%
Managers	17	13.5%
Professionals	32	25.4%
Support Staff	16	12.7%
Direct Service	40	31.7%
Missing	14	11.1%

Questionnaire

The questionnaire for the second study consisted of four major sections, three of which were relevant to the current research focus (see Omdahl & Fritz, this volume, for information on the other section): items addressing employee outcome variables; valence ratings of other employees; and demographic information.

Employee outcome variables. The first section of the questionnaire included indexes for eight employee outcome variables, three of which are relevant to the current study (contact lead author for information about the other variables). The measures of job satisfaction, organizational commitment, and workplace cynicism followed the first study. Coworker satisfaction was not evaluated, given its failure to achieve reliability as an index in the first study.

Valence ratings of other employees. The second section of the questionnaire asked for a listing of those people who directly supervise/manage the participant, the people who are directly supervised/managed by the participant, and other people whom the person interacts with for important job duties or for daily unimportant job duties. We allowed space for participants to list multiple supervisors/managers because many job types (e.g., waitrons, sales associates) work with different supervisors/managers on different days of the week/month. The questionnaire asked the participant to specify the relationship of the person to him/herself and then to rate the person from -3 (negative) to +3 (positive) with a neutral midpoint of 0. They were instructed to use this valence scale to indicate how they typically felt about the person.

Demographics. In the final section of the questionnaire, participants provided basic demographic information identical to that of the first study.

Procedure

The procedure for data collection followed that of the first study.

Results of Study 2

Index Reliabilities

Cronbach's alphas were computed for each of the indexes. All of the alphas were acceptable (see Table 4).

Table 4
Index Reliabilities for Study 2

Index	Alpha
Job Satisfaction	.82
Organizational Commitment	.75
Workplace Cynicism	.92

Relationships between Negative Peers and Outcome Variables

To examine the hypotheses, correlations between proportions of negative supervisors, co-workers, and subordinates as well as between total number of negative employees and the employee outcome variables were computed. Since participants listed negative relationships with supervisors, coworkers, and subordinates, t-tests for differences in correlations for non-independent groups were computed (Ferguson, 1959). Missing data for some cases reduced the number of cases. The correlations between proportions of negative peers and employee outcome variables replicated the findings from the first study and also revealed that negative supervisor relationships have a greater impact than negative subordinate relationships and that negative coworkers relationships have a greater impact than negative subordinates relationships (see Table 5).

Table 5
Correlations

	Supervisors	Co-workers	Subordinates	Combined
Job Satisfaction	-.41**a	-.40**a	.02b	-.39**
Org. Commit.	-.49**a	-.45**a	-.04b	-.51**
Cynicism	.52**a	.49**a	-.05b	.54**

* p<.01   **p<.001

Note: Correlations with differing subscripts within rows are significantly different at the p<.05 level.

Significance tests between correlations for supervisors and coworkers were computed for each outcome variable using the t-test for correlations between dependent samples (Ferguson, 1959) (see Table 5). No significant difference was found between correlations between proportion of negative supervisor relationships and job satisfaction and proportion of negative coworker relationships and job satisfaction, t(83)=.09, n. s., but the difference between correlations between proportion of negative supervisor relationships and job satisfaction and proportion of negative subordinate relationships and job satisfaction, t(83)=-3.10, p < .05, and the difference between the correlations between the proportion of negative coworker relationships and job satisfaction and the proportion of negative subordinate relationships and job satisfaction were significant, t(83)=-2.94, p < .05.

No significant difference was found between correlations between proportion of negative supervisor relationships and commitment and proportion of negative coworker relationships and commitment, t(83)=.39, n. s., but the difference between correlations between proportion of negative supervisor relationships and commitment and proportion of negative subordinate relationships and commitment (t(83)=-3.395, p<.05) and the difference between correlations between correlations between proportion of negative coworker relationships and commitment and proportion of negative subordinate relationships and commitment (t(83)=-2.87, p < .05) were significant.

No significant difference was found between correlations between proportion of negative supervisor relationships and cynicism and proportion of negative coworker relationships and cynicism (t(83)=.-.30, n. s.), but the difference between correlations between proportion of negative supervisor relationships and cynicism and proportion of negative subordinate relationships and cynicism (t(83)=4.39, p<.05) and the difference between correlations between correlations between proportion of negative coworker relationships and cynicism and proportion of negative subordinate relationships and cynicism (t(83)=3.88, p < .05) were significant.

In summary, for job satisfaction, organizational commitment, and workplace cynicism, no difference emerged in the correlational strength of supervisory relationships and coworker relationships with these variables. However, for every outcome variable, both supervisory relationships and coworker relationships had significantly greater correlations with outcome variables than did subordinates.

General Discussion

Proportion of Negative Supervisor, Peers, Subordinates and Outcome Variables

These studies revealed that proportion of negative work relationships correlated significantly and negatively with job satisfaction and organizational commitment, and significantly and positively with workplace cynicism. The second study replicated the first study's results and, additionally, sought to determine the relative effects of status of relationship partner. This study found partial support in that proportion of negative supervisors had a stronger effect on the outcome variables than did negative subordinates. The pattern emerging from these studies' focus on work-related outcomes indicates that affective variables such as cynicism, commitment, and satisfaction may depend on the affective quality, as measured by proportion of negative peers, of one's environment.

These studies add to our knowledge of work relationships by extending our knowledge of an important but neglected work relationship: The negative peer, boss, or subordinate. This research confirms the wisdom of taking organizational level and degree of relative power into account when doing organizational research. These findings further highlight the importance of role responsibilities organizational members have to one another.

This research also offers support for the development of a measure of cynicism about work. Organizational cynicism (Dean, et al., 1998) is a variable that is still in the first stages of research development, with various approaches to conceptualization and measurement (Wanous, Reichers, & Austin, 2000). The reliability and validity of the measure of workplace cynicism used in these studies should be developed further by examining the instrument's relationship to other relevant constructs and used in further research.

Although the research reported is correlational in nature, it is an important foundational contribution because of the lack of research in this area. These findings clearly establish connections between negative relationships at work and important personal and organizational outcomes in a variety of organizations and across power levels in organizations. Future work needs to build on the ideas presented here in several ways.

Theoretical Framework

The correlation of proportion of negative relationships at work to job satisfaction, commitment, and workplace cynicism may be explained by the social information processing model (Salancik & Pfeffer, 1978). One's perception of the organization as a good place to work, trustworthy, and worthy of one's commitment is likely to be influenced by the opinions and comments of others, which may in turn provide evidence that an employee may use to evaluate the extent to which the psychological contract with the organization was met (Nelson, et al., 1991). Alternatively, the influence of negative peers may operate through their effect on lessened social support.

The social information processing model, or social construction model (e.g., Sias & Jablin, 1995), would suggest that the mechanism through which social support (or lack thereof) from relationships at work operates is one of perception created through discourse. From literature on framing (e.g., Fairhurst & Sarr, 1996), we know that language has a powerful influence on how others construe organizational life. Perceptions of the organization as a community or as a war zone or political site would generate different expectations for the type of communication appropriate within them.

Implications for Future Research

One way in which communication-specific future research can give attention to the processes through which communication with others creates social reality is to follow Sias (1996) and Sias and Jablin's (1995) analysis of workers' discourse. Analysis of utterances typical in unpleasant work relationships through diary methods or through video or audio taping would be one method of tapping such discourse. Studies examining the extent to which different negative work relationship types (Fritz, 2002) affect job satisfaction, organizational commitment, and workplace cynicism and other outcomes, such as stress, would add to our understanding of problematic work relationships. Finally, longitudinal studies examining the effects of problematic interactions over time would be helpful in examining the long-term effects of problematic workplace relationships.

References

Argyle, M., & Furnham, A. (1983). Sources of satisfaction and conflict in long-term relationships. *Journal of Marriage and the Family, 45,* 481-493.

Arnett, R. C. (1999). Metaphorical guidance: Administration as building and renovation. *Journal of Educational Admistration, 37,* 80-87.

Ashforth, B. (1994). Petty tyranny in organizations. *Human Relations, 47,* 755-778.

Balshem, M. (1988). The clerical worker's boss: An agent of job stress. *Human Organization, 47,* 361-367.

Beach, S. R. H., Martin, J. K., Blum, T. C., & Roman, P. M. (1993). Effects of marital and co-worker relationships on negative affect: Testing the central role of marriage. *American Journal of Family Therapy, 21,* 313-323

Berger, P. L., & Luckmann, T. (1967). *The social construction of reality.* Garden City, NY: Doubleday & Co.

Bridge, K., & Baxter, L. (1992). Blended relationships: Friends as work associates. *Western Journal of Communication, 56,* 200-225.

Bryan, A., & Gallois, C. (1992). Rules about assertion in the workplace: Effects of status and message type. *Australian Journal of Psychology, 44,* 51-59.

Chapman, J. (1993). Collegial support linked to reduction of job stress. *Nursing Management, 24*(5), 52-56.

Cooper, C. L. & Cartwright, S. (1994). Healthy mind; health organization: A proactive approach to occupational stress. *Human Relations, 47,* 455-470.

Crosby, F. (1982). *Relative deprivation and working women.* New York: Oxford University Press.

Dean, J. W., Brandes, P., & Dharwadkar, R. (1998). Organizational cynicism. *Academy of Management Review, 23,* 341-352.

Fairhurst, G. T., & Sarr, R. A. (1996). *The art of framing: Managing the language of leadership.* San Francisco: Jossey-Bass.

Ferguson, G. A. (1959). Statistical analysis in psychology and education. New York: McGraw-Hill.

Fritz, J. M. H. (2002). How do I dislike thee? Let me count the ways: Constructing impressions of troublesome others at work. *Management Communication Quarterly, 15,* 410-438.

Fritz, J. M. H. (1997a). Men's and women's organizational peer relationships: A comparison. *Journal of Business Communication, 34,* 27-46.

Fritz, J. M. H. (1997b). Responses to unpleasant work relationships. *Communication Research Reports, 14,* 302-311.

Fritz, J. M. H., Williams, C., & Arnett, R. C. (November, 2004). Moving forward, looking back: Replication and extension of a study of the influence of communication and adherence to expectations for appropriate business conduct on recognition of organizational ethical standards and commitment to the organization. Paper presented at the annual meeting of the National Communication Association, Chicago.

Gant, L. M., Nagda, B. A., Brabson, H. V., Jayaratne, S., Chess, W. A., & Singh, A. (1993). Effects of social support and undermining on African American workers' perceptions of coworker and supervisor relationships and psychological well-being. *Social Worker, 38,* 158-164.

Gettman, D., & Pena, D. (1986). Women, mental health, and the workplace in a transnational setting. *Social Work, 31,* 5-11.

Giddens, A. (1984). *The constitution of society.* Berkeley, CA: University of California Press.

Hackman, J. R., & Oldham, G. R. (1980). *Work redesign.* Reading, MA: Addison-Wesley.

Jenner, J. R. (1986). A measure of chronic organizational stress. *Psychological Reports, 58,* 543-546.

Jorde-Bloom, P. (1988). Factors influencing overall job satisfaction and organizational commitment in early childhood work environments. *Journal of Research in Childhood Education, 3,* 107-122.

Kanter, R. M. (1977). *Men and women of the corporation.* New York: Basic Books.

Kanter, D. L., & Mervis, P. H. (1989). *The cynical Americans: Living and working in an age of discontint and disillusionment.* San Francisco: Jossey- Bass.

Kram, K., & Isabella, L. (1985). Mentoring alternatives: The role of peer relationships in career development. *Academy of Management Journal, 28,* 110-132.

Leiter, M. P. (1988). Burnout as a function of communication patterns. *Group and Organization Studies, 13,* 111-128.

Leiter, M. P., & Maslach, C. (1988). The impact of interpersonal environment on burnout and organizational commitment. *Journal of Organizational Behavior, 9,* 297-308.

Leiter, M. P., & Meechan, K. A. (1986). Role structure and burnout in the field of human services. *Journal of Applied Behavioral Science, 22,* 47-52.

Louis, M. R. (1980). Surprise and sense-making: What newcomers experience in entering unfamiliar organizational settings. *Administrative Science Quarterly, 25,* 226-251.

Marks, S. R. (1994). Intimacy in the public realm: The case of co-workers. *Social Forces, 72,* 843-858.

McAllister, D. J. (1995). Affect- and cognition-based trust as foundations for interpersonal cooperation in organizations. *Academy of Management Journal, 38,* 24-59.

Monroe, C., Borzi, M. G., & DiSalvo, V. S. (1992). Managerial strategies for dealing with difficult subordinates. *Southern Communication Journal, 58,* 247-254.

Morrill, C. (1989). The management of managers: Disputing in an executive hierarchy. *Sociological Forum, 4,* 387-407.

Morris, J. H., & Steers, R. M. (1980). Structural influences on organizational commitment. *Journal of Vocational Behavior, 17,* 50-57.

Mowday, R. T., Steers, R. M., & Porter, L. W. (1979). The measurement of organizational commitment. *Journal of Vocational Behavior, 14,* 224-247.

Meyer, J. P., & Allen, N. J. (1997). *Commitment in the workplace: Theory, research, and application.* Thousand Oaks, CA: Sage.

Nelson, D. L., Quick, J. C., & Joplin, J. R. (1991). Psychological contracting and newcomer socialization: An attachment theory foundation. *Journal of Social Behavior and Personality, 6,* 55-72.

Odden, C. M., & Sias, P. M. (1997). Peer communication relationships and psychological climate. *Communication Quarterly, 45,* 153-166.

O'Hair, D., & Cody, M. J. (1987). Machiavellian beliefs and social influence. *Western Journal of Speech Communication, 51,* 279-303.

Organ, D. (1988). *Organizational citizenship behavior: The good soldier syndrome.* Lexington, MA: D. C. Heath and Company.

Ratsoy, E. W., Sarros, J. C., & Aidoo-Taylor, N. (1986). Organizational stress and coping: A model and empirical check. *Alberta Journal of Educational Research, 32,* 270-285.

Repetti, R. L., & Cosmas, K. A. (1991). The quality of the social environment at work and job satisfaction. *Journal of Applied Social Psychology, 21,* 840-854.

Salancik, G. R., & Pfeffer, J. (1978). A social information processing approach to job attitudes and task design. *Administrative Science Quarterly, 23,* 223-253.

Schneider, B. (1987). The people make the place. *Personnel Psychology, 40,* 431-453.

Schuler, R. S. (1982). An integrative transactional process model of stress in organizations. *Journal of Occupational Behavior, 3,* 5-19.

Sias, P. M. (1996). Constructing perceptions of differential treatment: An analysis of coworker discourse. *Communication Monographs, 63,* 171-187.

Sias, P. M., & Perry, T. (2004). Disengaging from workplace relationships: A research note, *Human Communication Research, 30,* 587-602.

Sias, P. M., & Cahill, D. J. (1998). From coworkers to friends: The development of peer friendships in the workplace. *Western Journal of Communication, 62,* 273-299.

Sias, P. M., & Jablin, F. M. (1995). Differential superior-subordinate relations, perceptions of fairness, and coworker communication. *Human Communication Research, 22,* 5-38.

Solly, D. C., & Hohenshil, T. H. (1986). Job satisfaction of school psychologists in a primarily rural state. *School Review, 15,* 119-126.

Steers, R. M. (1977). Antecedents and outcomes of organizational commitment. *Administrative Science Quarterly, 22,* 6-56.

Stohl, C. (1995). *Organizational communication: Connectedness in action.* Thousand Oaks, CA: Sage.

Thomas, J. G., & Griffin, R. W. (1989). The power of social information in the workplace. *Organizational Dynamics, 18* (2), 63-75.

Wanous, J. P., Reichers, A. E., & Austin, J. T. (2000). Cynicism about organizational change. *Group and Organization Management, 25,* 132-153.

White, S. E., & Mitchell, T. R. (1979). Job enrichment versus social cues: A comparison and competitive test. *Journal of Applied Psychology, 64,* 1-9.

Whitener, E. M., & Walz, P. M. (1993). Exchange theory determinants of affective and continuance commitment and turnover. *Journal of Vocational Behavior, 42,* 265-281.

Emotion Management in
Dealing with Difficult People

Michael W. Kramer & Claire L. Tan

There is a long history of communication research on relationships in organizational settings. Much of this research has focused on superior-subordinate relationships (e.g. Fairhurst, 2001; Jablin, 1979) and somewhat less on peer relationships (e.g., Sias & Cahill, 1998; Sias & Jablin, 1995). Although this research has recognized that there are differential relationships in supervisor relationships from close, insider/partnership relationships to more distant, outsider/overseer ones (see Graen & Uhl-Bien, 1995), and in peer relationships from close or special relationships to information or polite ones (Kram & Isabella, 1985), only recently have scholars looked specifically at how individuals manage relationships with disliked or difficult others with whom they must maintain relationships as part of their work responsibilities (Fritz, 1997). Essays in this volume continue this vein of research.

The research on maintaining relationships with disliked others has generally examined how individuals strategically manage those relationships to minimize difficulties and discomfort, for example, through distancing behaviors (Hess, 2000). As such, it continues a general focus on rational examinations of organizational lives while limiting the discussion of the role of emotions (Fineman, 1993). Emotions are an integral part of interactions in general (Planalp, 2003) and in organizational life in particular (Ashforth & Humphrey, 1995). Emotions are particularly salient in relationships with disliked or difficult others. The label itself, disliked others, suggests a negative emotional aspect of the relationships. Most people would say that, regardless of the context, in relationships with disliked others, there is a tension between the need to maintain the relationship and a desire to escape it (Hess, 2002).

Although there is research on maintaining relationships with disliked others at work and research on emotion management at work, this study provides unique insights into relationships at work by examining emotion management with difficult or disliked others in the workplace. More specifically, it provides insights into the challenges of managing emotions while maintaining relationships with disliked others in the workplace by contrasting the emotional interactions with disliked others to those with liked others.

Review of Literature

Maintaining Relationships with Disliked Others

Much of the research on personal relationships has assumed that positive affect or liking is an essential component for relationship development. Popular relationship models explaining friendships and romantic relationships suggest that liking leads to relationship development and disliking leads to relationship dissolution (e.g., Knapp, 1984). Such assumptions seem unwarranted for certain types of relationships. Although attraction is a critical component in voluntary relationship development, people must create and maintain relationships with people for a variety of other reasons that have little to do with feelings toward each other (Berscheid, 1985). In work settings, individuals frequently must work with individuals with whom they would not choose to work or with people they do not like as part of their jobs. Often these relationships are not voluntary, since the employees may feel they have little choice but to maintain the relationships despite being dissatisfied (Hess, 2000). As a result, these unpleasant work relationships often affect workers and the organization adversely as the energy spent on managing these relationships interferes with the coordination of work and leads to stress, and in extreme cases, to employee turnover (Fritz, 1997).

As an alternative to turnover, employees may instead use a variety of strategies to maintain relationships with disliked others in their work settings. Hess (2000) examined a large number of individual tactics people use to distance themselves from relationships with disliked others and through cluster analysis identified five general strategies for managing these types of relationships. The five strategies include ignoring the person or his/her humanity, detaching psychologically from the person, reducing involvement with the person, depersonalizing the interaction with the person, or showing antagonism toward the person. By creating distance between the individual and the disliked other these strategies allow the relationship to be minimally maintained.

Approaching the topic somewhat differently, Rusbult and Zembrodt (1983) explored two dimensions of responses to relational problems, active versus passive, and constructive versus destructive. They viewed voice or addressing the issues as active-constructive, loyalty or waiting for things to change as passive-constructive, exit or leaving the relationship as active-destructive, and neglect or allowing the relationship to deteriorate as passive-destructive. These various options allow individuals to manage or end the relationship. Emotional reactions and emotion management are implicit in this research although not explicitly discussed.

Emotion Management

Seminal research in emotion management has focused primarily on frontline interactions between employees and customers or clients (Morris & Feldman, 1996). Much of this research has examined how employees must express positive emotions to others regardless of their actual felt emotions. In a variety of interactions, such as flight attendants serving their passengers (Hochschild, 1983), Disney "cast members" "performing" for their "guests" (Van Maanen & Kunda, 1989), or cruise ship crew members accommodating their passengers (Tracy, 2000), employees manage their emotions by expressing positive emotions even when they do not feel them. In contrast to these positive emotion management situations, a number of occupations involve expressing neutral or negative emotions. For example, 911 operators manage emotions by expressing a calm, neutral demeanor when dealing with chaotic circumstances (Shuler & Sypher, 2000), and bill collectors learn to express various levels of negative emotions in order to pressure clients to make payments (Sutton, 1991).

Because emotion management is often encouraged for the benefit of the organization rather than the employees, it is frequently viewed negatively as top down commodification of emotions for the financial gain of organizations (Mumby & Putnam, 1992; Putnam & Mumby, 1993). Emotion management is further viewed negatively when it involves deep acting where employees become so involved in presenting the organizationally prescribed emotions that they lose touch with their real or felt emotions (Hochschild, 1979). In contrast to these negative views of emotion management, some employees seem to enjoy the process of emotion management. Emergency 911 operatives report that maintaining a calm, neutral demeanor despite chaotic or comical circumstances provides them with an emotional rush that makes the job interesting and relieves boredom (Shuler & Sypher, 2000).

Although discussion of positive and negative effects of emotion management by frontline employees provides interesting insights into emotion management in the workplace, it fails to recognize that most emotional interactions occur between organizational members away from customers and clients (Waldron, 1994). A certain level of emotion management is necessary for organizational members to interact in a civil and effective manner. In every culture, the tension between spontaneously expressing emotions and strategically managing them is controlled by explicit or implicit rules for appropriate and inappropriate displays of emotion (Planalp, 1999). In the United States, the general rules for emotion management seem to suggest that individuals should behave professionally by masking negative emotions and expressing positive emotions at modest levels (Kramer & Hess, 2002). Abiding by social norms for appropriate emotion displays would seem particularly challenging in dealing with interactions with disliked others. By focusing on frontline employees, previous research has failed to concentrate on emotion management in ongoing workplace relationships.

Social Exchange Theory

The separate fields of research on relationship development and emotion management in the workplace can be integrated through social exchange theory. Through communication, individuals exchange resources to create relationships (Roloff, 1981). Individuals exchange a variety of resources in their relationships: love; status; information; money; goods; and services (Foa & Foa, 1980). Individuals consider the relative costs and benefits of the relationship, compare their experience with expectations for relationship, and they compare the current relationship with real or imagined alternatives. The outcome (rewards minus costs), as well as assessments of how the relationship compares with expectations and alternatives, determine whether people strive to develop, maintain, or end relationships (Thibault & Kelly, 1959).

This very rational explanation of relationships can be broadened to include an understanding of how positive and negative emotions influence social exchange processes. A primary outcome of exchanges is often an emotional reaction; it is often how an individual feels about an interaction, not the actual resources exchanged, that leads to positive or negative evaluations of relationships (Planalp, 2003). The way in which emotional interactions are managed are particularly likely to influence the overall evaluation of the relationships. As such, managing emotional events can be particularly important in organizational settings where people may have little choice but to maintain relationships. How individuals manage these emotional events with disliked others is likely to impact their overall evaluations of the relationships.

Emotions are frequently conceptualized as resulting from the discrepancy between expected and actual events (Mandler, 1975). These expectancy violations occur when events either exceed expectations, generally resulting in positive emotions, or when they fail to meet expectations, resulting in negative emotions (Omdahl, 1995). In social exchange terms, the exchange is evaluated as fair or unfair based on the resulting emotional reaction (Planalp, 2003). On one hand, this conceptualization of emotions might suggest that habituation would occur where expectations for interactions with disliked others would be normalized such that the inappropriate or unpleasant behaviors would be expected and not result in emotional reactions. On the other hand, since emotions can be generated on several levels simultaneously, interactions with disliked others will often still violate the general expectations for interactions, resulting in emotional responses (Fiebig & Kramer, 1998). Together, the evaluation of emotional exchanges may compel relational change by leading either to deterioration or further development of relationships (Planalp, 2003).

Research Questions

Social exchange theory considers how past exchanges influence the evaluation of current interactions (Thibault & Kelly, 1959). This suggests that exchanges with disliked others may begin with different situations and expectations than interactions with liked others. As a result, this study explored this first research question:

> *RQ1:* What types of events precipitate emotional episodes with disliked and liked others in the work setting?

Social exchanges result in a wide range of emotions from very positive ones such as joy to very negative ones such as anger. Some of these emotions are universally recognized (Ekman, 1973). Given that the expectations for the social exchanges with disliked and liked others are different, the emotional responses to those interactions should differ. Therefore, the second research question was:

> *RQ2:* What types of emotions are experienced in emotional episodes with disliked and liked others in the work setting?

Previous research suggests two general strategies for managing felt emotions: expressing the felt emotions or disguising/masking them (e. g., expressing neutrality when angry) (Fiebig & Kramer, 1998). Research on maintaining relationships indicates that most individuals minimize or avoid once they have evaluated their relationships negatively (Hess, 2000). This research does not, however, specifically address strategies used to manage emotions during interactions that lead to or support the negative evaluations. The strategies used to manage emotions may also differ for interactions with disliked others compared to liked others. In order to explore this possibility, this research addressed this question:

> *RQ3:* How do people manage their communication behaviors in emotional episodes with disliked and liked others?

Social exchange theory suggests that emotional interactions influence relationships by leading to positive or negative feelings about relationships (Planalp, 2003). However, previous research is equivocal on the impact of managing emotions on future relationships. Waldron and Krone (1991) found that expressing felt emotions often has no significant impact on future relationships, while masking often has a negative impact by lowering perceptions of openness. Fiebig and Kramer (1998) found that expressing positive emotions often leads to positive outcomes such as more open communication and positive relationships, while expressing negative felt emotions sometimes leads to more open communication, but just as often leads to closed communication and detachment. Kramer and

Hess (1998) found that expressing emotions in a socially appropriate manner (i.e., professionally) tends to improve relationships, but expressing emotions in a socially inappropriate manner (unprofessionally) tends to damage relationships. The reactions to social exchanges involving expressing or managing emotions may differ depending on whether the interactions are with disliked or liked others. Thus, this study explored this final question:

RQ4: What impact do emotion management episodes have on future relationships with disliked and liked others?

Methods

Respondents

Given an interest in exploring these questions in a broad range of occupations and organizations, a technique used elsewhere was followed (e.g., Teboul, 1995). Students in two upper level communication classes were offered extra credit if they had two adults who were full-time employees fill out questionnaires on their behalf. In order to verify that the students did not complete the questionnaires themselves, respondents provided their first name and either a daytime phone or email address. Approximately 20% of these were randomly contacted to confirm their participation and then identifying information was discarded.

This data collection technique resulted in 52 questionnaires representing a wide range of respondents. Respondents were 63.5 % female and 36.5% male. Their average age was 40.1 (*SD*=13.7). Approximately 54% were married, 36% were single, and 10% divorced or widowed. They were a fairly educated group with about 21% holding graduate degrees, 44% holding bachelor's degrees, 21% having attended some college, and 15% having only attended high school. The most common occupations reported were education (21%), retail sales (15%), management (11%), food service employees (8%), media employees (6%), construction (6%), health professions (6%), and office staff (6%).

Questionnaire

The questionnaire was modeled after ones used in other emotion research (e.g., Fiebig & Kramer, 1998; Waldron & Krone, 1991) (contact lead author for questionnaire). Respondents were asked to recall two situations at work in which they experienced either positive or negative emotions, one with a disliked other and one with a liked other. In response to open-ended questions for each situation, they described their relationship to the other person/people, the situation that elicited an emotional reaction to the other person, their emotions during the episodes, their behaviors during the event, the impact of the episodes on their relationships with the other people, and whether they did anything different in subsequent interaction with the person.

Analysis

Content analysis using a grounded theory approach permitted categories for responses to emerge from the data rather than being set by a predetermined coding scheme (Glaser & Strauss, 1967). First, responses to each question were examined to determine whether they represented a single response; responses were divided into separate units if they represented multiple responses. Through a constant comparison method, individual responses for each question were divided into categories that seemed to represent different responses to the questions. Once all the data were divided this way, responses within each category were examined again to verify that they represented a similar response. Then categories were compared to make certain that none of the categories overlapped. Finally, category labels were developed. Exemplars from each category are provided in the results section.

To assess intercoder reliability, one coder developed categories for the responses to the interactions with disliked others and the other for interactions with liked others. Then, each coder categorized approximately 20% of the data for the other interactions into the categories that had been developed by the other coder. Results indicated that simple agreement for the sets between the two coders for the categories in Tables 1-4 ranged from 87-93% and that kappa, which corrects for chance agreement, ranged from .78 to .91 (Fleiss, 1971).

Results

RQ1: *Events Precipitating Emotional Encounters with Disliked and Liked Others*

We analyzed two aspects of the situation to address RQ1. First we examined the nature of the organizational relationships for the people involved. Next, we examined the type of event or incident that caused the emotional episodes.

Table 1
Frequencies of Relationships and Events for Emotion Management with Disliked and Liked Others

Categories	Disliked Others	Liked Others
Relationships		
Coworkers/Peers	29	27
Supervisors	14	12
Subordinates	6	6
Customers/Clients	1	4
Volunteers/Others	1	2
No Response	1	1
Events		
Positive Events	*0*	*38*
Work related assistance or support	0	15
Personal assistance or support	0	7
Provide assistance or support	0	6
Received praise or recognition	0	5
Casual conversation at work	0	4
Gave praise or recognition	0	2
Personal good news	0	1
Negative Events	*51*	*13*
Target conduct	38	3
Target character trait	6	0
Differences between parties	5	4
Past event	1	0
Bad/disappointing news	0	5
Person leaving	0	1
No Response	*1*	*1*

Relationships. Results on the top of Table 1 indicate the number of emotional episodes with coworkers, supervisors, subordinates, and other organizational associates for the interactions with the liked and disliked others. A chi-square confirmed that although the majority of emotional interactions were with peers, there were no significant differences in the type of organizational relationships that individuals reported having emotional episodes with for disliked versus liked others, $\chi^2(4) = 3.02$, $p < .56$.

Events. The events that caused the emotional interactions with disliked and liked others are reported in two ways at the bottom of Table 1. First, the events were divided into ones that resulted in positive or negative responses. Emotional interactions with disliked were exclusively negative interactions with liked others were more often positive than negative. A chi-square indicated that this pattern was significant, $\chi^2(1) = 60.56$, $p < .001$.

Next, events were categorized into specific categories. For interactions with disliked others, the most commonly mentioned event (appearing in Table 1) was *target conduct* (38 instances, or 75%). This category included a number of subcategories of behaviors (not appearing in the table). Disrespect or rudeness (11 instances) generally involved some degree of verbal abuse. When a 53-year-old teacher went to inform his colleague that she had forgotten her duty for the day, instead of thanking him, he recounted how his colleague "lashed out at me, called me 'rude' and told me that I should have done her duty if I noticed the situation." A number of individuals reported unethical behaviors (10) such as when a 28-year-old electrician wrote about how his coworker "spoke of untrue actions to make himself look good." Supervisors sometimes abused their power (9). For example, a 22-year-old graduate student was told by her supervisor that "he was 'king' and had all the power to decide my fate in terms of my education and job." Other subcategories included individuals expressing negative work attitudes (3), making unreasonable demands (3), or working inefficiently (3).

The second most common category for emotional interactions with disliked others was *target character traits* (6 or 12%). These included a variety of persistent characteristics of the target. For example, a 30-year-old assistant manager was affected by his subordinate who "kept talking to me about his personal life. Things I don't need to know. Don't want to know," a behavior he started "after one day of working with him." The third category was *conflict or differences between parties* (5 or 10%). This involved situations in which respondents became aware that there were significant differences between them and another person. For example, a 41-year-old digital print operator could not understand why her coworker "thought it needed the input of our director" for a project that was "not that important." Finally, memories of *past events* sometimes evoked emotions. For one respondent, a 50-year-old self-employed contractor, the mere sight of the delivery man walking in the door the first time some years after a confrontation was enough to create a negative event for him.

For interactions with liked others, the majority of the events resulted in positive emotions. The most commonly mentioned events involved unexpected assistance. In a number of cases this was *work related assistance or support* (15 or 29%). In a typical example, a 29-year-old fitness director wrote that she "was putting together a program and this colleague helped me out even though they [sic] did not have to and it saved the day." Instead of work related support, in other cases respondents reported *receiving personal support* (7 or 13%). For example, a 57-year-old teaching assistant wrote that he was surprised when a supervisor "who I had only worked with briefly visited me in the hospital."

In contrast to receiving support, the opportunity to *provide assistance and support* (6 or 12%) caused positive emotional responses for a number of respondents. A 54-year-old contractor was initially surprised and later reassured when his supervisor "one day come to me to ask if I would do a part of his job that he was very good at but could no longer do by himself." He was pleased that he could help his supervisor. *Receiving praise or recognition* (5 or 10%) resulted in positive emotions such as when a 28-year-old electrician was excited when he received a large raise. *Giving praise or recognition* (2 or 4%) also resulted in positive emotions. A 50-year-old nurse in management was excited and proud of a subordinate and "gave her a very high evaluation and the highest pay raise I've ever given." Sometimes the positive emotions occurred during *casual conversation* at work, such as 23-year-old state highway department employee who felt great when he and a coworker were having "some conversations with each other about our personal lives (spirituality, hunting, family)." Hearing *good news* (1 or 2%) also caused positive emotions, like when a 25-year-old secretary was excited and happy when she found out a coworker had gotten engaged.

Interactions with liked others also resulted in negative emotions at times. Sometimes respondents heard *bad or disappointing news* (5 or 10%). A 64-year-old employee of a retail outlet was angry and disappointed when he heard that his friend who applied for an opening in another department had lost out to someone else. Sometimes respondents experienced *conflict or differences between parties* (4 or 8%) with liked others. For example, a 46-year-old production scheduler at a manufacturing plant was upset with her supervisor when the supervisor treated her and a coworker as if they had both equally contributed to a problem when it was really the coworker's problem. Finally, a few respondents experienced negative emotions because of *target conduct* (3 or 6%). A 25-year-old media relations employee became upset when he asked a coworker for assistance and did not receive any.

Overall, results related to *RQ1* indicate that organizational roles that resulted in emotional events did not differ for disliked or liked others. However, there were significant differences in the events that resulted in emotional responses. For disliked others, all of the events involved negative interactions, especially relating to the behaviors and traits of the other person. With liked others, most events were positive such as receiving or giving support or praise and recognition. The events with liked others that resulted in negative emotions were related to bad news, conflict, and personal conduct.

RQ2: Emotions Experienced with Disliked and Liked Others

Many respondents reported multiple emotions. The multiple emotions were categorized into specific categories (see Table 2). Many emotions were predominately associated with interactions with either disliked or liked others. For example, *resentment, disdain, fear, helplessness*, and *distrust* were experienced only with interactions with disliked others. *Angry/frustrated* and *hurt/disappointed* were experienced primarily in interactions with disliked others, although there were a few instances involving liked others. In contrast, most of the experiences of *empathy* or *negative emotions not directed at the other* were associated with interactions with liked others, although there were examples involving disliked others. All of the positive emotions (*happy/excited, grateful/relief, content/confident*) were associated with interactions with liked others.

In order to compare these results statistically, it was necessary to reduce multiple responses into single categories based on the first or predominate emotion listed. Therefore, five broad categories were created: positive emotions, empathy or sympathy, negative emotions about the situation but not the person, negative emotions directed at

the person, and surprise. A chi-square indicated that there were
significant differences between episodes with disliked and liked

Table 2

Emotion Reactions to Events with Disliked and Liked Others

Categories	Disliked Others	Liked Others
Positive Emotions	0	40
Happy/Excited	0	18
Grateful/Relieved	0	17
Content/Confident	0	5
Empathy/Sympathy toward the Others	1	8
Negative Emotions not Directed at the Other	2	7
Upset with the Situation	0	4
Embarrassment	2	2
Frightened	0	1
Negative Emotions Involving the Other	76	6
Angry/Frustrated/Upset	45	4
Hurt/Disappointed	10	2
Resentment	5	0
Disdain	5	0
Fear	5	0
Helpless/Depressed/Confused	5	0
Distrust	1	0
Surprise	1	5
Not applicable/Others	8	4

others, $\chi^2(4) = 75.68$, $p < .001$. This result was due to all of the positive
emotions and sympathy/empathy being associated with interactions
with liked others and the vast majority of the negative emotions
directed at the other person resulting from interactions with disliked
others.

RQ3: Emotion Management Behaviors with Disliked and Liked Others

Respondents reported a variety of behaviors in response to emotion

Table 3
Behaviors after Emotional Events with Disliked and Liked Others

Categories	Disliked Others	Liked Others
Discussion While Masking Felt Emotions	11	7
Accommodating While Masking Felt Emotions	20	0
Expressed Negative Emotions/Confrontation	15	1
Involved a Third Party in the Situation	7	0
Passive Disagreement	6	0
Discussion or Conversation	0	21
Express Thanks and Gratitude	0	15
Gave Praise and Recognition	0	5
Tears or Hugs	0	5
Other	1	6

events with disliked and liked others (see Table 3). With disliked others, the most common responses to emotion events were *accommodating while masking felt emotions*. As described by a 24-year-old advertising account coordinator, "I was extremely frustrated. I was mad. I felt my face warm up and I am sure my cheeks were red. I was squeezing my hands together under the table to help with the stress. I said nothing, as this was one of the many times he treated me this way." He tried to control his emotions and did nothing as he accommodated the disliked other. The second most common response to disliked others was to *express negative emotions* and confront the individual. In a typical example of this, a 35-year-old education employee wrote how he blatantly told his coworker, "That's the way we do it. If you want it differently, do it yourself." A smaller number of individuals responded to emotion events with disliked others with *discussion while masking emotions*. This was the case for a 23-year-old store manager who, despite feeling "very emotional after being attacked" by a more experienced peer, tried to control herself and "calmly tell him how he was making me feel" and "explained to him the reasoning behind the decisions." In a few instances, individuals *involved a third party in the situation*. For example, a 50-year-old teacher brought the matter up to her supervisor's superior when she was asked to compromise her personal ethics. The final behavior mentioned was *passive disagreement*. Examples include when a 52-year-old software engineer threw up his hands to indicate dissatisfaction, or a 21-year-old server simply huffed and walked off.

In emotion interactions with liked others, the most common response was *discussion or conversation*. Because these were often positive experiences to begin with, people often simply talked about the event. For example, when a 25-year-old recreational sports coordinator's supervisor relieved some of his anxiety as a new employee by talking to him in a straightforward manner, he "just sat and really listened to what his advice was and what I needed to do to succeed." But even when the emotions were negative, conversation often ensued. A 23-year-old manager felt sympathy and empathy when she found out a favorite coworker was being transferred to another store. She wrote, "To support her, I gave her the positives for the transfer and found ways to justify the move. I listened to her vent about her emotions and frustrations." Another response to positive emotion events was simply to *express thanks and gratitude*, sometimes including *tears or hugs*, as well. In a typical example, when a 48-year-old special education teacher was surprised and grateful that a coworker had organized her shelves, desk, and cabinets for her, she "gave her a big hug and teared up. I also expressed my gratitude by telling her how grateful I was." In a few other instances, the interaction provided an opportunity to *give praise and recognition*, such as when a 59-year-old supervisor was able to congratulate a subordinate who got a promotion after an interview for which he had helped prepare him. Because a few of the interactions were quite negative, respondents did sometimes respond with *discussion while masking emotions* or sometimes *confrontation*. For example, a 50 year-old-teacher, who was very angry at a school administrator, "went to his office and closed the door. In a loud and angry voice [did *I* yell?]," she told him that he should apologize for what he did.

Even though some respondents reported multiple behaviors, it is striking that only two categories of behaviors overlap between the liked and disliked others: respondents discussed their reactions while masking their negative emotions and they confronted someone while expressing negative emotions. Not surprisingly, when behaviors were reduced to the primary response, a chi-square indicated that there were significant differences depending on the type of relationship, $\chi^2(7) = 76.61, p < .001$.

RQ4: Impact on Relationships with Disliked and Liked Others

The short term impact of the emotion laden events is reported in the top of Table 4. Again, the difference in the impact of interactions with disliked versus liked others is clear and significant, as indicated by a chi-square, $\chi^2(5) = 45.26$, $p < .001$.

Table 4
*Short and Long Term Impact of Emotion Events with Disliked
and Liked Others on Relationship*

Categories	Disliked Others	Liked Others
Short Term Impact		
Relationship Deterioration	23	3
Neutral/Maintained Relationship	14	12
Relationship Dissolution	8	0
Avoidance	8	0
Improved Relationship	8	35
Cognitive Distancing	6	0
Wanted to Please Person	0	2
Other	1	2
Long Term Impact		
Neutral/No Impact	14	26
Physical Distancing	12	0
Psychological Distancing	12	0
Avoidance	7	0
Improved Relationship	7	14
No Further Interaction	3	2
Developed Relationship Outside Work	0	4
Worked Harder	0	2
Other	5	4

The most common short term result of these interactions with disliked others was *relationship deterioration*. A 57-year-old teaching assistant reported the negative interaction "further eroded an already tenuous relationship that had once been a positive one." The second most common category was *neutral or maintained relationship*. For example, a 25-year-old media relations employee wrote that he "basically agreed to disagree" without the relationship changing much. Other negative impacts included *relationship dissolution*, which typically involved respondents seeking some form of physical separation from the disliked other, such as a 44-year-old claims accountant who requested a job transfer after the situation became too stressful for her. *Avoidance* is also another response to negative interactions. As succinctly put forth by a 38-year-old assistant manager, "I avoid him like the plague." A few respondents reported *cognitive distancing* from disliked others, a mental strategy of minimizing or avoiding the relationship, often in conjunction with another response. In one such example, a 46-year-old production scheduler wrote how the event help "shed a new light" on the relationship and caused him to "back off." Finally, in a few instances respondents reported the impact created an *improved relationship* with disliked others. This was evident for a 23-year-old retail manager who described how even though the confrontation "was uncomfortable and emotional" for her, it "opened a new line of communication for the two of us...and increased the respect and understanding within the relationship."

For interactions with liked others, the most common short term impact was *improved relationships*. Even though these were positive relationships to begin with, often the emotional experience led to a stronger bond between the individuals. For example, when a business woman stood by a 50-year-old real estate appraiser during tough times, he was grateful and wrote that it "created more trust" in their relationship. Because the relationships were already positive, the second most common category indicated no real change, *neutral or maintained relationship*. In a typical response, a 21-year-old server, who was grateful to her busboy for helping out during a busy time, maintained the positive relationship because "he always gets large tips from me." In a few cases, despite negative interactions, the relationship remained the same. The previously mentioned media relations employee was temporarily upset with his coworker for not helping, but wrote that "after a day or two we were back to where we were prior to the disagreement." In a small number of very negative emotional interactions with liked others, the result was *relationship deterioration*. The teacher who was upset with her administrator wrote, "I never felt comfortable with him again. We never laughed together again. Actually I quit at the end of the year—but this was only one of many reasons that converged." Finally in two instances, respondents *wanted to please the person* after the event. A 33-year-old English teacher was very grateful for the support she received from a coworker during her divorce and wrote, "I work hard to keep her respect and to meet her expectations."

The long term impacts are reported in the bottom of Table 4. Again the differences in responses to disliked and liked others are apparent and a chi-square confirmed that these were significant, $\chi^2(7)=40.73$, $p<.001$. The categories for the long term impacts are quite similar to the short term impacts for both liked and disliked others.

With disliked others there was often *no impact*, as related by a 54-year-old self- employed contractor, "I continued to treat him as I wanted to be treated." Individuals also *physically distanced* themselves as seen when a 35-year-old educator substituted electronic mail for personal communication whenever he could. As with short term impacts, some respondents also *psychologically distanced* themselves from the disliked other in the long term. For example, a 24-year-old advertising accounts coordinator noted how she learned to "keep my opinions to myself instead of sharing them in meetings." Another long term impact was *avoidance* as practiced by a 29-year-old fitness director in her attempt to minimize interactions with the disliked coworker. In a few instances the long term impact was an *improved relationship*, such as the building of a "much better rapport" with her superintendent for a 52-year-old teacher. A final category identified as *no further interactions* also emerged. Frequently these are cases marked by one-time negative interactions or relationships that dissolved after one party left the job.

With liked others, almost half the time there was *no impact*, with the relationships continuing as before. Sometimes even when the incident was negative, such as the media relations employee not receiving help from a coworker, they continued their friendship and working relationship. In other instances there were *improved relationships*, such as a 46-year-old production scheduler whose former supervisor continued to help her advance in the company. A specific indication of improved work relationships was respondents sometimes *developed a relationship outside of work*. For example, a 47-year-old radiology technician was grateful that a volunteer visited her regularly after her operation and has maintained a relationship with the volunteer even though she quit her job there. The two individuals who wanted to please the other person in the short term *worked harder* to do the same in the long run. Finally, sometimes there were *no further interactions*. For example, the upset teacher moved to another school and no longer interacted with him.

Post-hoc Analysis of Behaviors to Outcomes

Given the previous results, it seemed valuable to explore whether the behaviors in *RQ3* were associated with short and long term outcomes in *RQ4* depending on whether the relationship was with a liked or disliked other. This post-hoc analysis revealed some interesting patterns, although small cell sizes made statistical comparisons problematic. As might be expected in interactions with liked others, discussion (n = 13) and expressing thanks (n = 13) were strongly associated with short term improved relationships and neutral or improved long term relationships. There were so few interactions with liked others that resulted in deterioration (n = 3) that there was no observable pattern. For interactions with disliked others, masking emotions by either accommodation (n = 11) or discussion (n = 6) was associated with relationship deterioration or dissolution. In contrast, expressing or confronting the disliked other often had a neutral (n = 8) or positive (n = 2) short and long term impact on the relationship, although expressing the emotions could also lead to relationship deterioration (n = 2). A few instances of discussion while masking emotions (n = 3) also showed some association with improved long term relationships with disliked others. Together, these results suggest that masking emotion may have a negative impact on relationships with disliked others while expressing them or discussing them may have a negative, neutral or positive impact.

Discussion

This study examined emotional interactions with disliked and liked others in work settings. The contrasts that emerged from the results for emotional episodes with disliked versus liked others are quite striking. Although the results indicated that the interactions were equally distributed across organizational roles (e.g., with supervisors, peers, etc.) for liked and disliked others, there were significant differences in the types of events that precipitated emotional responses, in the emotions experienced, in their emotion management behaviors, and in the short and long term impacts of the interactions.

With disliked others, the pattern that emerged in the results suggests that respondents typically experienced a negative spiral of relationship deterioration as part of emotional episodes. With disliked others, respondents most often reported negative episodes, such as inappropriate behaviors. Not surprisingly, the resulting emotions were typically negative as well, usually anger and frustration or disappointment. Then they frequently masked their emotions whether they accommodated the disliked other, passively disagreed with them, or discussed it with them, or they expressed their negative emotions to the disliked other. The impact of these emotion management behaviors was that the relationships with disliked others tended to remain negative or deteriorated further. In the long term, they typically minimized their relationships with disliked others through avoidance or by creating physical and psychological distance. In social exchange theory terms, the exchange basis of the relationships with disliked others became increasingly costly compared to alternative relationships.

In contrast, with liked others, a positive spiral of relationship development was the most common pattern. Respondents primarily reported positive episodes, such as receiving or providing assistance and praise with liked others. As a result, the emotions were typically positive as well, usually happiness or relief. In most of the instances in which respondents felt negative emotions in interactions with liked others, it was because they felt sympathy or empathy for the other person; they were not upset at the other person. Respondents also managed their emotions differently with liked others. Instead of masking their emotions, they typically expressed their positive emotions or sympathy for the liked other. These responses usually maintained or improved the relationships and sometimes included developing relationships outside of work. From a social exchange theory perspective, the relationships became more beneficial and developed further over time.

While downward relational spirals for disliked others and upward relational spirals for liked others were typical results of emotional episodes, the results indicate that emotional episodes can also be turning points in organizational relationships (e.g., Bullis & Bach, 1989). In a number of instances, emotional interactions with disliked others brought about significant positive changes and improved relationships. For example, a 23-year-old retail manager was involved in a major disagreement with another manager over their different management styles. Although it was an emotional exchange in which she felt hurt and misunderstood, by discussing the issues, the negative event actually helped to open up a new line of communication for them, one that would otherwise not have been possible. Not only were they eventually able to laugh and joke about it without any hard feelings, but their respect for each other also grew as both understood the other better after the incident. As suggested by the post-hoc analysis, in this case expressing the emotions and discussing the issues led to a positive outcome and ended the negative spiral. From a social exchange perspective, the discussion changed the cost-benefit ratio of the exchange from a negative to a positive one so that the evaluation of the relationship also changed to more positive. Had the manager masked emotions, it is likely that the relationship would have continued in a negative spiral because there would not have been any change in the exchange ratio.

The results for negative interactions with liked others also served as possible turning points. Often these episodes were brushed aside. When a liked peer did not give the requested assistance, a respondent was upset at him, but later dismissed it as a one-time event and the relationship returned to the same after a day or two. But if the event was severe enough, emotional episodes turned positive relationships into negative ones. For example, when a teacher confronted her liked supervisor for mistreating her and he did not apologize or back down from his position, she lost respect for him and began avoiding him. Eventually she took a position elsewhere in the organization to reduce interaction with him. In social exchange terminology, the severity of the emotional episode changed the relationship to one that was too costly to maintain and so the relationship ended. These examples suggest that strong emotional encounters have the potential to change workplace relationships with disliked or liked others.

Collectively, emotion management episodes in which emotions are masked rather than expressed are most frequently associated with disliked others rather than evenly distributed among organizational acquaintances. Previous research on emotion management has considered the impact of role (e.g., customer), but not the type of relationship (disliked, liked) in examining emotion management. The findings here suggest that emotion management with liked others is relatively easy; felt emotions are typically positive, or supportive such as sympathy, and can be expressed. With disliked others, the emotions are typically negative and so decisions to manage emotions by expressing or masking felt emotions become problematic. Managing emotions with disliked other is critical given the general organizational norm against expressing strong negative emotions;

expressing emotions inappropriately is likely to be considered unprofessional (Kramer & Hess, 2002).

Results suggest that expressing emotions rather than masking them may help change relationship trajectories with disliked others. Masking emotions was associated with relationship deterioration, but expressing emotions or at least discussing the issues while masking the feelings could lead to neutral or positive relationship development. Although this is a very tentative conclusion given the small sample and the potential negative impact as well, other research finds similar results. Waldron and Krone (1991) found that masking emotions generally had a negative impact on relationships while expressing them at least prevented further deterioration. Fiebig and Kramer (1998) found that expressing negative emotions could lead to either positive or negative relational outcomes. It appears that expressing emotions has greater potential for changing relationships with disliked others compared to masking those emotions, although it does not always have this impact. Together this suggests that managing emotions with coworkers, especially disliked coworkers, is a complex and difficult task.

These results here for the emotion management decision clarify previous research concerning the impact of masking or expressing emotions. Previous research that found that masking negative emotions frequently impacts relationships negatively (Waldron & Krone, 1991) or that expressing can have a positive or negative impact (Kramer & Hess, 2002) did not consider the nature of the relationship in which the emotions occurred. These results suggest that the negative impacts of masking or expressing emotions are most often associated with interaction with disliked others. Expressing emotions to liked others tends to have a positive impact on relationships.

The short and long term impacts reported by respondents are consistent with the general strategies for dealing with relational problems (Rusbult & Zembrodt, 1983) and with the types of distancing behaviors identified elsewhere (Hess, 2000; 2002). Respondents reported a range of active and passive strategies to distance themselves physically or psychologically from their disliked others. The results add to this research by suggesting that respondents recognize that these work relationships are somewhat voluntary since some chose to change positions to avoid interacting with disliked others.

Limitations

As with most emotion research, this study is limited by its reliance on self-report recall data. For example, it is impossible to know if these respondents were actually masking their emotions as they claimed to do. However, respondents were arguably the most accurate source for reporting their own emotions and the impact the events had on their perceptions of their relationships. It is also possible that respondents more readily recalled negative interactions with disliked others and positive interactions with liked others. Similarly, the results may be due to self-fulfilling prophecies in which respondents expect negative interactions with disliked others and positive interactions with liked others, and as a result interpret the interactions that way with little regard for the actual behaviors. However, the fact that the respondents included a number of examples in which relationships turned around as a result of emotional episodes suggests this is not an important issue. Future research using multiple data collection techniques such as diaries and observation may address these concerns.

Application

The results are applicable to organizational members. Since emotional responses are generally the result of discrepancies between expectations and experiences (Mandler, 1975), it is valuable for organizational members to expect that interactions with disliked others are likely to result in negative emotions. Anticipating negative encounters may minimize the emotions and help prevent relationships from following a negative spiral, although it will not eliminate the negative response. Also it is valuable to know that expressing the emotions or at least discussing the issues rather than masking and avoiding them has the potential for improving relationship. Given the norms of professionalism, individuals may believe that masking emotions and avoiding issues is the most appropriate way to handle emotional encounters. Results suggest that this often leads to relationship deterioration. Expressing the feelings and addressing the issues can lead to positive outcomes. However, since it does not always do so, it is important to carefully select the times and places for such expressions. On the positive side, the results point to the importance of expressing emotions to liked others. Expressing thanks, giving praise, and being sympathetic help to solidify and deepen relationships. While such behavior is probably second nature for many individuals, this study reinforces the value of such emotional expression and support in relationship development.

Conclusion

By comparing emotional episodes with disliked and liked others, this study contributes to our understanding of communicating with difficult people in work settings. With liked others, emotions are typically positive, so felt emotions can be expressed with little or no management. With disliked others, negative emotions are frequently part of the interactions. This makes managing emotions a particularly important part of the communication process for interacting with disliked others.

References

Ashforth, B. E., & Humphrey, R. H. (1995). Emotion in the workplace: A reappraisal. *Human Relations, 48,* 97-125.

Berscheid, E. (1985). Interpersonal attraction. In G. Lindzey & E. Aronson (Eds.), *Handbook of Social Psychology* (Vol. 2, pp. 413-484). New York: Random House.

Bullis, C., & Bach, B. W. (1989). Are mentor relationships helping organizations? An exploration of developing mentee-mentor-organizational identification using turning point analysis. *Communication Quarterly, 37,* 199-213.

Ekman, P. (1973). Cross-cultural studies of facial expression. In P. Ekman, (Ed.), *Darwin and facial expression: A century of research in review* (pp. 169-222). New York: Academic Press.

Fairhurst, G. T. (2001). Dualisms in leadership research. In F. M. Jablin & L. L. Putnam (Eds.), *The new handbook of organizational communication: Advances in theory, research, and methods* (pp. 379-439). Thousand Oaks, CA: Sage.

Fiebig, G. V., & Kramer, M. W. (1998). A framework for the study of emotions in organizational contexts. *Management Communication Quarterly, 11,* 536-572.

Fineman, S. (1993). An emotional agenda. In S. Fineman (Ed.), *Emotion in organizations* (pp. 216-224). Newbury Park, CA: Sage.

Fritz, J. M. H. (1997). Responses to unpleasant work relationships. *Communication Research Reports, 14,* 302-311.

Fleiss, J. L. (1971). Measuring nominal scale agreement among many raters. *Psychological Bulletin, 76,* 378-382.

Foa, E. B., & Foa, U. G. (1980). Resource theory: Interpersonal behavior as exchange. In K. J. Gergen, M. S. Greenberg, & R. H. Willis (Eds.), *Social exchange: Advances in theory and research* (pp. 77-94). New York: Plenum Press.

Glaser, B., & Strauss, A. (1967). *The discovery of grounded theory: Strategies for qualitative research.* Chicago: Aldine.

Graen , G. B., & Uhl-Bien, M. (1995). Relationship-based approach to leadership: Development of leader-member exchange (LMX) theory of leadership over 25 years: applying a multilevel multidomain perspective. *Leadership Quarterly, 6,* 219-247.

Hess, J. A. (2000). Maintaining nonvoluntary relationship with disliked partners: An investigation into the use of distancing behaviors. *Human Communication Research, 26,* 458-488.

Hess, J. A. (2002). Maintaining unwanted relationships. In D. J. Canary & M. Dainton (Eds.), *Maintaining relationships through communication: Relational, contextual, and cultural variations* (pp. 103-124). Mahwah, NJ: Lawrence Erlbaum.

Hochschild, A. R. (1979). Emotion work, feeling rules, and social structure. *American Journal of Sociology, 85,* 551-575.

Hochschild, A. R. (1983). *The managed heart.* Berkeley: University of California Press.

Jablin, F. M. (1979). Superior-subordinate communication: The state of the art. *Psychological Bulletin, 86,* 1201-1222.

Knapp, M. L. (1984). *Interpersonal communication and human relationships.* New York: Allyn & Bacon.

Kram, K. E., & Isabella, L. A. (1985). Mentoring alternatives: The role of peer relationships in career development. *Academy of Management Journal, 28,* 110-132.

Kramer, M. W., & Hess, J. A. (1998, November). *Emotion display norms: Rules for emotion management in organizational settings.* Paper presented at the NCA Annual Convention in New York.

Kramer, M. W., & Hess, J. A. (2002). Communication rules for the display of emotions in organizational settings. *Management Communication Quarterly, 16,* 66-80.

Mandler, G. (1975). *Mind and body: Psychology of emotion and stress.* New York: Norton.

Morris, J. A., & Feldman, D. C. (1996). The dimensions, antecedents, and consequences of emotional labor. *Academy of Management Review, 21,* 986-1010.

Mumby, D. K., & Putman., L. L. (1992). The politics of emotions: A feminist reading of bounded rationality. *Academy of Management Review, 17,* 465-486.

Omdahl, B. L. (1995). *Cognitive appraisal, emotion, and empathy.* Mahwah, NJ: Lawrence Erlbaum.

Planalp, S. (1999). *Communicating emotion: Social, moral, and cultural processes.* Cambridge, UK: Cambridge University Press.

Planalp, S. (2003). The unacknowledged role of emotion in theories of close relationships: How do theories feel? *Communication Theory, 13,* 78-99.

Putnam, L. L., & Mumby, D. K. (1993). Organizations, emotion and the myth of rationality. In S. Fineman (Ed.), *Emotion in organizations* (pp. 36-57). Newbury Park, CA: Sage.

Roloff, M. E. (1981). *Interpersonal communication: The social exchange approach.* Beverly Hills, CA: Sage.

Rusbult, C. E., & Zembrodt, I. M. (1983) Responses to dissatisfaction in romantic involvements: A multidimensional scaling analysis. *Journal of Experimental Social Psychology, 19,* 274-293.

Shuler, S., & Sypher, B. D. (2000). Seeking emotional labor: When managing the heart enhances the work experience. *Management Communication Quarterly, 14,* 50-89.

Sias, P. M., & Cahill, D. J. (1998). From coworkers to friends: The development of peer friendships in the workplace. *Western Journal of Communication, 62,* 273-299.

Sias, P. M., & Jablin, F. M. (1995). Differential superior-subordinate relations, perceptions of fairness, and coworker communication. *Human Communication Research, 22,* 5-38.

Sutton, R. I. (1991). Maintaining norms about expressed emotions: The case of bill collectors. *Administrative Science Quarterly, 36,* 245-268.

Teboul, J. C. B. (1995). Determinants of new hire information-seeking during organizational encounter. *Western Journal of Communication, 59,* 305-325.

Thibault, J. W., & Kelley, H. H. (1959). *The social psychology of groups.* New York: Wiley.

Tracy, S. J. (2000). Becoming a character for commerce: Emotion labor, self-subordination, and discursive construction of identity in a total institution. *Management Communication Quarterly, 14,* 90-128.

Van Maanen, J., & Kunda, G. (1989). "Real feelings": Emotional expression and organizational culture. *Research in Organizational Behavior, 11,* 43-103.

Waldron, V.R. (1994). Once more, with feeling: Reconsidering the role of emotion in work. In S.A. Deetz (Ed.), *Communication Yearbook* (Vol. 17, pp. 388-416). Thousand Oaks, CA: Sage.

Waldron, V. R., & Krone, K. J. (1991). The experience and expression of emotion in the workplace. *Management Communication Quarterly, 4,* 287-309.

9 | Should I Stay or Should I Go Now? The Role of Negative Communication and Relational Maintenance in Distress and Well-Being

> I am trapped in this relationship. If I elect to change advisors, I will damage, or throw away, an opportunity to parlay my degree into a tenure-track job. My advisor's letter of recommendation is critical to an academic job. I have been betrayed, but I must swallow her egregious behavior in order to move on. To change advisors in the final stages of my dissertation would be professional suicide.
>
> Anonymous 5th year Ph.D. student

Maintaining a professional relationship in the face of adversity is often required to gain the benefits accrued by that relationship. So it is not surprising that an array of interpersonal strategies are used to maintain relationships (Canary & Stafford, 1994; Lee & Jablin, 1995) and we expend much effort doing so (Dindia & Baxter, 1987). The effort expended on a relationship is especially prominent when one is forced to choose to maintain or to dissolve a distressed relationship. Each approach potentially poses a set of costs to one's personal and social well-being, and the process of choosing may also take energy. The current study examines the extent to which enacting relational maintenance or disengagement strategies in response to receiving negative messages from a superior in a workplace context is related to distress and well-being.

Rationale

Maintaining a workplace relationship requires effort and strategic communication (Canary & Stafford, 1994; Daly & Wiemann, 1994; Seibold, Cantrill, & Meyers, 1985). Therefore, individuals use communication in ways that balance their needs with the needs of their partner. As a result, influence messages often revolve around principles of appropriateness, politeness, or other-orientation (cf., Bippus, 2001; Brown & Levinson, 1978; Burleson, 1994; Roskos-Ewoldsen, 1997).

However, at times, co-workers and superiors are compelled to evaluate or to be critical of others either as part of their professional responsibilities or based on personal inclination. These messages hold the potential to be perceived as threatening, even if the source uses the linguistic structures of politeness. This is due, in part, to the core of the message, which informs individuals that they have not acted appropriately, have not met some obligation or responsibility, or possess a deficit. Thus, in response, receivers may enact behavioral strategies to protect themselves (Hess, 2000) and/or express dissatisfaction publicly (Fiebig & Kramer, 1998; Kramer & Hess, 2002) or privately (Meares, Oetzel, Torres, Derkas, & Ginossar, 2004; Sias & Jablin, 1995); any of these behaviors may hold negative consequences for the receiver and for the relationship.

The Process of Self-Protection

Self-protection consists of an array of cognitive and behavioral strategies that function to maintain the integrity of the self (Rosenberg, 1965, 1979). Thus, individuals tend to self-protect when they receive information that is perceived to be inconsistent with current conceptions of self (e.g., negative evaluations or criticism). Because self-protection requires action such as an attitude or belief change (Brehm, 1966), affect regulation (Higgins, 1987), and/or coping (Lazarus, 1993; Lazarus & Folkman, 1984) to neutralize the threat, it can manifest as psychological, affective, and social responses.

Psychological Response Mechanisms

The notions of self-discrepancies can be used as an explanatory mechanism in situations where individuals perceive a threat (Higgins, 1987, 1989; Higgins, Klein, & Strauman, 1985). Higgins (1987) defined self-discrepancies as cognitive states created by the perception of not meeting expectations. Thus, communication allows individuals to assess the extent to which they are meeting expectations (Kinch, 1967; Mead, 1934), implying that "negative" communication is self-discrepant and threatening.

According to Higgins and others (Bruch, Rivet, & Laurenti, 2000;

Gonnerman, Parker, Lavine, & Huff, 2000), self-discrepancies activate negative affect, which signals that a threat to the self has been encountered and that the threat *should* be dealt with to reduce or eliminate the discrepancy to protect the self. Thus, receiving negative communication should activate a self-discrepancy, prompting cognition, affect, and behavior to protect the self.

Research shows that negative behavior from a relational partner prompts individuals to think about the behavior to understand its causes (Camper, Jacobson, Holtzworth-Munroe, & Schmaling, 1988; Holtzworth-Munroe & Jacobson, 1985; Orvis, Kelley, & Butler, 1976) and can result in dislike for the person displaying the negative behavior (Beatty & Dobos, 1992; Ilgen, Peterson, Martin, & Boeschen, 1981), both of which are indications of self-protection. Further, given that self-discrepancies activate negative affect (Cohen, Tyrrell, & Smith, 1993; Friedman, 1992; Herbert & Cohen, 1993; O'Leary, 1990; Suls & Wan, 1993), it is reasonable to assume that receiving and thinking about negative messages may elicit various forms of distress. Thus:

> *H1*: Receiving messages that are perceived to be negative will be related positively to cognitive and affective states indicative of distress.

In addition to the creation of self-discrepancies, under conditions of recurrent thoughts or repeated exposure to negative messages, potentially harmful psychological and physiological states related to negative affect may emerge. These include psychological and behavioral dysfunction (e.g., Fiscella & Campbell, 1999; Savin-Williams, 1994) and physiologic states such as acute blood pressure and heart rate increases (Levenson & Gottman, 1983), pituitary and adrenal hormone activation (Malarkey, Kiecolt-Glaser, Pearl, & Glaser, 1994), and down-regulated immune system responses (Ewart, Burnett, & Taylor, 1983; Kiecolt-Glaser et al., 1993). Thus, psycho-somatic symptoms indicative of decreased well-being may surface in those who experience repeated negative affective states. Thus:

> *H2:* Within the context of significant interpersonal relationships, interaction that elicits negative affective states will be related positively to psychological conditions and psychosomatic symptoms indicative of decreased well-being.

The Effects of Social Power

Social power influences how information flows and how interactions are perceived and understood (Henderson, 1981), but it also sets up boundary conditions within relationships. Therefore, when subordinates interact with a superior they may interpret and react to the interaction with a heightened sense of importance. Several social contexts with clear power differentials have been examined for the effects of negative messages on subordinates including parent-child (Beatty, Zelley, Dobos, & Rudd, 1994; Gelles & Harrop, 1991; Rohner & Rohner, 1980), coach-athlete (Kassing & Infante, 1999; Sinclair & Vealey, 1989), supervisor-employee (Ilgen, Mitchell, & Fredrickson, 1981; Ilgen, Peterson, Martin, & Boeschen, 1981) and instructor-student (Myers, 1998; Myers & Knox, 1999) contexts.

Three conclusions follow from this research. One, individuals exposed to negative messages from a superior report various forms of distress, which is consistent with the research reviewed earlier. Two, the studies show that hostility toward self, the powerholder, and the social context may surface (e.g., Beatty, Zelley, Dobos, & Rudd, 1994; Kassing & Infante, 1999; Savin-Williams, 1994). Three, the studies also reveal that individuals take various forms of action against the powerholder, including relational disengagement in the form of decreased motivation and participation (e.g., Ilgen, Mitchell, & Fredrickson, 1981; Myers & Knox, 1999), and in some cases, direct confrontation against the powerholder (e.g., Rohner & Rohner, 1980; Savin-Williams, 1994).

These social reactions are illustrated in Baron's (1988) work on criticism. In a series of laboratory studies using undergraduates, Baron found that in response to destructive criticism, undergraduates indicated that they would be more likely to handle future conflict with the source through "resistance or avoidance and less likely to handle future disagreements through collaboration or compromise" (p. 199). This suggests that the "preferred" social reaction to negative messages may be biased toward relational dissolution and disengagement rather than preservation/maintenance. However, as has been alluded to above, in an organizational setting dissolution and disengagement may not be beneficial or possible.

Social Response Mechanisms

Given the complexity of social responses (see Hess, 2000; Kalbfleish,

1997; Keltner, Young, & Buswell, 1997), how one reacts to a perceived threat within the context of a relationship can be a strategic decision, meaning that one may decide to maintain or to disengage. Under certain conditions, however, individuals may be blocked from disengagement, forcing them to deal with the threat in ways other than by avoiding or withdrawing. Under these conditions, it is likely that those who are threatened will engage responses that maintain the relationship, but these responses may not be self-protective. Thus, the discrepancies produced by this situation should elicit distress and affect aspects of one's well-being.

Higgins (1987) delineated two types of self-discrepancies (actual-ideal, actual-ought), suggesting that each may motivate a different class of reactions. Messages that call into question one's performance or competencies tend to activate an actual-ideal self-discrepancy, which has been linked to agitation-type affects (Bruch et al., 2000; Gonnerman et al., 2000). In terms of social responses, agitation affects should prompt approach, confrontation, or rejection (e.g., hostility) responses. Messages that call into question one's social skills or obligations tend to activate an actual-ought self-discrepancy, which has been linked to dejection-type affects (Bruch et al., 2000; Gonnerman et al., 2000). In terms of social responses, dejection affects should prompt withdrawal, avoidance, or denial responses.

Regardless, according to self-discrepancy theory, these two classes of responses should function to reduce the self-discrepancy and, as a result, reduce distress. Thus, it is reasonable to conceptualize these responses as attempts to protect one's self. Thus:

H3: Responding to negative messages from a powerful relational partner by avoiding, rejecting, confronting, or defying that partner will be related negatively to distress and psychosomatic symptoms.

However, deciding to disengage or dissolve a relationship to protect oneself from future exposure to negative messages could be costly. Thus, subordinates who desire to avoid these costs must preserve the relationship, which may put them in a bind. Interestingly, none of the studies reviewed in this section assessed the effects of relational maintenance (e.g., making amends or appeasing) on subordinates. This is a curious oversight because appeasement often reduces conflict within hierarchical relationships (Baron, 1990;

Kalbfleish, 1997; Keltner et al., 1997).

Relational repair often requires one of the interactants to appease (see Kalbfleish, 1997) to signal that relational preservation is desired. The individual who appeases may need to justify to him/herself that maintaining the relationship is beneficial in spite of its current harm(s). As a result, enacting maintenance strategies may foster the formation of an additional self-discrepancy or re-activate the original self-discrepancy to the extent that individuals: 1) were actually wrong and accept their wrongdoing; 2) believe that they were not at fault, but feel forced to preserve the relationship for it's benefits; or 3) believe they have apologized simply to avoid relational dissolution and its consequences. Thus:

> *H4:* Responding to negative messages from a powerful relational partner by appeasing that partner will be related positively to distress and psychosomatic symptoms.

Selection of Relational Context

Examining the link between messages and well-being involves selection of a context. While extant work in this area has examined several contexts, the context chosen for the current study was selected based on two criteria: 1) there is a high motivation to preserve the relationship because of its importance and benefits, and 2) the relationship holds clearly specified roles of unequal power. Therefore, this investigation examined the academic advisor-graduate student relationship because graduate students are motivated to preserve the relationship with their advisor, the relationship demonstrates a clear power differential, and the relationship is couched within an organizational setting that serves to frame notions of appropriateness.

Method

The following method tested the four hypotheses identified above.

Participants and Procedures

Participants (N=434) were randomly chosen graduate students who were currently enrolled in a variety of graduate programs at a large midwestern university. Participants were mailed a packet containing a cover letter, a survey, and a self-addressed, stamped return envelope. This procedure was reviewed, approved, and considered exempt from written consent procedures by the Institutional Review Board of the university at which the study was conducted.

Descriptive analyses revealed that the sample consisted of 64.3% female (n=279), the average age was 30 years (SD=6.7; range=20-55 years), and 76% of the sample was white/Caucasian. The average time spent enrolled in graduate school was 2.5 years (SD=1.4). The average reported GPA was just below an "A."

Measures

Based on prior work that has modeled the process of threat assessment and its relationship to distress (e.g., Lazarus & Folkman, 1984; Higgins, 1987), the variables used in the current study fell into three broad categories: 1) perceptions of a "negative" communication event, 2) affective, behavioral, and cognitive reactions attributed to the reported event, and 3) the experience of psychosomatic symptoms subsequent to the reported event.

Perception measures. All participants were asked to indicate if their academic advisor had ever said or done anything to them that they perceived as "negative." If a participant indicated that s/he had experienced a negative event (n=136), s/he was then asked to describe the nature of the most salient or most recent event and was instructed to complete four 9-point Likert-type scales (anchored by 1="A little" to 9="A great deal") that assessed the extent to which the event was 1) uncomfortable, 2) hurtful, 3) severe, and 4) stressful. Following these judgments, participants were asked to indicate why they thought the event occurred, how long ago the event occurred, and how often these types of events occur.

Distress measures. The distress variables were drawn from the cognitive, affective, and physical/physiological domains, which when combined, composed our conception of well-being (see Feist et al., 1995) and represented the three major outcomes revealed within the literature on the effects of receiving negative messages reviewed above.

To assess participants' *cognitive reactions* to the reported negative event, five 9-point Likert-type items (anchored by 1="not very often" to 9="very often") asked participants to indicate how often they thought about the event, how intense those thoughts were, and whether or not they thought about "getting even" with their advisor, "changing advisors," or "dropping out" of the program. Based, in part, on Horowitz, Wilner, and Alvarez's (1979) work, the first two of these five items were combined to form an "intrusiveness" scale, which tapped the extent to which each participant thought about the event (α=.87). The remaining three items were used as single item indicators to assess the extent to which each participant thought about enacting specific behavioral strategies in response to the reported event (e.g., "getting even," "changing advisors," "dropping out").

To assess participants' *affective reactions*, seven 7-point Likert-type items (anchored by 0="none of this feeling" to 6="a lot of this feeling") asked participants to indicate the extent to which they generally felt irritated, scared, confused, angry, calm, sad, or happy during or after the reported negative event. Based on prior research on affective experiences (Russell, 1980; Watson, Clark, & Tellegen, 1988), when appropriate, the seven affect items were combined to form positive (happy, calm; α=.76) and negative (irritated, scared, confused, angry, sad; α=.86) affect scales.

Based, in part, on research that has examined the nature of relational maintenance and avoidance strategies (e.g., Hess, 2000; Kalbfleish, 1997; Lee & Jablin, 1995; Roloff & Cloven, 1994), *social reactions* were assessed using 12 9-point Likert-type items (anchored by 1="NO!!" to 9="YES!!"). These items assessed how participants actually responded during or after the reported negative event (quit talking to, tried to make better, picked fights with, less friendly toward, same as usual, talked to about situation, quit doings things for, criticized, argued with, worked out a compromise, never discussed, told I was sorry).

In addition to the 12 single item measures, sets of items were combined to form four social response indices, including the extent to which participants 1) avoided, withdrew, or distanced themselves from their advisor (e.g., "quit talking to," "quit doing things for," "less friendly toward"), 2) approached their advisor in an actively negative manner (e.g., "picked fights with," "argued with"), 3) approached their advisor in an actively positive manner (e.g., "tried to make the relationship better," "talked about the situation," "worked out a compromise," "told advisor I was sorry"), or 4) ignored the situation (e.g., "I have been the same as usual toward my advisor," "the situation has never been discussed"). Responses to each behavioral reaction index were totaled to form a composite score for each.

Perceptions of the *hostility of the environment* in which the reported negative event took place were assessed by asking participants to indicate the extent to which they agreed or disagreed with six 9-point Likert-type statements (anchored by 1="strongly agree" to 9="strongly disagree") concerning the nature of the academic department in which they were enrolled. Sample items included "the atmosphere in my department is stressful," "graduate students in my department are competitive," and "I do not feel safe in my department." These six items were combined to form a perceptions of environment/department scale (α=.73).

Perceptions of the academic advisor were assessed using six 9-point semantic-differential scales. Participants were asked to indicate the extent to which their advisor is "reliable-unreliable," "valuable-worthless," "honest-dishonest," "friendly-unfriendly," "pleasant-unpleasant," and "trustworthy-untrustworthy." These six items were combined to form a perceptions of advisor scale (α=.86).

A modified[1] version of the Hopkins symptoms checklist (Derogatis et al., 1974) was used to examine *psychosomatic symptoms*. The modified checklist contained 32 7-point Likert-type items (anchored by 0="None" to 6="A lot") that tapped physical, physiological, or psychological conditions experienced subsequent to the reported negative event.[2]

The measured psychosomatic conditions included: 1) general anxiety (e.g., somatization: "headaches," "dizziness;" physical anxiety: "trembling," "tenseness or being upset;" α=.92); 2) depressive tendencies (e.g., "blaming self," "loneliness;" α=.90); 3) social paranoia (e.g., "feeling critical of others," "feeling that others are unfriendly or that they dislike me;" α=.92); and 4) trouble concentrating (e.g., "trouble remembering things," "difficulty in making decisions;" α=.93).

Results[3]

Testing H1

Hypothesis 1 stated that messages that are perceived as negative will be related positively to cognitive and affective states indicative of distress. Regression analyses were conducted to test H1 within the negative sub-set of questionnaires (n=136). This analysis consisted of entering the sub-set of perceptual measures (discomfort, hurtful, stressful, severity) to account for the variance in each of the relevant measures of distress. To streamline the results, non-significant findings are not discussed and discussion of specific predictors is limited.

Thinking about the event (intrusive thoughts). As a set, the perceptual measures were able to account for a significant portion of the variance due to thought intrusiveness (R^2=.62, $F(3, 130)$=41.92, p<.0001).

Thinking about options. A significant portion of the variance due to thinking about what to do in response to receiving the negative communication was accounted for by the perceptual variables, including "getting even" (R^2=.17, $F(3, 130)$=4.99, p<.001), "changing advisors" (R^2=.21, $F(3, 130)$=6.88, p<.0001), and thinking about "dropping out" (R^2=.31, $F(3, 130)$=11.26, p<.0001).

Affective states. The perceptual measures were able to account for a significant amount of variance in six of the seven single item affect measures and in both of the combined affect scales. In terms of single items affective indices, a significant amount of variance was accounted for due to irritated (R^2=.31, $F(4, 130)$=11.37, p<.01), scared (R^2=.12, $F(4, 130)$=3.47, p<.01), angry (R^2=.26, $F(4, 130)$=9.06, p<.01), calm (R^2=.12, $F(4, 130)$=3.39, p<.01), sad (R^2=.21, $F(4, 130)$=6.73, p<.01), and happy (R^2=.12, $F(4, 130)$=3.54, p<.01) by the perceptual measures. In addition, the perceptual measures were also able to account for a significant amount of variance due to the negative (R^2=.34, $F(4, 130)$=14.55, p<.01) and positive (R^2=.18, $F(4, 130)$=6.15, p<.01) affective indices.

Social responses. The perceptual measures accounted for a significant amount of the variance due to eight of the 12 social response items.[4] In terms of the social response indices, the set of perceptual measures was able to account for significant variance in three of the four indices, including withdrawal (R^2=.23, $F(4, 111)$=8.35, p<.0001), actively negative (R^2=.19, $F(4, 111)$=6.38, p<.0001), and actively positive (R^2=.13, $F(4, 111)$=4.10, p<.003).

Hostility. The perceptual measures were able to account for a significant amount of variance in both hostility measures (toward advisor: R^2=.26, $F(4, 111)$=10.04, p<.001; toward department: R^2=.15, $F(4, 111)$=4.90, p<.01).

Psychosomatic symptoms. The perceptual measures were also able to account for a significant amount of variance due to all four psychosomatic factors: general anxiety (R^2=.20, $F(4, 111)$=7.03, p<.001), depressive tendencies (R^2=.21, $F(4, 111)$=7.38, p<.0001), social paranoia

(R^2=.18, F(4, 111)=6.21, p<.0001), and trouble concentrating (R^2=.14, F(4, 111)=4.59, p<.0003).

Testing H2

Hypothesis 2 stated that interaction with significant others that elicits negative affective states will be related positively to psychological conditions and psychosomatic symptoms indicative of decreased well-being. Regression analyses were conducted to test H2 within the negative sub-set of questionnaires (n=136). This analysis tested the relationship between affective reactions experienced after interacting with one's advisor and reported hostility and psychosomatic symptoms in the graduate students. To avoid multicollinearity (Haitovsky, 1969; Rockwell, 1975), the affect scales rather than the individual affect items were used to explain variance in each of the dependent measures.

Hostility. Affective reactions experienced after interacting with one's advisor accounted for one's level of reported hostility toward one's advisor (R^2=.48, F(2, 113)=52.63, p<.0001). Both affect scales emerged as significant predictors in the expected manner.

Affective reactions also related significantly to perceptions of the environment/department (R^2=.09, F(2, 113)=5.50, p<.01). The negative affect scale emerged as a significant predictor in the expected direction.

Psychosomatic symptoms. The relationship between affective experience and reported psychosomatic symptoms was significant and consistent across all four psychosomatic factors. A significant amount of variance was accounted for by the negative affect scale in the general anxiety (R^2=.44, F(2, 113)=43.61, p<.0001), depressive symptoms (R^2=.41, F(2, 113)=38.51, p<.0001), social paranoia (R^2=.44, F(2, 113)=43.86, p<.0001), and trouble concentrating (R^2=.40, F(2, 131)=37.74, p<.0001) factors. Positive affect had no significant relationship with any of the psychosomatic factors.

Testing H3

Hypothesis 3 stated that responding to negative messages by avoiding, rejecting, confronting, or defying the relational partner would be related negatively to distress and psychosomatic symptoms. Regression analyses were conducted to test H3 within the negative sub-set of questionnaires (n=136). This set of analyses was conducted by entering the set of negative social response measures simultaneously to explain the variance in each dependent measure.

Hostility and Affect. The relationship between the negative social response strategies and several of the distress measures were found to be inconsistent with H3. A significant portion of variance due to hostility toward one's advisor (R^2=.24, $F(6, 109)$=5.67, p<.0001) was accounted for by "I quit talking to my advisor" ($ß$=.23, F=5.97, p<.01) and "I picked fights with my advisor" ($ß$=.38, F=16.25, p<.0001), indicating that individuals who employed these strategies adopted a more negative view of their advisors and hence experienced increased distress.

Similarly, the affective measures also demonstrated relationships opposite to that predicted by H3. A significant portion of variance due to positive affect (R^2=.15, $F(6, 109)$=3.27, p<.003) was accounted for by "I quit talking to my advisor" strategy ($ß$=-.28, F=7.40, p<.007), indicating that individuals who chose this social response experienced less positive affect. In addition, a significant amount of variance due to negative affect (R^2=.22, $F(6, 109)$=5.15, p<.0001) was accounted for by "I quit doing things for my advisor" ($ß$=.21, F=3.79, p<.05), indicating that individuals who selected this strategy experienced more negative affect.

The actively negative and withdrawal social response indices were able to account for a significant amount of variance due to hostility and affect. The actively negative index was able to account for a significant amount of variance in the hostility toward advisor (R^2=.06, $F(1, 117)$=7.71, p<.01), but not hostility toward the department (ns), positive affect (R^2=.04, $F(1, 117)$=5.14, p<.05), and negative affect (R^2=.09, $F(1, 117)$=12.14, p<.01) measures. The withdrawal index was able to account for a significant amount of variance in the hostility toward advisor (R^2=.12, $F(1, 116)$=15.74, p<.01), hostility toward the department (R^2=.05, $F(1, 116)$=6.19, p<.01), positive affect (R^2=.11, $F(1, 116)$=14.71, p<.01), and negative affect (R^2=.16, $F(1, 116)$=21.93, p<.01) measures. However, the nature of the relationships did not support H3.

Psychosomatic symptoms. A significant portion of variance due to the generalized anxiety factor was accounted for by the negative social response strategies (R^2=.31, $F(6, 109)$=7.98, p<.0001). Four strategies (less friendly, quit doing things for, criticize, pick fights) emerged as significant predictors, only one of which was consistent with H3 (criticizing the advisor).

Opposite to H3, "picking fights with" (ß=.23, F=6.73, p<.01), "quit doing things for" (ß=.24, F=5.37, p<.02), and "being less friendly toward" (ß=.27, F=5.39, p<.02) one's advisor after exposure to a negative event all related positively to decreased well-being. However, consistent with H3, "criticizing" one's advisor was related negatively and significantly to decreased well-being (ß=-.29, F=9.39, p<.002).

A significant portion of variance due to depressive symptoms was accounted for by the negative social response strategies (R^2=.16, F(6, 109)=3.56, p<.002). Supporting H3, criticizing one's advisor was related negatively and significantly to depressive symptoms, and it emerged as the only significant predictor for this dependent measure (ß=-.23, F=4.86, p<.02).

A significant amount of variance due to social paranoia was accounted for by the negative social response strategies (R^2=.20, F(6, 109)=4.59, p<.0002). Opposite to H3 however, "quit talking to" (ß=.20, F=4.16, p<.04) and "quit doing things for" (ß=.28, F=6.44, p<.01) both emerged as significant, positive predictors. Although criticizing one's advisor was not significant in this case, it demonstrated a relationship in support of H3 (ß=-.11, *ns*).

A significant portion of variance due to the trouble concentrating factor was accounted for by the set of negative social response strategies (R^2=.17, F(6, 109)=3.79, p<.001). Opposite to H3, "I quit doing things for my advisor" emerged as a significant, positive predictor (ß=.29, F=6.79, p<.01). Consistent with H3, however, "I criticize my advisor whenever I can" emerged as a significant, negative predictor (ß=-.23, F=4.77, p<.03).

Using the social response indices to account for the psychosomatic factors revealed that the actively negative indices were able to account for a significant amount of variance in only the social paranoia measure (R^2=.03, F(1, 117)=4.04, p<.05), while the withdrawal indices were able to account for a significant portion of variance due to all four of the psychosomatic factors (anxiety: R^2=.17, F(1, 116)=24.16, p<.01; depressive tendencies: R^2=.07, F(1, 116)=9.14, p<.01; social paranoia: R^2=.16, F(1, 116)=21.53, p<.01; trouble concentrating: R^2=.06, F(1, 116)=7.55, p<.01). However, the nature of the relationships was opposite to those predicted by H3.

Overall, this test revealed a consistent pattern of support for H3 within the psychosomatic symptoms measures when individuals chose to be "passive aggressive" by criticizing their advisor, but not when they confronted, avoided, or defied their advisor directly. Further, opposite to H3, individuals who chose to engage negative behavioral strategies were more likely to report being more hostile and experiencing more negative affect rather than less.

Testing H4

Hypothesis 4 stated that responding to negative messages by appeasing the relational partner will be related positively to distress and psychosomatic symptoms. Regression analyses were conducted to test H3 within the negative sub-set of questionnaires (n=136). This set of analyses was conducted by entering the positive social responses as a set to account for the variance in each dependent measure.

Consistent with H4, a significant amount of variance due to the general anxiety (R^2=.09, $F(4, 111)$=2.71, $p<.05$), depressive symptoms (R^2=.14, $F(4, 111)$=4.51, $p<.005$), social paranoia (R^2=.13, $F(4, 111)$=4.11, $p<.007$), and trouble concentrating (R^2=.12, $F(4, 111)$=3.71, $p<.01$) factors was accounted for by the appeasement social response strategies. Attention to the beta weights indicated that "trying to make the relationship better" and the "I told my advisor I was sorry" strategies emerged as significant predictors in the predicted direction.[5]

Interestingly, the actively positive index was not able to account for a significant amount of variance in three of the four psychosomatic factors, or the hostility and affect factors. The only psychosomatic factor that was accounted for by the actively positive index was trouble concentrating (R^2=.04, $F(1, 114)$=4.77, $p<.03$).

In summary, regression analyses revealed a pattern consistent with H4 within the psychosomatic factors. No support for H4 was found within the hostility and affect measures, where the relationships were non-significant.

Discussion

Social interaction can be a powerful source for positive and negative effects on interactants. The current study revealed the extent to which interactions that are characterized by a power differential in which subordinates experience at least one instance of negativity have significant negative effects on the subordinates.

Self-Protection, Distress, and Well-Being

This study held that self-protection, manifest through the activation of self-discrepancies, is an important psychological mechanism that links negative messages to distress and well-being. The results based on testing H1 show that negative perceptions prompted by negative messages related positively to intrusive thinking, thoughts of revenge and of escaping the situation, and to negative affect. Negative perceptions also related positively to social strategies that function to change the nature of the relationship through avoiding or punishing the individual whom delivered the negative message, or through relational maintenance strategies, which presumably are attempts to reduce exposure to future negativity. Finally, negative perceptions generally related positively to hostility and psychosomatic symptoms. These findings suggest that the act of labeling an interaction as "negative" holds significant implications for one's cognitions, affects, behaviors, and well-being, which is consistent with Feist et al.'s (1995) models of subjective well-being.

The results from testing H2 suggest that negative affect, or in some cases a decrease in positive affect, is related significantly to measures of distress and decreased well-being. These findings verify extant work that has revealed a link between negative affect and decreased psychological and physical health. One implication that follows from these results is that the effects of interaction on one's hostility and psychosomatic symptoms may be mediated by one's affective reactions to one's relational partner.

The results from testing H3 suggest that social response strategies that are confrontational, defiant, or avoidant generally are related positively to levels of distress and decreased well-being. However, deciding to be passive aggressive by criticizing the powerholder behind that person's back is related negatively to decreased well-being and demonstrated a non-significant relationship to hostility and negative affect. These findings indicate that expressed passive-aggressiveness may serve a self-protective function.

The results from testing H4 suggest that some of the relational maintenance strategies are related to decreased well-being. Of note are the positive relationships between "I tried to make the relationship better," "I told my advisor I was sorry," and psychosomatic symptoms. The results indicate that relational maintenance may hold negative consequences.

Of special note is the finding that criticism is related to

psychosomatic symptoms. Criticizing the powerholder related consistently and *negatively* to the psychosomatic symptoms measured in this study. This indicates that passive-aggressiveness may function as a psychological and emotional energizer that alleviates distress. This relationship supports the findings of Keller, Shiflett, Schleifer, and Bartlett (1994), who found that verbal aggression directed at others enhanced the immune system functioning of those who were verbally aggressive, and Kinney (1997), who found that verbal aggressiveness was associated negatively with depressive tendencies. In addition, Lapinski and Boster (2001) have recently found that under conditions of ego-threat individuals derogated the source of the threat as a way to protect themselves.

Two theoretical explanations can be advanced regarding criticism. One explanation suggests that criticism gives individuals a voice and a sense of control, which may be important mechanisms that allow for effective coping. Thus, criticism becomes a way to gain power and to re-affirm one's self-concept and self-worth. This social response may be of great importance within organizational settings to the extent to which the act of criticism is valued by the culture of the organization.

Another explanation suggests that criticism is a social event and, as such, allows individuals to justify to themselves and others why the negative event was "unjust," "wrong," or "unwarranted." Thus, social support and the formation of an "in-group," which is defined as those who are against the powerholder, may result. Psychological and physiological benefits may very well result from these processes. The fact that criticism is common within and across many social contexts (if not all) is an indication that it serves a critical social-emotional function. Future studies must determine the long-term consequences of this behavior.

Another finding that deserves discussion is the relationship between saying "sorry" and psychosomatic symptoms. When students told their advisors that they were sorry for what had happened between them, this social response related positively to psychosomatic symptoms. One explanation for this finding is that taking responsibility elicits distress because telling another that you are sorry implies that you were wrong and broke an established norm. Higgins's (1987, 1989) work on self-discrepancy theory provides a theoretical grounding for this finding. Applied to an organizational context, apologizing (or expressing regret) is a normal part of organizational ethics that fosters relational maintenance. The possibility that it may promote distress is a finding that must be examined in future work.

Limitations

Several limitations place boundary conditions on the findings of this study. First, the fact that anonymous self-report methodology was used makes verification of the students' responses impossible. It may well be the case that students who were angered by their academic advisors inflated the intensity of their responses as a way to cope or to get even. Second, only one side of the interaction was examined, meaning that in future work researchers should examine both the student's and advisor's perceptions to examine how each corresponds.

Conclusion

This investigation found that 30% (136 out of 434) of the graduate students sampled reported at least one negative interaction with their academic advisor. This confirms the findings of mass surveys (e.g., Gelles & Straus, 1979; Vissing, Straus, Gelles, & Harrop, 1991) which indicate that negativity occurs in many types of relationships. This suggests that negative messages serve a function; however, the result may be opposite to what was desired by the powerholder. More importantly, given the symptoms that the graduate students reported as a result of exposure to negative interactions, even a minority is worth noting in this case. When these results are extended to more abusive relationships, the severity of the accompanying symptoms is likely to rise. Thus, the consequences of social interaction can be significant, especially if relational maintenance processes are taken into account.

This study also found that subordinates exposed to a "negative" interaction subsequently adopted non-productive behaviors. Graduate students who experienced discomfort with their academic advisors reported that they avoided work, quit talking to their advisor, and adopted a hostile attitude toward their advisor. These findings suggest that to maximize work efficiency and productivity, taking steps to avoid perceptions of negativity may serve well both the subordinate and the powerholder. Future research is needed to explore how communication can be used effectively in evaluative and/or critical organizational contexts to avoid negative perceptions and accompanying non-productive reactions (Albrecht, Adelman, & Associates, 1987; Applegate, 1980; Cutrona & Suhr, 1994; Goldsmith & Fitch, 1997; Novack, Volk, Drossman, & Lipkin, 1993; Quill & Townsend, 1991). The fact that individuals are motivated to maintain professional relationships in the face of adversity makes the study of reactions to critical and negative messages in organizational settings of import for communication scholars. Understanding how we react and cope with adversity in organizational settings may provide insight into helping individuals maintain professional relationships without experiencing harm and decreased productivity.

Notes

1. Items within factors were eliminated randomly to reduce instrument length. The 58-item Hopkins Symptoms Checklist (HSCL) demonstrates good internal consistency, test-retest reliability, and construct and discriminate validity (Derogatis et al., 1974; Steketee & Doppelt, 1986), suggesting that its five factors are unique. Kleijn, Hovens, and Rodenburg (2001) assessed the psychometric properties of five language versions of a modified HSCL and found high internal consistencies (ranging from .83 to .92) within the two factors examined (anxiety and depression) across all five language translations.

2. Confirmatory factor analyses conducted on the modified five factors of the Hopkins symptoms checklist suggested that in this data set the somatic and physical anxiety factors should be combined. A structural equation model test of parallelism initially failed to fit using the five factor model ($X^2(5)=16.48$, $p<.01$). However, when the somatic and physical anxiety factors were allowed to co-vary the parallelism test indicated excellent model fit ($X^2(4)=1.78$, $p<.78$). Thus, for the current study, the somatic and physical anxiety items were combined to form a general anxiety factor ($\alpha=.92$), which reduced the psychosomatic checklist from a five to a four factor model and resulted in an excellent fit ($X^2(2)=0.68$, $p<.71$).

3. For the sake of brevity and efficiency, detailed presentation of the results can be obtained by contacting the author directly.

4. Contact the author for a detailed presentation of these results.

5. See note 4.

References

Albrecht, T., Adelman, A., & Associates (1987). *Communicating social support.* Newbury Park, CA: Sage.

Applegate, J. L. (1980). Adaptive communication in educational contexts: A study of teachers' communicative strategies. *Communication Education, 29,* 158-170.

Baron, R. A. (1988). Negative effects of destructive criticism: Impact on conflict, self-efficacy, and task-performance. *Journal of Applied Psychology, 73,* 199-207.

Baron, R. A. (1990). Countering the effects of destructive criticism: The relative efficacy of four interventions. *Journal of Applied Psychology, 75,* 235-245.

Beatty, M. J., & Dobos, J. A. (1992). Adults sons' satisfaction with their relationship with fathers and person-group (father) communication apprehension. *Communication Quarterly, 40,* 162-176.

Beatty, M. J., Zelley, J. R., Dobos, J. A., & Rudd, J. E. (1994). Fathers' trait verbal aggressiveness and argumentativeness as predictors of adult sons' perceptions of fathers' sarcasm, criticism, and verbal aggressiveness. *Communication Quarterly, 42,* 407-415.

Bippus, A. M. (2001). Recipients' criteria for evaluating the skillfulness of comforting communication and the outcomes of comforting interactions. *Communication Monographs, 68,* 301-313.

Brehm, J. W. (1966). *A theory of psychological reactance.* New York: Academic Press.

Brown, P., & Levinson, S. (1978). Universals in language usage: Politeness phenomena. In E. Goody (Ed.), *Questions and politeness: Strategies in social interaction* (pp. 56-289). Cambridge, MA: Cambridge University Press.

Bruch, M. A., Rivet, K. M., & Laurenti, H. J. (2000). Type of self-discrepancy and relationships to components of the tripartite model of emotional distress. *Personality & Individual Differences, 29,* 37-44.

Burleson, B. R. (1994). Comforting messages: Features, functions, and outcomes. In J. A. Daly, & J. M. Wiemann (Eds.), *Strategic interpersonal communication* (pp. 135-161). Hillsdale, NJ: Lawrence Erlbaum Associates.

Camper, P. M., Jacobson, N. S., Holtzworth-Munroe, A., & Schmaling, K. B. (1988). Causal attributions for interactional behaviors in married couples. *Cognitive Therapy and Research, 12,* 195-209.

Canary, D. J., & Stafford, L. (1994). Maintaining relationships through strategic and routine interaction. In D.J. Canary, & L. Stafford (Eds.), *Communication and relational maintenance* (pp. 3-22). NY: Academic Press

Cohen, S., Tyrrell, D. A. J., & Smith, A. P. (1993). Negative life events, perceived stress, negative affect, and susceptibility to the common cold. *Journal of Personality and Social Psychology, 64,* 131-140.

Cutrona, C. E., & Suhr, J. A. (1994). Social support communication in the context of marriage: An analysis of couples' supportive interactions. In B.R. Burleson, T. L. Albrecht, & I. G. Sarason (Eds.), *Communication of social support: Messages, interactions, relationships, and community* (pp. 113-135). Newbury Park, CA: Sage.

Daly, J. A., & Wiemann, J. M. (1994). *Strategic interpersonal communication.* Hillsdale, NJ: Lawrence Erlbaum Associates.

Derogatis, L. R., Lipman, R. S., Rickels, K., Uhlenhuth, E. H., & Covi, L. (1974). The Hopkins Symptoms Checklist (HSCL): A self report symptom inventory. *Behavioral Science, 19,* 1-15.

Dindia, K., & Baxter, L. A. (1987). Strategies for maintaining and repairing marital relationships. *Journal of Social and Personal Relationships, 4,* 143-158.

Ewart, C. K., Burnett, K. F., & Taylor, C. B. (1983). Communication behaviors that affect blood pressure: An A-B-A-B analysis of marital interaction. *Behavior Modification, 7,* 331-344.

Feist, G. J., Bodner, T. E., Jacobs, J. F., Miles, M., & Tan, V. (1995). Integrating top-down and bottom-up structural models of subjective well-being: A longitudinal investigation. *Journal of Personality and Social Psychology, 68,* 138-150.

Fiebig, G. V., & Kramer, M. W. (1998). A framework for the study of emotions in organizational contexts. *Management Communication Quarterly, 11,* 536-572.

Fiscella, K., & Campbell, T. L. (1999). Association of perceived family criticism with health behaviors. *The Journal of Family Practice, 48,* 128-134.

Friedman, H. S. (Ed.) (1992). *Hostility, coping, and health.* Washington, DC: American Psychological Association

Gelles, R. J., & Harrop, J. W. (1991). Verbal aggression by parents and psychological problems of children. *Child Abuse and Neglect, 15,* 223-238.

Gelles, R. J., & Straus, M. A. (1979). Determinants of violence in the family: Toward a theoretical integration. In W. Burr, R. Hill, F. I. Nye, & I. Reiss (Eds.), *Contemporary theories about the family* (pp. 549-581). New York: Free Press.

Goldsmith, D. J., & Fitch, K. (1997). The normative context of advice as social support. *Human Communication Research, 23,* 454-476.

Gonnerman, M. E. Jr., Parker, C. P., Lavine, H., & Huff, H. (2000). The relationship between self-discrepancies and affective states: The moderating roles of self-monitoring and standpoints on the self. *Personality & Social Psychology Bulletin, 26,* 810-819.

Haitovsky, Y. (1969). Multicollinearity in regression analysis: A comment. *Review of Economics and Statistics, 51,* 486-489.

Henderson, A. H. (1981). *Social power: Social psychological models and theories.* New York, NY: Praeger Publishers.

Herbert, T. B., & Cohen, S. (1993). Depression and immunity: A meta-analytic review. *Psychological Bulletin, 113,* 472-486.

Hess, J. A. (2000). Maintaining nonvoluntary relationships with disliked partners: An investigation into the use of distancing behaviors. *Human Communication Research, 26,* 458-488.

Higgins, E. T. (1987). Self-discrepancy: A theory relating self and affect. *Psychological Review, 94,* 319-340.

Higgins, E. T. (1989). Self-discrepancy theory: What patterns of self-beliefs cause people to suffer? *Advances in Experimental Social Psychology, 22,* 93-136.

Higgins, E. T., Klein, R., & Strauman, T. (1985). Self-concept discrepancy theory: A psychological model for distinguishing among different aspects of depression and anxiety. *Social Cognition, 3,* 51-76.

Holtzworth-Munroe, A., & Jacobson, N. S. (1985). Causal attributions of married couples: When do they search for causes? What do they conclude when they do? *Journal of Personality and Social Psychology, 48,* 1398-1412.

Horowitz, M., Wilner, N., & Alvarez, M. A. (1979). Impact of event scale: A measure of subjective stress. *Psychosomatic Medicine, 41,* 209-218.

Ilgen, D. R., Mitchell, T. R., & Fredrickson, J. W. (1981). Poor performers: Supervisors' and subordinates' responses. *Organizational Behavior and Human Performance, 27,* 386-410.

Ilgen, D. R., Peterson, R. B., Martin, B. A., & Boeschen, D. A. (1981). Supervisor and subordinate reactions to performance appraisal sessions. *Organizational Behavior and Human Performance, 28,* 311-330.

Kalbfleish, P. J. (1997). Appeasing the mentor. *Aggressive Behavior, 23,* 389-403.

Kassing, J. W., & Infante, D. A. (1999). Aggressive communication in the coach-athlete relationship. *Communication Research Reports, 16,* 110-120.

Keller, S. E., Shiflett, S. C., Schleifer, S. J., & Bartlett, J. A. (1994). Stress, immunity, and health. In R. Glaser, & J. Kiecolt-Glaser (Eds.), *Handbook of human stress and immunity* (pp. 217-244). San Diego, CA: Academic Press.

Keltner, D., Young, R. C., & Buswell, B. N. (1997). Appeasement in human emotion, social practice, and personality. *Aggressive Behavior, 23,* 359-374.

Kiecolt-Glaser, J. K., Malarkey, W. B., Chee, M., Newton, T., Cacioppo, J. T., Mao, H., & Glaser, R. (1993). Negative behavior during marital conflict is associated with immunological down-regulation. *Psychosomatic Medicine, 55,* 395-409.

Kinch, J. W. (1967). A formalized theory of self-concept. In J.G. Manis, & B.N. Meltzer (Eds.), *Symbolic interaction: A reader in social psychology* (pp. 232-240). Boston: Allyn & Bacon.

Kinney, T. A. (1997). Verbal aggression and well-being. *Psychosomatic Medicine, 59,* 88.

Kramer, M. W., & Hess, J. A. (2002). Communication rules for the display of emotions in organizational settings. *Management Communication Quarterly, 16,* 66-80.

Lapinski, M. K., & Boster, F. J. (2001). Modeling the ego-defensive function of attitudes. *Communication Monographs, 68,* 314-324.

Lazarus, R. S. (1993). Coping theory and research: Past, present, and future. *Psychosomatic Medicine, 55,* 234-247.

Lazarus, R.S., & Folkman, S. (1984). *Stress, appraisal and coping.* New York: Springer.

Lee, J., & Jablin, F. M. (1995). Maintenance communication in superior-subordinate work relationships. *Human Communication Research, 22,* 220-257.

Levenson, R. W., & Gottman, J. M. (1983). Marital interaction: Physiological linkage and affective exchange. *Journal of Personality and Social Psychology, 45,* 587-597.

Malarkey, W. B., Kiecolt-Glaser, J., Pearl, D., & Glaser, R. (1994). Hostile behavior during marital conflict alters pituitary and adrenal hormones. *Psychosomatic Medicine, 56,* 41-51.

Mead, G. H. (1934). *Mind, self and society.* Chicago, IL: University of Chicago Press.

Mears, M. M., Oetzel, J. G., Torres, A., Derkas, D., & Ginossar, T. (2004). Employee mistreatment and muted voices in the culturally diverse workplace. *Journal of Applied Communication Research, 32,* 4-27.

Myers, S. A. (1998). Instructor socio-communicative style, argumentativeness, and verbal aggressiveness in the college classroom. *Communication Research Reports, 15,* 141-150.

Myers, S. A., & Knox, R. L. (1999). Verbal aggression in the college classroom: Perceived instructor use and student affective learning. *Communication Quarterly, 47,* 33-45.

Novack, D. H., Volk, G. Drossman, D. A., & Lipkin, M. (1993). Medical interviewing and interpersonal skills teaching in US medical schools: Progress, problems, and promise. *Journal of the American Medical Association, 269*, 2101-2105.

O'Leary, A. (1990). Stress, emotion, and human immune function. *Psychological Bulletin, 108*, 363-382.

Orvis, B. R., Kelley, H. H., & Butler, D. (1976). Attributional conflict in young couples. In J. H. Harvey, W. J. Ickes, & R. F. Kidd (Eds.), *New directions in attribution research* (Vol. 1, pp. 353-368). Hillsdale, NJ: Lawrence Erlbaum Associates.

Quill, T. E., & Townsend, P. (1991). Bad news: Delivery, dialogue, and dilemmas. *Archives of Internal Medicine, 151*, 463-468.

Rockwell, R. C. (1975). Assessment of multicollinearity: The Haitovsky test of the determinant. *Sociological Methods & Research, 3*, 308-320.

Rohner, R.P., & Rohner, E.C. (1980). Antecedents and consequences of parental rejection: A theory of emotional abuse. *Child Abuse and Neglect, 4*, 189-198.

Roloff, M. E., & Cloven, D. H. (1994). When partners transgress: Maintaining violated relationships. In D. J. Canary, & L. Stafford (Eds.), *Communication and relational maintenance* (pp. 23-43). NY: Academic Press

Rosenberg, M. (1965). *Society and the adolescent self-image.* Princeton, NJ: Princeton University Press.

Rosenberg, M. (1979). *Conceiving the self.* New York: Basic Books.

Roskos-Ewoldsen, D. R. (1997). Implicit theories of persuasion. *Human Communication Research, 24*, 31-63.

Russell, J. A. (1980). A circumplex model of affect. *Journal of Personality and Social Psychology, 57*, 848-856.

Savin-Williams, R. C. (1994). Verbal and physical abuse as stressors in the lives of lesbian, gay male, and bi-sexual youths: Associations with school problems, running away, substance abuse, prostitution, and suicide. *Journal of Consulting and Clinical Psychology, 62*, 261-269.

Seibold, D. R., Cantrill, J. G., & Meyers, R. A. (1985). Communication and interpersonal influence. In M. L. Knapp and G. R. Miller (Eds.), *Handbook of Interpersonal Communication* (pp. 551-611). Beverly Hills, CA: SAGE.

Sias, P. M., & Jablin, F. M. (1995). Differential superior-subordinate relations, perceptions of fairness, and coworker communication. *Human Communication Research, 22*, 5-38.

Sinclair, D. A., & Vealey, R. S. (1989). Effects of coaches expectations and feedback on self-perceptions of athletes. *Journal of Sport Behavior, 12*, 77-91.

Suls, J., & Wan, C. K. (1993). The relationship between trait hostility and cardiovascular reactivity: A quantitative review and analysis. *Psycho-physiology, 30*, 615-626.

Vissing, Y. M., Straus, M. A., Gelles, R. J., & Harrop, J. W. (1991). Verbal aggression by parents and psychosocial problems of children. *Child Abuse and Neglect, 15*, 223-238.

Watson, D., Clark, L. A., & Tellegen, A. (1988). Development and validation of brief measures of positive and negative affect: The PANAS scales. *Journal of Personality and Social Psychology, 54*, 1063-1070.

Part III:
Dealing with
Problematic Work Relationships

10 Distancing from Problematic Coworkers

Jon A. Hess

Troublesome relationships are a universal aspect of human social interaction (Levitt, Silver, & Franco, 1996). Perhaps nowhere besides the family are problematic relationships so commonplace as in the workplace. Although relationship research primarily focuses on positive relations and thorny problems that occur even in the best of relationships, virtually everyone who has worked in an organization can relate stories of problematic relationships. In class, students usually talk more enthusiastically about these difficult workplace relations than about positive and easier to manage relationships. The challenges these relationships pose resonate with people's deepest feelings and most significant experiences at work. Problematic work relationships are often as memorable as they are challenging.

Workplace relations are largely nonvoluntary relationships. They are created when people with diverse backgrounds, reasons for working in a company, different work styles, values, and incompatible personal and career goals must all work with each other. Such an environment should create conditions where personal differences and conflicts are commonplace. If negative relationships had little impact on workers, they would not be of much concern to researchers despite their prevalence. Unfortunately, these relationships have significant negative effects on those who experience them. Fritz and Omdahl (1998) found that the greater the proportion of negative peers people have at work, the greater their workplace cynicism and the lesser their job satisfaction and organizational commitment. Furthermore, problematic relationships can have detrimental effects on people's well-being. In Kinney's (1998) study of graduate students as well as the study presented in the preceding chapter, respondents who experienced negative interactions with their advisors reported that they experienced more aches and pains, anxiety, depression, and trouble in concentrating than did those who reported no such negative experiences.

If people are to be successful at work and find their jobs satisfying, they must learn how to deal with these difficult relationships. One of the most important ways people cope with negative relationships is by distancing themselves from the problematic partner (Hess, 2002a). In this chapter I provide a detailed review of what distance is, the role it plays in problematic workplace relationships, how the organizational setting may impact people's use of distancing tactics, and why people use distance in such relationships. A careful reading of the literature suggests that underlying the act of maintaining relationships with problematic coworkers is a more general process of using affiliation (closeness and distance) to regulate arousal in personal relationships. The end of the chapter delineates this model and discusses its implications for problematic relationships in the workplace.

Distance in Problematic Workplace Relationships

Nonvoluntary Relationships

In the workplace, problematic relationships are almost always nonvoluntary relationships. The term "nonvoluntary relationship" is normally used to describe relationships that people wish they did not have and would discontinue if given the opportunity. Typical of this approach was Thibaut and Kelley's (1986) classic definition. They described a nonvoluntary relationship as "a relationship in which the person is forced to stay even though he [or she] would prefer not to" (p. 169). Using their social exchange theory, they defined the nonvoluntary relationship in terms of comparison level (CL, what a person believes he or she is entitled to get out of a relationship) and outcomes (O, what costs and rewards a person is actually getting out of a relationship). Thibaut and Kelley formulated a nonvoluntary relationship as a relationship in which $CL > O$.

The prevalence of this definition is based upon its intuitive appeal. Thibaut and Kelley (1986) further noted, "[if] a person would... voluntarily choose the very relationship to which he [or she] is constrained, it does not seem reasonable to describe it as nonvoluntary" (pp. 169-170). Yet, it *is* reasonable to describe such a relationship as nonvoluntary. That definition confounds choice and satisfaction. A person who cannot afford a new car retains her present vehicle nonvoluntarily, even if she does like it. And while her positive feelings toward that vehicle make her satisfied, the fact that she cannot replace it may still be relevant to the way she maintains the automobile. Likewise, a person's happiness in a relationship does not make the relationship voluntary in nature.

A more accurate definition of a nonvoluntary relationship disentangles choice and satisfaction. One such definition states that a nonvoluntary relationship is "a relationship in which the actor believes he or she has no choice but to maintain it, at least at present and in the immediate future" (Hess, 2000, p. 460). In Thibaut and Kelley's (1986) terms, this means that $O > CL_{alt}$ (CL_{alt}, comparison level of alternatives, is the level of costs and rewards that a person would get from any available alternative to that relationship, which can range from a relationship with someone else to no relationship at all).

It is important to note that in this definition perceptions about choice refer to a *reasonable* degree of confinement to a relationship. While a person could leave a job to escape a problematic workplace relationship, other comparable jobs may not be available or might require unacceptable compromises in other facets of that person's life (e.g., relocating a family or losing pension benefits). As long as the alternatives feel sufficiently unacceptable, the relationship is nonvoluntary to that person.

One way to discern reasonable degree of confinement is to consider a person's choices based on factors intrinsic and extrinsic to the relationship. If people feel that factors unrelated to the relationship itself preclude the relationship's dissolution, then the relationship is nonvoluntary (Hess, 2002a). Obviously, most germane to this discussion is the factor of working together in an organization. Unless a person feels he or she could easily get another job and is willing to do so, any relationship made necessary by a person's job is a nonvoluntary relationship.

Although the majority of nonvoluntary relationships are entirely satisfactory, those relationships that are unsatisfactory are the ones that become problematic workplace relationships. Because of their nonvoluntary nature, workers must find ways to deal with the other person. Success in the workplace requires that people not let bad relationships prevent them from accomplishing their goals (Poitras, Bowen, & Byrne, 2003). Thus, the challenge for workers is how to keep these relationships from being obstructive. With regard to interpersonal communication with problematic coworkers, one of the most common ways people cope is by distancing themselves from the other person.

The Nature of Distance

Definition of distance. The term "distance" has been used many different ways throughout the literature. For example, it has been used in some cases to refer to physical space between people (e.g., Hall, 1959) and in other cases to refer to perceptual judgments of affiliation (e.g., Jacobson, 1989; Johnson et al., 2004). Some literature uses the term to refer to both physical and perceptual qualities (e.g., Kantor & Lehr, 1975). Furthermore, among the articles which use distance to refer to perceptions of affiliation, the referents have varied from relational partners (e.g., Salzmann & Grasha, 1991; Pistole, 1994) to a quality of the organization or even the organization itself (e.g., Fink & Chen, 1995). Micholt (1992) used "psychological distance" to refer not only to perceived affiliation, but also to "clarity in the relationship" between parties. Park (1924) and Bogardus (1925) included "degrees of understanding" as part of their definition of distance. Goffman (1961) used the term "role distance" to refer to a person's ability to separate her- or himself from a social role. Somewhat similarly, Delsol and Margolin (2004) used psychological distance in the context of adults who grew up in violent families to describe the ability of some people to be more disengaged from their parents and from the conflict they had, so that they do not perpetuate that cycle in their own families.

The conceptual confusion resulting from the inconsistency in definition makes it difficult to acquire a coherent picture of what distance is and what role it plays in relational communication. Because scholars have studied different, but often overlapping, constructs using the same term, readers must go beyond the label and look at what specific construct was studied and what the study found. The commonality shared by most of these definitions is the idea of distance being a sense of separation from someone, or a rift in the relational ties that bind people together. Thus, the definition of distance I use in this chapter is "a feeling of separation from another" (Hess, 2002b, p. 664). Distance is a perceptual judgment, which is "a subjective measure, of sociometric origin, as experienced by each person" (Micholt, 1992, p. 228). Although distance is created by a specific set of interactive behaviors, it is how people interpret these actions that creates the perception of distance.

Aside from how this definition seems to encompass the most common uses of the term, the definition also fits well with prevalent definitions of closeness (e.g., Kelley et al., 1983). The conceptual fit with closeness is important, because closeness and distance are both part of the same relationship quality, affiliation. The inherent link between closeness and distance are reflected in Helgeson, Shaver, and Dyer's (1987) observation that "distance, in contrast with obliviousness, arises from closeness or expected closeness and requires some prior connection that is noticeably strained" (p. 199). Kelley et al. (1983) defined closeness as resulting from relational ties that are strong, diverse, and frequent. In like manner, distance results from relational ties that are weak, limited in scope, and infrequent in occurrence (Hess, 2003).

Distancing strategies: Types of distancing behaviors. One way to understand distance better is to examine the ways people distance themselves from others. Several studies have examined these processes. Work by Kreilkamp (1981) and Helgeson et al. (1987) formed the foundation for comprehensive studies done more recently (Hess, 2000, 2002b). The cumulative result of these studies is a complete yet parsimonious typology of distancing strategies people use in personal encounters. Although closeness and distance are opposite ends of the same continuum, they are not simply the absence of one another. Instead, a different set of behaviors seems to cause closeness and distance (Hess, 2002b). Thus, when a person reduces distancing behaviors, that change can move the relationship toward a neutral mid-point, but the relationship will not become "close" until that person enacts closeness-enhancing behaviors.

Distancing can be divided into general strategies that people employ to separate themselves from others, and the specific tactics they use to accomplish their strategies. There are three general strategies available to people who wish to make a relationship more distant (Hess, 2002b):

Avoidance. This strategy entails behaving in ways that prevent an interaction from happening, or if interaction is inevitable, minimizing the amount of contact between the two people. Interactions can be prevented by avoiding contact (such as not being where the other person is) or simply ignoring the other if the two people do end up in the same place. If the two do interact, there are three basic tactics people can use to reduce the amount of interaction: being reserved (not say much); shortening the duration of the interaction (such as by not asking unnecessary questions); and getting others involved with the interaction, thus avoiding one-on-one time.

Disengagement. A second strategy for distancing oneself from others does not entail any reduction in interaction but instead functions by communicating in a less personal way. When using this strategy, people hide some of who they are by not making themselves fully present in the encounter. There are three basic methods that can be used. First, people my hide information about themselves, either by restricting conversation to more superficial topics, or by deceiving others about personal qualities or intentions. Second, people can use a disengaged communication style. This method may involve less immediate verbal and nonverbal messages (decreasing eye contact, standing further away, smiling less, etc.) or paying less attention to the other person (focusing on someone else, or just "zoning out" during conversation). Third, people can be disengaged by interacting less personally. This method might involve withholding social pleasantries that are part of relationship building (e.g., joking with the person or using nicknames), treating the other impersonally, or treating her or him as a lesser person who is merely an object to be tolerated.

Cognitive dissociation. The final strategy involves changes in perception, rather than interactive behaviors. These changes generally involve a negative judgment of the other person and their actions, or just a sense of detachment from that individual. The result of the negative attributions is that the other person cannot be strongly associated with the self because of the difference in personal characteristics between that individual's negative qualities and the actor's own more positively perceived qualities (an explanation for this effect can be found in Heider's (1958) Balance Theory, described later in this chapter). People cognitively dissociate themselves from others by discounting others' messages (that is, interpreting a message in a way to minimize its importance), mentally degrading the other person, or simply feeling a sense of separation, such as by reducing emotional involvement in the relationship.

Behaviors or strategies? One question that naturally arises about affiliation is the degree to which people are consciously strategic in their interactions. Much of the early work on distancing uses language that describes it as a generalized behavior more than as a premeditated strategy. Descriptors for distancing included "processes" (Kreilkamp, 1981), "features" of a distant relationship (Helgeson et al., 1987), and "behaviors" (Hess, 2000).

There are reasons to believe that at least some, if not much, of people's distancing messages are subconscious responses rather then carefully crafted plans. Given that disclosure and openness involves risk (Altman & Taylor, 1973), it seems plausible that people who were acting strategically might hold back a little more in nonvoluntary relationships than in those relationships they could easily exit. However, one comparison in a study of distancing in different relationships showed that there was no difference in how much people distanced themselves from liked partners based on relational choice (Hess, 2000). It appears that affiliative choices were governed by affect rather than strategy.

Nonetheless, it is also clear that a substantial amount of people's distancing behavior *is* intentional. Affiliation is a subjective experience that exists only in people's perceptions of the relational messages they or others are sending. Thus, there has to be a conscious component to it, and people's accounts of how they maintain nonvoluntary relationships with disliked partners and their explanations for why they act as they do show a conscious intent to distance themselves (Hess, 2000). In this chapter, I use both terms. The term "behavior" is more inclusive, because it does not address whether or not a person acted with intent. However, the term "strategy" is used whenever it is the term used in literature cited or whenever I want to focus on mindful choices.

Why People Distance Themselves From Problematic Coworkers

If we accept the fact that people distance themselves as much as possible from problematic coworkers, the natural question is why. Research on psychological distance suggests a number of reasons why people distance themselves in workplace relationships. Three reasons that seem most prevalent are reviewed in this section: differences in status; face management; and stress reduction.

Status differences. Salzmann and Grasha (1991) studied psychological size (a reflection of a person's status within an organization) and psychological distance, and found that lower and middle level managers saw those above them in the organizational hierarchy to be of greater stature within the company. They also found that managers perceived a degree of distance between themselves and their higher-ups relative to their difference in authority.

What is interesting about their findings was that this perception of distance was not equally reciprocated. The managers who were lower in the hierarchy saw a greater distance between themselves and their supervisors than the supervisors saw in those same relationships. So, it is clear that people who are lower in organizational rank perceive that power differential as something that inherently decreases closeness between two people. One possible explanation is that the subordinate's lack of authority and the lack of access to some information that superiors have creates anxiety and insecurity that can inhibit the subordinate's ability to feel close to the superior. After all, this uncertainty makes trust difficult, and whenever one person cannot fully trust another, he or she is likely to feel distant. Although this dynamic is not inherent in all negative relationships, it has the potential to problematize any hierarchical relationship in the workplace.

Face management. A second reason why people distance themselves from problematic coworkers has less to do with the target person and more to do with other peers in the workplace. If the person believes that others in the organization also hold a negative opinion of the problematic coworker, then that person may try to avoid close personal ties to prevent "guilt by association." Thus, people may distance themselves from unpopular coworkers not for reasons relating to the relationship with the coworker, but for reasons pertaining to relationships with others in the organization.

The theoretical explanation for this involves a combination of facework (Goffman, 1967) and balance theory (Heider, 1958). Research is clear that people are generally motivated to maintain face with those who are important to them (Cupach & Metts, 1994). Close ties with unpopular members of an organization can hurt both positive face and negative face. Positive face (the desire to be liked and respected) can be damaged because others may interpret an association with someone as endorsement of that person's views, work habits, or other personal qualities. Thus, the negative affect that people hold towards an unpopular coworkers may also transfer to those close to that individual. Heider's balance theory explains why this transfer of judgment may happen. Balance theory explains how people form perceptual units involving the relationship between two people (the person, p, and the other, o) and some other entity (x). That entity can be anything, including attributes of o's personal qualities. Balance theory posits that people are motivated to make their perceptions fit together harmoniously. Because the relationship between o and x is positive by definition (an individual is assumed to positively associate with her or his own personality), then the relationship between p and o determines others' perceptions of p's personality. If p has a close relationship with o, then the triad can only be balanced by assuming that p shares or endorses those same attributes as o has. Conversely, if p is distant from o, then the triangle is better balanced by assuming that p does not share o's qualities. Thus, p's distancing can prevent o's unpopularity from extending to p as well.

Negative face refers to the desire to have autonomy. It stands to reason that the threat to positive face posed by a close relationship with an unpopular coworker will also threaten a person's negative face. One of the most important sources of power within an organization is the support of others. Bormann (1990) characterized agreement as the "currency of social approval" (p. 141), because people will often agree with others' ideas not so much out of sharing a similar perspective but as a way to support that individual's initiative. Likewise, group members will often disagree with or fail to support a person's ideas as a means of preventing that person from assuming power within the organization. If a person loses positive face, then that person may also find that loss of social approval to be an impediment to accomplishing her or his goals within the organization. Thus, disapproval from others can also result in loss of negative face.

It is certain that people do indeed distance themselves from unpopular coworkers as a way of winning or maintaining the approval of others. Anecdotally, I have seen references to such tactics in accounts that participants in some of my studies have written. However, what is not known is the extent to which this strategy is prevalent or the relationships among the colleagues when it occurs. The desire for approval from others is a powerful form of motivation (Schutz, 1958), and it may be the case that approval from certain others is a more powerful motivator than the approval of others. It is plausible such actions are commonplace, and that the opinions of those who have more status or are better liked engender more of these actions. However, in the absence of empirical data, we can only speculate whether this strategy is the exception or the rule.

Stress reduction. The most common reason why people distance themselves in the workplace is to cope with the stress of a difficult relationship. Interacting with a problematic coworker is a stressful situation, so people need to find ways of reducing the stress to a more comfortable level. Again, Heider's (1958) balance theory provides an explanation. Balance theory can be applied not only to a triadic relationship of two people and an entity as discussed previously, but also just to the two people. Assuming that problematic coworkers elicit negative feelings from a person, then a close relationship (positive unit formation) matched to negative sentiment produces an unbalanced situation. This imbalance creates stress that people are motivated to reduce. The way people can reduce this stress is by changing the unit-formation to a weaker connection—that is, by distancing themselves from the other person. Evidence from studies of nonvoluntary relationships with disliked partners shows that distancing is a primary means of coping with the stress created by such relationships and it is used nearly universally (Hess, 2000). So, distancing is an active strategy used as a way of reducing the stress caused by working with troublesome coworkers.

Impact of Workplace on Distance in Problematic Relationships

Because the organization is a unique environment, it is likely that some aspects of people's behavior will be different in organizational settings than in other contexts. Thus, scholars must ask what specific impact the workplace has on how people respond to problematic relationships, and how these responses may differ from interaction in non-work environments. The sections that follow address that issue.

Distancing in the workplace versus distancing in social settings. Almost no research has directly compared people's distancing behaviors in the workplace with their distancing behaviors in non-work settings. However, there is one data set that allows such a direct comparison. A secondary analysis of data (Hess, 1996) shows one interesting difference in distance between work and social relationships. In this study, participants (n = 94) were asked to respond to questions about two nonvoluntary relationships with disliked partners: one in a work setting and one in a social setting. The order of relationship context was counter-balanced to prevent order effects. One of the questions asked respondents to rate the frequency of 26 distancing behaviors, using a 9-point Likert-type scale. Of those 26 distancing behaviors, there were significant differences in amount of distancing across the contexts in 14 of them.

For 13 distancing behaviors, the reported use was greater in the workplace relationships, while only one behavior was reported as being used significantly more in social settings. Distancing tactics reported more in workplace relationships than social relations were as follows: acting strictly according the social norms rather than personalizing the interaction, perceiving no association between the self and other, using a less immediate channel, describing self and other as separate, avoiding asking questions, excluding the other from a gathering, ignoring the other when in each other's presence, treating the other impersonally, perceiving the other as less than human, avoiding touch or eye contact, avoiding jokes or intimate conversation, ignoring the other's thoughts or feelings, and using superficial politeness. The only distancing tactic for which respondents reported greater use in social relations was deceiving the partner about personal information.

Finding patterns in the types of distancing behaviors proved more difficult than discerning overall difference in use. In general, the highest *t* values were for tactics that fit into the disengagement strategy, followed by the avoidant tactics, followed by the one cognitive dissociation tactic, but there were many exceptions to this pattern. Furthermore, the one tactic reported more in social settings was also from the disengagement strategy. So, little can be concluded about patterns of specific tactics.

In general, we can conclude that these data showed people using distance as a coping strategy even more in the workplace than they did in non-work relationships. While these data do not indicate why people distanced themselves more or why they relied more on certain tactics than others, the results speak to the importance of examining distance in problematic workplace relationships.

Eliminating non-work interactions. Although many problematic relationships came into existence as negative relations, some problematic relationships were desirable relations at some point in their existence. In fact, it is sometimes the fact that such relationships used to be close that causes them to be problematic later. For example, friendships that have deteriorated or romantic relationships that have been broken off are often problematic *because of* the awkwardness two people feel in encountering their former friend or lover.

In a study of workplace friendships gone awry, Sias et al. (2004) found that when workplace friendships deteriorated, people minimized their time together by eliminating interaction outside the workplace. Although they could not necessarily reduce contact in the workplace, reducing contact outside of the workplace helped people distance themselves and de-escalate the intensity of the relationship. This change in interaction patterns distances people in two ways. Obviously, the decreased contact is avoidance (strategy one, discussed previously). Furthermore, by redefining the relationship as strictly a task-oriented interaction, the partners were distanced through disengagement (strategy two).

Norms for appropriate behavior. In any profession and in any organization, unwritten norms emerge that govern behaviors in the workplace. Norms are assumptions or expectations held by members of the organization about what behaviors are appropriate or inappropriate (Schein, 1969). In some cases, norms are not entirely clear or strongly enforced, but in other cases, norms can be very strong and powerfully enforced. Wahrman (1972) noted that with some norms, "members of a group...believe that they have a right to demand that other people abide by them" (p. 205). Regardless of how clear or how strong the norms are, they impact the range of behavior choices that an organization's members can choose from.

Clarity of relational definitions. One way in which norms may impact relationships in the workplace is in how clearly relationships are defined. Although workplace relationships exist for the purpose of accomplishing a task, the task and social dimensions of group work are inseparable (Bormann, 1990). Thus, every relationship has a social dimension. In many cases, the social nature of friendships in the workplace is clearly defined, but in some cases there may be more ambiguity as to the exact nature of two people's relationship.

A situation in which this ambiguity has been documented is when workplace friendships deteriorate. Sias et al. (2004) found that when friendships in the workplace deteriorated, people tried to avoid talking about non-work topics. But, in contrast with social relationships where taboo topics might sometimes be negotiated, coworkers simply stopped talking about such topics without explicitly acknowledging the change. In fact, they generally avoided talking about their relationship as well. Sias et al. (2004) found that concerns about the ability to do their job created a "chilling effect" which led to a reduction in the communication, and they concluded that this "chilling effect may be unique to the workplace" (p. 336). The study by Sias et al. (2004) suggests that some relational variables may be left more implicit or ambiguous in work settings than might be the case in relationships emerging in social settings.

Emotion management. Another area in which norms play an important role is the display of emotions in the workplace. Problematic workplace relationships create a range of emotions for those involved, and this leads to the issue of which emotions are appropriate to display and which emotions must be concealed. Because people must decide whether to reveal, mask, or change a felt emotion, emotion management is an important issue people must address in problematic workplace relationships (Hochschild, 1983).

A recent study revealed a variety of display rules that could have bearing on emotion management in problematic work relationships. Kramer and Hess (2002) found that employees are expected to display emotions professionally, in ways that improve situations and help others, and that negative emotions are most often expected to be masked rather than directly expressed. Because these display rules are more restrictive of emotion expression than what people sometimes experience in personal and family relationships (where people may feel more free to show their felt emotions as they experience them), it seems likely that coping with problematic workplace relationships may be more difficult. The results from this study suggests that the ability to effectively use distancing behaviors may be highly important in work settings as a socially skilled method of reducing unpleasant arousal arising in problematic work relationships. Those who are more adept at distancing may find themselves better able to control arousal, and thereby, be more effective in the workplace.

Questions Yet Unanswered

The foregoing review shows that people in problematic workplace relationships use distance as a means of coping with the stress these nonvoluntary relations place on them. Although the research reviewed thusfar offers clues as to why people select strategies and what impact the workplace context has on these relations, the answers are far from definitive.

A close examination suggests that distancing strategies use affiliation (either distance or closeness) as a means of regulating arousal in personal relationships. A closer look at this process of regulating arousal sheds light on questions yet unanswered. The remainder of the chapter is devoted to offering a preliminary sketch of a model which explains distancing in terms of intimacy regulation.

The model proposed is in the initial stages of its development and is designed to offer only a general overview.

The Underlying Process: Distancing as Arousal Regulator

The basic premise of this theory is that distancing is used to regulate a person's arousal in a relationship. The idea of arousal impacting relational behaviors has been explored in many studies, and the model presented in this chapter has much in common with previous arousal models, particularly Cappella and Greene's (1982) and Patterson's (1973) models. It should be noted that the model presented in this chapter is meant to explain people's behavior during the maintenance phase of a personal relationship. Although these same processes may take place during relationship development or dissolution, these stages of the relationship life course may differ in significant ways. Such differences are beyond the scope of my initial overview of this theory.

Existing Equilibrium or Arousal Models

Three models of equilibrium or arousal in personal relationships provide the conceptual foundation for the regulatory theory of affiliation in this chapter. These models are Argyle and Dean's (1965) Equilibrium Model, Patterson's (1976) Arousal Labeling Model, and Cappella and Greene's (1982) Discrepancy-Arousal Model.

Argyle and Dean (1965) were interested in explaining how people use nonverbal cues to maintain equilibrium in intimacy in any given interaction. In particular, Argyle and Dean focused on gaze and physical distance, finding that when people sense too much or too little intimacy in one of those channels, that they compensate with the other. Argyle and Dean's equilibrium model has gained much attention from researchers, and its basic idea is sound. However, Argyle and Dean's model made no attempt to explain people's use of matching responses (to move away from the set equilibrium point to a new level of intimacy), nor did they consider speech or other nonverbal channels such as touch or body movement.

To address these and other limitations, Patterson (1976) proposed an Arousal-Labeling Model. This model introduced arousal as the critical factor in causing people to behave in the way they did. His idea was that both compensation and matching responses were driven by the type of arousal that people experienced from their relational involvement. He believed that when people detected a change in their partner's intimacy level, that they experienced a noticeable change in their own arousal level. Depending upon what attributions the person made, this arousal might be viewed as either positive or negative. If the arousal elicited a positive emotion, then the people would reciprocate the partner's behaviors to create more intimacy; if the arousal elicited a negative emotion, the person would compensate to offset the change in intimacy.

In response to this model, Cappella and Greene (1982) proposed the Discrepancy-Arousal Model. They were concerned that Patterson's model required too much cognitive load and was not able to account for non-conscious, micro-momentary responses across the age spectrum. In Cappella and Greene's Discrepancy Arousal model, the process begins with an expectation for the other's behavior which arises from norms, preferences, and experiences. Insofar as the other's behavior is consistent with that expectation, there is no arousal. However, when the other violates that expectation, the person experiences a discrepancy. The magnitude of the discrepancy determines the level of arousal, and the arousal level determines affect (positive or negative). Positive affect results in reciprocation of the intimacy of the other, while negative affect engenders compensation for the other's intimacy.

Arousal Regulation Theory of Distancing

Using some of the key principles for the aforementioned theories, I propose a model to explain how people use distancing to manage relationships with difficult others. I offer an overview of the model followed by a discussion of how it differs from prior theories and the implications it has for interactions with problematic others in the workplace.

Perceptions about relationship. As shown in Figure 1, this process has four basic steps. The process begins at the very top when a person, *P*, has a perception about the nature and quality of the relationship with another person, *O*. These perceptions are influenced by at least three factors. First, *P*'s personality traits influence the perception he or she has of the relationship with *O*. Specifically, such qualities as extraversion, self-esteem level, and exchange orientation (e.g., Murstein, Cerreto, & MacDonald, 1977) will affect perceptions of a relationship. Second, the frequency with which two people interact is likely to influence perceptions about the relationship. For example, if two people rarely see each other, they are likely to perceive a distant and impersonal relationship as appropriate. However, if organizational changes bring them into constant contact, the distance and impersonality may be perceived as unnatural. Third, the nature of the situation will affect relational perceptions. For example, the type of behaviors expected (normed) at that time, in that setting, and the configuration of people in the context in most cases will impact perceptions of the relationship. Greeting another with a hug when they meet at church might be appropriate, but it might be perceived as problematic in the workplace. With the combined influence of personality traits, frequency of interaction, the situation, the person observes the behavior of the other and notes deviations from a satisfactory relationship.

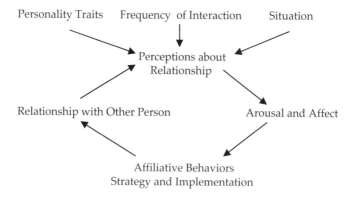

Figure 1. Arousal Regulation Model of Distancing

Arousal and affect. The assessment of level of deviation determines affect. Two aspects of the experienced arousal are significant in understanding P's affiliative reaction (discussed in the next step). The first of these is the valence of the affect produced by interacting with the partner. Consistent with Patterson's (1976) and Capella and Greene's (1982) models, the arousal regulation model suggests that the valence of the affect determines the nature of the response (increased or decreased affiliation).

The second important aspect is the magnitude of the arousal. The magnitude of arousal determines the degree of impact it has on P, and thus, the extent of P's response. The size of the discrepancy between perceived and desired relationship definitions is proportional to the amount of arousal. If the difference between these two perceptions is small, the situation will not lead to much arousal and P will minimally adjust existing patterns of affiliation. On the other hand, if the difference is considerable, then P will enact changes that he or she sees as more significant in order to move the relationship to a status that will allow P to restore optimal arousal.

Another factor influencing the magnitude of arousal is the importance of the relationship to P. If the relationship is of little importance, then it will lead to less arousal than if the relationship is very important. For example, a subordinate who a supervisor rarely sees, a client with a very small account, or a coworker from another unit that a person spends a day with at a company training seminar but who will not be seen much after that day, are all examples of people who are of little relational significance. In contrast, a direct supervisor, a client whose account keeps the company afloat, or a coworker with whom P has a strong romantic attraction are all examples of people who are of great relational significance. For these relationships, the magnitude of arousal will be significantly greater.

Affiliative response. Once people have perceived the relationship and assessed arousal and affect, they respond to that assessment through affiliation strategies. If the degree of arousal evokes unpleasant feelings, then people will respond with changes in affiliation in attempt to reshape the nature of the relationship and thus, to restore a comfortable level of arousal from interactions with O. If the arousal engenders positive affect, then P will respond by reciprocating the affiliative behaviors of the other.

If people experience a generally comfortable level of arousal, then they can be expected to continue enacting the same affiliative behaviors as they have been doing recently. Readers should keep in mind that because affiliation is a relational message, it is impossible for people to stop communicating closeness or distance. Thus, people will still respond to desired arousal (neither under-aroused nor over-aroused) with affiliative messages; these messages will simply communicate the same amount of closeness or distance as before.

Factors impacting affiliative strategy choices. When people make affiliative changes to attenuate unpleasant arousal, many factors influence which tactics are used. The specific tactics people use may vary dramatically based on personality traits, their relationship with the other person, and the situation. Although further research is needed to determine which qualities are most influential, some factors can be anticipated based on extant research. Figure 2 illustrates the key factors.

Personality characteristics. Whenever people change the nature of a relationship, they take some degree of risk. In the case of making a relationship closer, the risks often involve the possibility that the other person could hurt them (Altman & Taylor, 1973) or that they may be violating an organizational boundary (e.g., Peterson, 1992). In the case of making a relationship more distant, the risk is that such a move could increase conflict or create antagonism from the other. Thus, it stands to reason that people who are more self-confident would be more likely to enter such transitions boldly than people with high social anxiety (Leary, 1991) or risk aversion (Kahneman & Tversky, 1984). These more anxious people might even rely on more of the cognitive tactics, and less obvious behavioral tactics. For example, someone with high social anxiety might be more likely to derogate a message as a means of distancing than to actively ignore that person when in the same location.

Relational factors. Among the many relational factors that could influence the types of messages people send, foremost is the person's relationship history with the other. The past experiences the two have shared and the perceptions P has of O provide the background that P takes into account when selecting strategies and messages. In group settings, norm violations are met with corrective actions from other group members first with subtle hints, then with gradually more explicit and blatant messages if the hints go unheeded (Bormann, 1990). This progression gives the offending person a chance to change behaviors and still save face. The same type of progression should be evident in dyadic relations as well. People would be expected to begin with subtler relational messages, and move to more explicit directives only as needed. P's past encounters with O and P's perceptions of how socially sensitive and responsive O is may dictate what tactics P is most likely to use.

Research also suggests P's relational goals and perceptions of O's orientation toward the relationship might influence strategy choice.

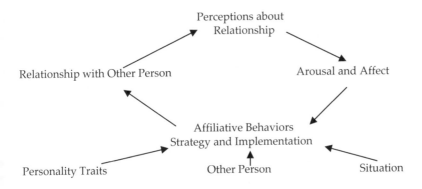

Figure 2. Regulatory Model of Relational Affiliation

Fritz (1997) found that if a person wanted a problem to be solved and perceived that the other wanted the same, then the person was more open to discussion about the issues. Likewise, if a person sees a problematic coworker as sharing the same goals, that person may be more likely to initially use subtler distancing tactics to reduce arousal and try to work through the issue with that individual.

Another significant relational factor that will likely impact strategies is the power differential between the two people. Power is an omnipresent aspect of organizational interactions, and a considerable amount of organizational involvement is affected by people's quest for and exercise of power (Frost, 1987). Thus, it is likely that power will impact many interactions between members of an organization. However, the impact of different types of influence and magnitudes of power may require further research. Evidence suggests that people of lower power are likely to amplify their closeness responses and mitigate their distancing tactics where possible, as a way of strengthening their ties with people who have the ability to offer rewards and punishments to them (Berger, 1985). However, the impact on people who are higher in power or on those with equal power is less certain.

More clear in the nature of its impact on affiliation tactics is the perception a person has of the other person's affiliation behaviors. People tend to reciprocate the relational messages that others send.

We tend to like those who like us, and dislike those who dislike us (Backman & Secord, 1959). Thus, O's messages of closeness are more likely to generate positive arousal in P and O's distancing messages are more likely to generate negative emotions in P. The exception to this is if other information is more important to P than O's messages. For instance, if O is trying to increase closeness with P, but P finds O annoying, then the arousal will generate a negative emotion and lead to compensatory distancing.

Situation norms. The final set of factors that will influence what affiliative strategy choices a person makes are situational influences. As with the other sets of factors, research is needed to discern if there are certain factors that are particularly powerful in their influence. Several situational factors would seem salient. First, workplace rules and norms concerning behavior. For closeness behaviors, organizational rules placing limits on personal relationships (e.g., limits on gift-giving, restrictions on romantic relations, etc.) may affect people's behaviors in some situations. For distancing, such factors as norms for emotion displays (e.g., Kramer & Hess, 2002) seem relevant.

In addition to rules and norms, the presence or involvement of other people may influence what messages a person sends. For example, the presence of a third party may make people more reluctant to send certain relational messages (perhaps showing less affection when others are around and flirting more when they are not) or more inclined to send certain messages (e.g., dissociating her- or himself from someone as a display to a third party).

Other person's responses. Once people have maintained or changed affiliative behaviors, then they monitor the partner's behaviors to see how they respond. If P does not make any changes, then a similar lack of affiliative changes from O would be expected; any changes on O's part are a stimulus for P's reflection on the relationship. However, if P makes changes, O's responses are very important. In the language of Watzlawick, Beavin, and Jackson (1967), O may choose to confirm, reject, or disconfirm P's new definition of the relationship. That is, O may choose to accept the new level of affiliation and reciprocate such behaviors (confirm), he or she might attempt to compensate by reacting in the opposite way (e.g., meeting increased closeness with distancing tactics; reject), or O might simply ignore P's changes and continue behaving in the same way (disconfirm).

All of these responses are significant stimuli for P's ongoing assessment of the relationship. It is important to bear in mind, of course, that people process their perceptions of the other's response through their own perceptual filters, and so people's new perceptions about the relationship will be based not only on the other's responses to their behaviors, but also on anything else that might impact a person's preferences about the relationship. In other words, not only O's behaviors but the other factors discussed in reviewing the first step of this cycle impact P's perceptions about the relationship, and thus, subsequent arousal.

Differences from previous models. The arousal regulation model of affiliation I propose shares the basic notion that people's perceptions lead to arousal, and the resulting affect motivates a response from that individual. However, there are some differences from the models reviewed above. In general, the previous models are more focused on micromomentary nonverbal behaviors, whereas the model I propose addresses global communication strategies, for both verbal and nonverbal behaviors. Rather than focusing on specific nonverbal cues that people enact during a conversation, this model explains people's general relationship strategies which may be enacted through many difference tactics that can be played out over lengthy periods of time. What are pertinent in these strategies are not only the behaviors people do, but also the behaviors they do not do. For instance, a decision *not* to talk about a particular topic with a certain person can be very significant, even though it does not result in any observable behavior changes to the relational partner or a researcher.

Additionally, the arousal regulation model is less focused on the partner's behaviors than the previous models. Although the nuances are complex and beyond the scope of this chapter, the existing models generally focus more on how people respond to changes in the partner's behaviors. That is not the case in this model. Although changes in partner behavior are sufficient to cause arousal, they are not necessary. A person may undergo a change in perceptions or expectations related to the relationship, which are independent of anything the partner does. One situation leading to this would be changes in a relationship with a third party. For example, if an individual is rejected by one dating partner, then he or she might suddenly begin to see another person, who had previously just been an acquaintance or friend, as a potential romantic partner. Another way that a person might change expectations for a relationship independent of anything that partner does would be the discovery of new information about the partner. Learning of an impressive talent or past accomplishment might make an individual a more appealing relational partner than he or she had previously been seen.

Implications for Theory and Practice

The foregoing review suggests several implications for theory and practice, as related to problematic workplace relationships. These implications focus on the centrality of affiliation in understanding workplace relationships, the role of social skills in career success, and the conceptualization of organizational communication competence.

Centrality of relational affiliation. The processes of relational affiliation--enhancing closeness and increasing distance--may be the most fundamental quality of personal relationships, in the workplace or outside of work. These processes are perhaps *the* essential barometer of how people feel about a relationship. It is through affiliation that people regulate arousal, and thus, affiliative behaviors are the key indicator of how a person feels about a relationship at any given point in time. Although affiliation garners considerable attention in the research on personal relationships (e.g., Dillard, Solomon, & Palmer, 1999; Mashek & Aron, 2004), it has not been given much attention in the organizational literature. Organizational communication scholars should find it valuable to pay more attention to those processes and their outcomes than has been done in the past.

Social skills and career success. One of the business world's worst kept secrets is the importance of good social skills in career success. People who excel at their tasks but cannot get along with others are rarely successful in their professions. Research has shown that people with better developed socio-cognitive abilities are more successful at work, getting more frequent and higher promotions than less developed peers (Sypher & Zorn, 1986; Zorn & Violanti, 1996). This finding is intuitive. People with strong social skills are more likely to make friends and garner support from those with whom they work, and such positive relationships often pay dividends in evaluations, promotions, and leadership ability. Furthermore, such people are more likely to cope successfully with problematic relationships, preventing such interpersonal problems from becoming a major career obstacle. People with less social abilities are more likely to mishandle such relationships and increase the problematic nature of the relationship.

Another benefit gained by people with better social skills is that dealing with problematic relationships can be easier and less stressful for them, leaving more cognitive resources available for other tasks. Those with lesser social skills are likely to invest more of their cognitive resources to dealing with and worrying about such relationships, or simply be overwhelmed by such relations sufficiently that the situation impedes their ability to be effective. These negative situations can also lead to further problems for people who have difficulty handling them constructively. In their study of troublesome relationships, Levitt, Silver, and Franco (1996) found that people sometimes reported dysfunctional ways of coping, such as use of alcohol or drugs. In cases like these, what began as one problem can then lead to further problems that may also be detrimental to one's career.

Organizational communication competence. A third implication of this regulatory theory is the need to expand the conceptualization of organizational communication competence. Although scholars are widely aware of the importance of interpersonal skills in the workplace, studies of communication skills required for competence in the workplace typically focus on task-related communication. For example, Jablin and Sias (2001) summarized the communication skills most often discussed in the organizational competence literature as follows: "listening, giving feedback, advising, persuading, instructing, interviewing, and motivating" along with "enhanced self-confidence, persuasiveness, ability to clearly express ideas, and control of [speech] communication anxiety" (p. 822). Although some of these can go beyond task communication (e.g., listening, giving feedback, motivating), in general these communication skills are related to transmitting information, rather than building and maintaining personal relationships. Non-task relational skills need to be added to the list of essential elements of organizational communication effectiveness. It is not hard for most people to think of a person who can clearly express ideas, control speech anxiety, and craft a persuasive argument, but who is abrasive enough to others that the individual has not achieved the workplace success he or she might otherwise have.

Directions for Future Research

The arousal regulation theory offers an explanation of how people use distance as a means of dealing with problematic coworkers. Although the purpose in delineating this process was to explain how people cope with problematic coworkers, the model is equally adept at explaining people's maintenance of less problematic relations as well. Furthermore, it is not bound by negative affect in defining problematic relationships. A relationship that is problematic for positive reasons (e.g., a relationship in which two people are romantically attracted to each other but prohibited from engaging in such relations due to organizational restrictions) fits with the processes described in this model as well. Duck (1994) argued that scholars studying personal relationships need to do a better job of integrating the positive side and dark sides of personal relationship by advancing perspectives that apply to both extremes. This model does that task.

What is needed in future research is to further refine the model and test the premises posited in this article. Although there is plenty of corroborative evidence from other studies that support the ideas proposed in this theory, the theory itself has not been directly tested. Such tests would provide valuable support or refutation for the model as a whole, or for parts of it. Furthermore, the list of personality, relationship, and situation variables that influence people's perceptions and strategy choices is preliminary and needs closer examination. Clarifying those factors would refine the model as presented in this chapter, and better help us understand how and why people act as they do in these difficult workplace relationships.

Another research focus needed is to examine applied questions related to this model. What types of distancing or closeness-enhancing strategies are most effective in dealing with various workplace relational challenges? Can people be trained to recognize these behaviors and use them to increase their effectiveness at work? What other strategies (such as assertiveness) might be used in conjunction with affiliation to further improve a person's workplace success? These and other questions could provide valuable information.

Problematic workplace relationships pose a major source of stress and difficulty for almost all people working in organizations. Although problematic relationships often need to be addressed with in some task-related manner, the distancing reactions that people have are the "first line of defense" people take in such relationships. Furthermore, the degree of closeness or distance in a relationship not only impacts how people deal with the task issues at hand, but can also impact future responses by people involved. Thus, any study of problematic relationships would do well to take affiliation into account in its explanation of communication dynamics and suggestions for how to manage or improve the situation.

References

Altman, I., & Taylor, D. A. (1973). *Social penetration: The development of interpersonal relationships.* New York: Irvington.

Argyle, M., & Dean, J. (1965). Eye contact, distance, and affiliation. *Sociometry, 28,* 289-304.

Backman, C., & Secord, P. (1959). The effect of perceived liking on interpersonal attraction. *Human Relations, 12,* 379-384.

Berger, C. R. (1985). Social power and interpersonal communication. In M. L. Knapp & G. R. Miller (Eds.), *Handbook of interpersonal communication* (pp. 439-499). Newbury Park, CA: Sage.

Bogardus, E. S. (1925). Measuring social distances. *Journal of Applied Sociology, 9,* 299-308.

Bormann, E. G. (1990). *Small group communication: Theory and practice* (3rd ed.). New York: Harper & Row.

Capella, J. N., & Greene, J. O. (1982). A discrepancy-arousal explanation of mutual influence in expressive behavior for adult and infant-adult interaction. *Communication Monographs, 49,* 89-114.

Cupach, W. R., & Metts, S. (1994). *Facework.* Thousand Oaks, CA: Sage Publications.

Delsol, C., & Margolin, G. (2004). The role of family-of-origin violence in men's marital violence perpetuation. *Clinical Psychology Review, 24,* 99-122.

Dillard, J. P., Solomon, D. H., & Palmer, M. T. (1999). Structuring the concept of relational communication. *Communication Monographs, 66,* 49-65.

Duck, S. (1994). Stratagems, spoils and a serpent's tooth: On the delights and dilemmas of personal relationships. In W. R. Cupach & B. H. Spitzberg (Eds.), *The dark side of interpersonal communication* (pp. 3-24). Hillsdale, NJ: Lawrence Erlbaum.

Fink, E. L., & Chen, S. (1995). A Galileo analysis of organizational climate. *Human Communication Research, 21,* 494-521.

Fritz, J. M. H. (1997). Responses to unpleasant work relationships. *Communication Research Reports, 14,* 302-311.

Fritz, J. M. H., & Omdahl, B. L. (1998, November). *Effects of negative peer interaction on organizational members' outcomes.* Paper presented at the meeting of the National Communication Association, New York, NY.

Frost, P. J. (1987). Power, politics, and influence. In F. M. Jablin, L. L. Putnam, K. H. Roberts, & L. W. Porter (Eds.), *Handbook of organizational communication* (pp. 503-548). Newbury Park, CA: Sage.

Goffman, E. (1961). *Encounters: Two studies in the sociology of interaction.* Indianapolis: Bobbs-Merrill.

Goffman, E. (1967). *Interaction ritual: Essays on face-to-face behavior.* New York: Pantheon.

Hall, E. T. (1959). *The silent language.* Garden City, NY: Doubleday.

Heider, F. (1958). *The psychology of interpersonal relations.* New York: John Wiley & Sons.

Helgeson, V. S., Shaver, P., & Dyer, M. (1987). Prototypes of intimacy and distance in same-sex and opposite-sex relationships. *Journal of Personal and Social Relationships, 4,* 195-233.

Hess, J. A. (1996). *Maintaining nonvoluntary relationships with disliked partners: Balance and distance.* Unpublished doctoral dissertation, University of Minnesota, Minneapolis, MN.

Hess, J. A. (2000). Maintaining nonvoluntary relationships with disliked partners: An investigation into the use of distancing behaviors. *Human Communication Research, 26,* 458-488.

Hess, J. A. (2002a). Maintaining unwanted relationships. In D. J. Canary & M. Dainton (Eds.), *Maintaining relationships through communication: Relational, contextual, and cultural variations* (pp. 103-124). Mahwah, NJ: Lawrence Erlbaum.

Hess, J. A. (2002b). Distance regulation in personal relationships: The development of a conceptual model and a test of representational validity. *Journal of Social and Personal Relationships, 19,* 663-683.

Hess, J. A. (2003). Measuring distance in personal relationships: The Relational Distance Index. *Personal Relationships, 10,* 197-215.

Hochschild, A. R. (1983). *The managed heart.* Berkely: University of California Press.

Jablin, F. M., & Sias, P. M. (2001). Communication competence. In F. M. Jablin & L. L. Putnam (Eds.), *The new handbook of organizational communication: Advances in theory, research, and methods* (pp. 819-864). Thousand Oaks, CA: Sage.

Jacobson, N. S. (1989). The politics of intimacy. *Behavior Therapist, 12,* 29-32.

Johnson, A. J., Wittenberg, E., Haigh, M., Wigley, S., Becker, J., Brown, K., & Craig, E. (2004). The process of relationship development and deterioration: Turning points in friendships that have terminated. *Communication Quarterly, 52,* 54-67.

Kahneman, D., & Tversky, A. (1984). Choices, values, and frames. *American Psychologist, 39,* 341-350.

Kantor, D., & Lehr, W. (1975). *Inside the family.* San Francisco: Jossey-Bass.

Kelley, H. H., Berscheid, E., Christensen, A., Harvey, J. H., Huston, T. L., Levinger, G., McClintock, E., Peplau, L. A., Peterson, D. R. (1983). *Close relationships.* New York: W. H. Freeman.

Kinney, T. A. (1998). The psychosomatic effects of negative interactions. *Psychosomatic Medicine, 60,* 114.

Kramer, M. W., & Hess, J. A. (2002). Communication rules for the display of emotions in organizational settings. *Management Communication Quarterly, 16*(1), 66-80.

Kreilkamp, T. (1981). Psychological distance. In J. de Rivera (Ed.), *Conceptual encounter: A method for the exploration of human experience* (pp. 273-342). Washington, DC: University Press of America.

Leary, M. R. (1991). Social anxiety, shyness, and related constructs. In J. P. Robinson, P. R. Shaver, & L. S. Wrightsman (Eds.), *Measures of personality and social psychological attitudes* (Vol. 1, pp. 161-194). San Diego: Academic Press.

Levitt, M. J., Silver, M. E., & Franco, N. (1996). Troublesome relationships: A part of human experience. *Journal of Social and Personal Relationships, 13,* 523-536.

Mashek, D. J., & Aron, A. (Eds.). (2004). *Handbook of closeness and intimacy.* Mahwah, NJ: Lawrence Erlbaum.

Micholt, N. (1992). Psychological distance and group interventions. *Transactional Analysis Journal, 22,* 228-233.

Murstein, B. I., Cerreto, M., & MacDonald, M. G. (1977). A theory and investigation of the effect of exchange-orientation on marriage and friendship. *Journal of Marriage and the Family, 39*, 543-548.

Park, R. E. (1924). The concept of social distance as applied to the study of racial attitudes and racial relations. *Journal of Applied Sociology, 8*, 339-344.

Patterson, M. L. (1973). Compensation in nonverbal immediacy behaviors: A review. *Sociometry, 36*, 237-252.

Patterson, M. L. (1976). An arousal model of interpersonal intimacy. *Psychological Review, 83*, 235-245.

Peterson, M. R. (1992). *At personal risk: Boundary violations in professional-client relationships.* New York: W. W. Norton & Company.

Pistole, M. C. (1994). Adult attachment styles: Some thoughts on closeness-distance struggles. *Family Process, 33*, 147-159.

Poitras, J., Bowen, R. E., & Byrne, S. (2003). Bringing horses to water? Overcoming bad relationships in the pre-negotiating stage of consensus building. *Negotiation Journal, 19*(3), 251-263.

Salzmann, J., & Grasha, A. F. (1991). Psychological size and psychological distance in manager-subordinate relationships. *Journal of Social Psychology, 131*(5), 629-646.

Schein, E. (1969). *Process consultation.* Reading, MA: Addison-Wesley.

Schutz, W. G. (1958). *FIRO: A three-dimensional theory of interpersonal behavior.* New York: Holt, Rinehart, and Winston.

Sias, P. M., Heath, R. G., Perry, T., Silva, D., & Fix, B. (2004). Narratives of workplace friendship deterioration. *Journal of Social and Personal Relationships, 21*, 321-340.

Sypher, B. D., & Zorn, T. (1986). Communication-related abilities and upward mobility: A longitudinal investigation. *Human Communication Research, 12*, 420-431.

Thibaut, J. W., & Kelley, H. H. (1986). The social psychology of groups. New Brunswick, NJ: Transaction Books. (Original work published in 1959)

Wahrman, R. (1972). Status, deviance, and sanctions: A critical review. *Comparative Group Studies, 3*, 203-224.

Watzlawick, P., Beavin, J., & Jackson, D. D. (1967). *Pragmatics of human communication: A study of interactional patterns, pathologies, and paradoxes.* New York: W. W. Norton & Company.

Zorn, T. E., & Violanti, M. T. (1996). Communication abilities and individual achievement in organizations. *Management Communication Quarterly, 10*, 139-167.

11 | Professional Civility: Reclaiming Organizational Limits

Ronald C. Arnett

Load sixteen tons and what do you get
Another day older and deeper in debt
St. Peter don't you call me 'cause I can't go
I owe my soul to the company store.
                                        Merle Travis

Upon reflection on the events of a demanding day at work, one might charitably call the workplace the home of "unnecessary crises." Christopher Lasch (1991) penned an even more apt phrase, the "trivialization of crisis" (p. 62). The "trivialization of crisis" differentiates genuine crises from the manufactured, the unnecessary. Neil Postman (1985) stated that we use media to "amuse ourselves to death." It is possible to use feigned crises to amuse ourselves, lessening our obligation to engage in productive work.

Conflict theory reminds us of the importance of the helpful benefits of active engagement of conflict (Simmel, 1955). However, without differentiating real conflict from trivial conflict we permit the trivial to trump the genuine. The cost of the trivialization of crisis (Lasch, 1991) is the loss of discernment of the genuine. One reason for the loss of knowledge of a genuine crisis is the wholesale move of private life into the public space of an organization. The notion of professional civility, although not a remedy for organization confusion, offers a metaphor that has practical implications for discernment. We must discern what impacts the public life of an organization, a place where many who do not like one another must work together. Professional civility is a metaphor that admits that an organization is neither a family nor a place of friendship. Organizations may engender feelings akin to both feelings at times, but the fundamental necessity of public space in an organization is to give those who do not like one another guidelines for contributing to the organization, even to the point of advancing the person one does not like.

What Is Professional Civility?

Professional civility (Arnett & Fritz, 2004) is a "fuzzy metaphor" (Arnett, 2001) offering general guidelines for task and social interpersonal interaction in organizational contexts. Professional civility assumes an orientation to organizations as public places, the importance of coordinated roles, and the need for boundaries protecting pubic and private life. Professional civility assumes limits for expectations of persons and their employing organizations: organizations are not designed as places of self-fulfillment, and employees are not designed to give the totality of their lives to organizations, permitting the public to replace or overwhelm the private sphere. Organizations have a responsibility for public articulation of mission or guiding narrative that has fidelity, in which word and deed are connected. Professional civility rejects a human relations model in which organizations attempt to meet individual needs as a means to increase production. Professional civility embraces a human resource model, elevating ideas, creativity, and productivity as the focus of organizational life. Professional civility involves respect for others in the workplace and a willingness to work with those whom one may not like. Professional civility suggests following good ideas, from whatever source, whether a colleague, a person with a work style different from one's own, a secretary, or a CEO. Ideas, not the individual, propel professional civility in an organization.

Professional civility revisits the unexamined premises of modernity, the conflation of private life in the public sphere of organizational life. The crises of an organization need to have public consequences for an organization, consequences that impact the productive life of people working together. For example, imagine a university whose finances have failed and faces imminent closing. Professional civility takes off the table the obligation to fix relationships of "dislike," focusing on the public mission and operation of a place. Public life in organizations is not described by family or friendship vocabulary. Just as Robert Bellah and colleagues (1985) called into question the misuse of therapeutic vocabulary in the pursuit of community, this essay questions the misuse of family and friendship vocabulary in organizational life. Public life requires argumentative parameters larger than an individual self and one's own versions of family and friendship. Professional civility assumes three basic communicative commitments. First, an organization must state its professional mission and the communicative practices necessary to enhance such a mission. Second, a public organization must protect the public space of the organization and the private lives of employees. Finally, a public organization must admit limits: public obligations to one another do not assure private fulfillment. Private lives outside the workplace need support and encouragement. An organization committed to professional civility states its limits in mission, engagement of the mission, and the fact that a complete life needs much from outside the workplace.

Professional civility reclaims differentiation of public and private life and the difference between genuine and unnecessary crises. Professional civility does not lessen conflict or crisis, but places works to shape contentions within the public sphere of communicative interaction. Professional civility counters an ironic communicative crisis in the workplace, the crisis of unnecessary crises, embracing a basic assumption: when private and public spaces co-mingle there are two forms of loss. One is the loss of the public character of an organization, and the other is the loss of a rich and diversified private life. The next section addresses these issues.

Confusing Public and Private Life

Sometimes an organization engages in "bad faith" (Sartre, 1953, pp. 86-116) and lies about the scope of its commitment, using language of family and friendship. An organization that promises benefits such as reimbursement for further education for employees but is unsupportive of those educational efforts, a CEO espousing an open-door policy but is never available, and a manager that promises a family atmosphere only to engage in massive layoffs shortly thereafter are all engaging in bad faith. At that point, the blurring of public and private life takes on the label of "problematic." Such an insight is not new or novel, only largely ignored. The danger of the blurring of public and private life is at heart of Hannah Arendt's work. The collapse of modernity as a project of constant growth rests within the failed effort to unite public and private life within a single domain that Arendt termed the "social" (Arendt, 1958).

The sphere of the "social" collapses public and private life, permitting one to manufacture crises that do not genuinely impact a public place. The term "manufacture" is fitting in that the collapse of public and private life is a shadow consequence of an industrial revolution that lost its way in profit, confusing productivity with profit alone. Productivity involves something other than more work at longer hours. Productivity is the key to life, as Arendt frames in her work on labor (Arendt, 1958). Public and private lives are enhanced by productivity. Public organizations that emphasize productivity for the sole end of short-term profit by, for example, decreasing the number of full-time employees and expecting more than can be done with excellence, minimize public and private differentiation. Only the pragmatic necessity of creativity in the workplace opens the conversation to differentiated public and private life once again. Working longer doing the same thing does not permit paradigmatic change. Only creativity enhanced by a life enriched by more than the workplace opens such a door of opportunity and change.

The confusion of public and private life into the social leads to social comparison, not creative enhancement. Simmel, writing at the beginning of the 20th century, offers an example of such confusion in social spaces: the wrongful introduction of envy and jealousy into the workplace. "The feeling of the envious individual turns more around possession, that of the jealous person more around the possessor." (Simmel, 1955, p. 51). It is not that we can eliminate envy and jealousy, but the collapsing of public and private life puts all one's eggs in one basket. Imagine a work colleague who has no life outside of work. For her, work becomes all-consuming, and being an admired performer takes on unrealistic proportions. The success of others begins to rankle, and energy becomes focused on how to prevent others from gaining credit instead of how to make the organization better. When the organization is one's only source of fulfillment, success is limited to a single sphere, which enhances the probability of fostering an environment of jealously and envy.

Professional civility does not eliminate such feelings; however, the admission of limits of what is possible in a organization encourages all to seek meaningfulness in more than one place. Additionally, the communicative practices of professional civility seek to discourage comments of envy and jealousy; one needs to take their legitimacy off the table as much as possible. The power of discourse to construct perceptions of organizational life is illustrated in Sias's (1996) research on workplace conversations about equity. Professional civility works to make the workplace a safe place for enhancing public life in an organization by simultaneously calling for a rich and meaningful private life. The more public and private life remain distinct, each with its appropriate focus, the more one appreciates both spheres and the more each can enhance, if indirectly, the other. In a work sphere in which productivity is the focus, individual differences become a rich tapestry, and a rich private life permits rejoicing with others' successes. In addition, a separate private sphere can be celebrated without intrusion of work demands and cares.

The Loss of Differentiation

The work of Hannah Arendt (1958) frames the importance of differentiating public and private space, in order to avoid expansion of the "social," a place of lost definition. The loss of public and private difference leads to crises and conflicts that work within the horizon of a public organization and those that fall outside a public arena. Professional civility works as a metaphor that embraces conflict and crisis within public space, lessening the impulse to blur public and private communicative life. Conflict is, indeed, necessary and healthy. The key is to minimize private crises that invade a public space. Professional civility works with the assumption that organizational role trumps personal preference in an organization that lives within public space.

An organization must meet crises that challenge a given public direction. Such public challenges test a given direction, assuring pragmatic clarity of the "why," the "how," and the "wherefore" of a given direction, permitting necessary change. This essay affirms such public crisis points. However, when a crisis emerges from private communicative space, invading public space, decision-making by personal preference, identified by MacIntyre (1981) as "emotivism" (pp. 23-35), moves the definition of the crisis to the feigned. Private crises make sense in our personal lives. The task of professional civility is to keep communication appropriate in a public space. Professional civility works to reclaim public space within the workplace. As a by-product, such differentiation works to minimize confusion between genuine and feigned crisis in the workplace.

Discourse about professional civility is at best a reminder of the difference between genuine crises and the trivialization of crisis. The notion of professional civility works as a third construct, in addition to the employee and the organization. Professional civility is a call to something other than me, the employee, and the organization. Professional civility reminds us of something more important than me or the organization—preserving space where public engagement with one another for the good of an organization functions as a communicative background in everyday life of work.

"Do you know why they asked us to make that change? I know. They want to give the appearance of change with nothing of consequence altered. I am going to tell them the document was lost and did not get to us."

"Do you know why she is so unhappy? Have you met her children? I think they look like danger on legs. I am not going to do this work to try and please someone who is always so unhappy. The first chance I get I am telling everyone just how unreasonable this person is. I hate having such an unhappy boss."

"Did you see the car that he is driving? I cannot believe it. They must have given him a raise. I will not help him again. Just wait until he is in need of help. I will tell him I have just too much to do. I do not care that I report to him."

Each conversation frames conflict/disagreement within a private sphere. Each conversation begins one down a path of professional undermining by privatizing the discourse. Professional civility as its most basic level of engagement must counter professional undermining carried through the misuse of private discourse, making a "social" place where Arendt believed everyday evil lurks in the "banality" of collapsed public and private space (Arendt, 1977, p. 252). An example of this understanding of the social is the office party everyone is required to attend and at which persons feign intimacy with those one knows very little. The social tempts one to engage in a community of gossip and complaint to establish common ground at little cost or investment. Professional undermining works at this level of banality. Such simple comments lead to social deconstruction in the workplace. One deconstructs another when private motivations are tied to public acts and when one asks the question, "Would I do this the same way?"

There is, of course, a place for the deconstructive move. Nietzsche moved us from blind confidence in modernity to awareness of multiplicity. He called into question allegiance to the inevitability of progress and faith in the self. Such a move warranted attention and applause. Both organizations and employees are accountable to multiple stakeholders, including each other. However, to continue to deconstruct each moment and each person turns deconstruction into a self-fashioned technique in which only the self, oneself, remains as the final standing place of truth. Such a move turns us once again to modernity and confidence in the self. The postmodern organization must minimize allegiance to the self alone, the moral cul de sac of modernity, and to the organization alone, a form of tribalism/tradition located in the very local and the very particular, in the house of one's employment.

Professional civility frames the metaphorical and communicative praxis center of this essay. The term is a natural extension of theoretical work on dialogic civility (Arnett & Arneson, 1999). This essay outlines the lineage between dialogic civility and professional civility in intentionally modest, small steps pragmatically responsive to the postmodern rejection of the universal. The postmodern appetite for multiplicity of options reminds us of that it is unwise to adhere to grand schemes, to a meta-narrative, a framework or worldview assumed to be adhered to by everyone (e.g., the scientific meta-narrative, or a religious meta-narrative; see Lyotard, 1984). However, a postmodern moment lives with competing narrative remnants and petite narratives (Arnett & Fritz, 2004); humble narratives (Arnett, 2001) are central to this moment. Without competing narrative possibilities we return to the modern project of progress and a false confidence in a self capable of standing above history, tradition, and bias of socio-cultural standpoint. Meta-narrative absolutes do not drive this moment, but neither does confidence in the Enlightenment "I" that stands disembedded from particular circumstances. This essay enters this conversation with professional civility functioning pragmatically as one narrative option in a time of collapsed enlightenment confidence.

Just as the notion of dialogic civility is but one metaphor for understanding interpersonal engagement in the public domain (Arnett, 2001), professional civility is one small contribution to understanding organizational life in a postmodern era of narrative and virtue contention in which those who do not share virtue structures or work styles must labor together. Professional civility, like the notion of dialogic civility, is an alternative to a therapeutic emphasis on the self, suggesting instead the importance of a third party, a sense of the neighbor that keeps our organizational communicative lives tempered with concern beyond our own individual demands. Therapeutic discourse is the heart of the modern project, in which the self becomes the sacred. This premise is at the heart of the work of Reiff (1987). Postmodernity takes to task the overindulged importance of the agent, moving us from the focus on the self to a time of competing traditions. From the eyes of modernity, narrative projects such as professional civility look conservative, due to limited categories of freedom of the agent and oppressive traditions. However, from a postmodern standpoint, traditions are inevitable, and they contend for public space. It is not the agent or the self that propels the importance of a given tradition, but guidance by what Bakhtin (1981, 1986) called "the third." Professional civility is but one way to invite conversation with a third party outside the organization and the agent without assuming that this linkage is the privileged final answer

Modernity's Disdain for Traditional Life

Modernity's disdain for traditional life rests at the heart of Weber's argument (Weber, 1958). He assumed that the more commitment one had to a tradition and a community the less one would commit to the spirit of capitalism. He was correct. This essay turns this assumption on its head in a postmodern age. More of the same will not compete. Postmodernity assumes not one but many traditions that can guide us. It is these traditions that give us the bias out of which creativity emerges. This is the major thesis of Gadamer in his work on philosophical hermeneutics (Gadamer, 1975). Weber and many committed to the workplace asked us to find too much meaning in the workplace, only to put the creativity and longevity of our workplaces at risk in a postmodern era of paradigmatic change as normative action.

This essay suggests that organizations must differentiate between real and feigned/contrived crises, reclaiming a commitment to public communicative space and reclaiming limits. The workplace is a public place of engagement on a common task. Private life permits renewal, and public life permits contribution to organizations and communities. The two spheres complement when each is distinct.

In a traditional (premodern) society, differentiation of public and private life is unneeded. Rather, an organic sense of community is based upon common tasks and proximity. People do not reflect on identity and belonging in this traditional/premodern realm. Instead, people go about tasks working alongside family members (for example, the family farm) (Arnett & Fritz, 2004). However, modernity gives us disenfranchised persons, persons displaced from their traditional communities. It is in this moment of modern displacement of persons that organizations increasingly attempt to meet the public and private needs of persons. Modernity is the metaphor of amalgamation; it is the experiment that sought, and still seeks, to pull public and private life together. Yet, there have always been those questioning such efforts. The legendary coal mining song is such a reminder: "Saint Peter don't you call me, 'cause I can't go; I owe my soul to the company store" (Travis, 1947). The song reminds us of a "kept" community where one works and buys all one's items, only to fall short of money, finding oneself ever in debt.

Organizations and the connected community, controlled by what some might call "robber barons," emulated traditional life, only to find that imitation is just that: imitation. Yet, we still insist on trying to turn a public organization into a traditional place of blurred public and private life. The radical move in postmodernity is not to seek amalgamation of difference, but to reclaim difference. Professional civility is not a call to organizational appeasement, but to appropriate lessening of importance of public organizational life, countered by a rich and thoughtful private life. The blurring of public and private lives in the inability to go home from work, finding within one's head the noise of the day for the remainder of the evening: "Saint Peter, don't you call me, 'cause I can't go; I owe my soul to the company store."

We have too often given our personal souls to an organization. The radical move is not to perfect the organization with our private lives, but to take the flaws of organization life as a reminder of the pragmatic necessity of life outside the workplace. The key move of Arendt in her differentiation of public and private space is to stop a banality of evil that kills the soul, specifically the expectation of private nurture from public places and public accommodation from private places. To fail to differentiate public and private life is to give robber barons the ability to shape a life. As we fight to bring into the workplace more and more private support, we give over to a new set of robber barons the ability to find meaning outside the workplace. Professional civility is a call to put the public life of the workplace within limits that cannot claim all of our lives. The key element of professional civility is limitation, not progress or perfection. The modern experiment assumes that progress and perfection must guide our actions. However, to work to eliminate all flaws within an organization at a private level moves our focus of attention from a private life to an emotional form of "Sixteen Tons." Professional civility is an assertive cry to put the significance of organizations back in their proper place. They are public places calling for us to find community, family, or aesthetic life outside the workplace. Organizations are flawed, and they will continue to be flawed. Organizational imperfection reminds us of the importance of finding a community, family support, and aesthetic enrichment outside the workplace. Professional civility is a rejection of an organization's becoming "Pleasantville." The key test is to ask: "If I were independently wealthy, would I worry about this or that issue? Would I continue to work here?" If not, then one must reclaim the limits of influence that the public workplace has on one's life by nurturing a private life.

Traditional life dwells within an unreflective pre-division moment of public and private. Such discussion makes no sense in a traditional society. Modernity, however, lives on the Cartesian mind/body dichotomy, separating public and private, then moving to reunite them with the blurring of private and public life within the workplace (e.g., Ashcraft, 2000). Modernity works on the move of division that rests in denial of such a division. Modernity tries to "spin" an alternative to the reality presented. The separation of mind and body permits the separation of private and public, and when one attempts reflective reunion of the separated spheres, one ends in an unreflective place of "bad faith," doing spin that all know is false. Our claims about the modern workplace as a family are at best ceremonial rhetoric and at worse lies to keep us loading sixteen tons.

From Modern Magic to Postmodern Limits

Professional civility does not offer *the* answer to communicative life in organizations, but is one way to invite conversation that includes the importance of the third, the neighbor. Professional civility is a metaphor that signals a call to responsibility beyond our own demands and beyond the scope of the organization. Levinas stated that he was not a humanist, because humanism is not human enough (Levinas, 1998, p. 85). Humanism centered on the individual self misses the embedded, situated, and temporal nature of communicative life. Protection of the self or discussion of the organization as a private form of self-fulfillment is a humanistic model rejected by this author, who is in agreement with Levinas: it is not human enough. The human task in a time of competing traditions and recognized situatedness is more akin to Martin Buber's phrase, "the mud of everyday life" (Arnett & Arneson, 1999). We walk with mud up to our ankles and often to our knees, and at time we find life, like quicksand, sucking us down toward an unknown vacuum. All one needs to do to imagine such a moment is to remember a crisis in a family, an organizational, or a friendship. Humanism provided solidity of ground for the self to walk over, and postmodernity re-embeds the person in the mud(s) of everyday life.

This essay accepts the position that to be human requires foregoing a commitment to magic. The enlightenment project of confidence in the self walking upon the firmament of progress brings a shock to the postmodern writer similar to that experienced by anthropologists encountering animism in the 20th century and philosophers questioning a view of Deity that assumed the power and inevitability of *deus ex machina*. Humanism looks as primitive and as anachronistic to postmodern writers as past practices did to those committed to the eyes of progress. Interestingly, postmodernity then makes space for each—animism, deus ex machina, and humanism, but now each vies for narrative space, each working as a particular, not as a universal tradition.

Professional civility as framed in this essay rejects humanism as a moral cul de sac based on narrative assurance no longer available in a postmodern world. Often one will accept the limits of meta-narrative and agree that there is no one or final answer (a postmodern position) and then supply a modern answer of the importance of self. We have extended the life span of therapeutic discourse by permitting a modern answer to supply insight into a postmodern moment of multiplicity.

The notion of professional civility is a strident alternative metaphor that seeks to displace overemphasis on the self with the simultaneous action of knowing that the metaphor is inadequate and not a final answer. However, this metaphor is one way to address a failed project, the emphasis on the self as the identity basis of modernity. The postmodern deconstruction of agency calls for ways to engage human life contrary to a humanistic model based upon the self. A humanistic ethic of organizational life makes the desire for "my" happiness the criterion of organizational success. Professional civility works with a modest assumption: the criteria for success rests with adherence to a third, something outside the person and the organization, a commitment to the neighborhood, to the professional neighborhood that guides one's life. In pragmatic adherence to the reality of multiplicity, this essay concludes with a reminder that communication with others in the mud(s) of everyday life by necessity complicates the importance of any guiding metaphor or narrative; there are important multiple commitments beyond professional civility that embed this conversation within a postmodern commitment to multiple petite narratives (Lyotard, 1984). Simmel (1955) foreshadowed this position. He suggested that multiple webs of association govern communicative lives with professional civility being but one strand or connecting link. He understood life as a web of associations. This essay takes the notion of a web of associations with a linking assumption: how we understand the importance of the third party or the neighbor recasts our understanding of a given organization and our communicative life within an organization. This essay calls not for one, but for many strands that serve to connect us to the notion of the third.

This essay is a public think piece about the notion of the third, the neighbor, played out in modest scale with a single metaphor, with full knowledge of the necessity of additional strands that connect us to life beyond the immediacy of our own convictions. This essay invites conversation about the notion of professional civility, its kinship with the idea of the third and its connection to dialogic civility, and finally connects professional civility to the idea of the third. This essay outlines how this author links professional civility to the notion of the third: commitment to the unseen neighbor: in Levinas's words, to communicative action that keeps before one that "I am my brother's keeper" (1998, p. 98). This sense of justice, of the third, of the neighbor, relies upon a non-humanistic model defined neither by self-protection nor by organizational survival. The notion of the third reminds one of something more important than immediacy of organization or self. It is the background meaning of the third that situates and frames the significance of self and organization. Finally, this essay will end with a reminder that needs to function as a pragmatic commonplace in a time of narrative and virtue contention: one cannot place final trust in the notion of professional civility; it is but one call, one strand that connects oneself to the neighbor; it is not "the" call. This communicative move from offering "the" answer to conversation about an idea of limited utility that points toward an answer beyond self and organizational preoccupation is a space where professional civility and communicative praxis unite to offer a glimpse of an "I" called forth by an alterity other than self or organization. In the message of Nuremburg, there is something greater than following orders and self-protection at risk, something greater carried in the arms of the unseen third.

Bakhtin discusses the importance of "the third" in communication between persons. His reminder of someone/ something beyond the immediate nature of the interaction is a central contribution to dialogic theory and to those wanting to navigate life beyond the modern confines of the self. A postmodern era is simply a reminder of multiplicity and differentiation, a time in which one finds touchstones (Friedman, 1975) of petite narratives that keep us connected beyond the self. To frame professional civility as an answer is to fall into the modern abyss of the universal: singularity of answer. To omit professional civility is to ignore a tradition that has potential for conversation in a postmodern era of tradition(s). The notion of professional civility can too quickly be forsaken/rejected as a return to a traditional era. Its value rests with its position as a tradition competing with other traditions for space in the postmodern marketplace of ideas. A postmodern reading from a constructivist hermeneutic does not fear a tradition, only the claim to "the" tradition. Deconstruction offers its most potent contribution in dismantling false confidence in a universal, but when it continues to deconstruct every narrative and tradition it begins to fall within in its own grasp as a universal technique. Postmodernity from a constructivist perspective that accepts the deconstruction of modernity becomes open to differentiation and what Levinas refers to as "joy," not agreement, but the joy of life different than one's own.

One can make the case that any understanding of "the third" can take on meta-narrative status. The answer to that suggestion is, "Of course!" Postmodernity does not eliminate the possibility of another meta-narrative emerging. It simply states that at this point there is no common agreement on such a position. Postmodernity opens the door to a multiplicity of traditions that remind the "self" that life is lived as an embedded agent, not as a person standing on the universal assumptive ground of progress. The notion of the third becomes important in such a communicative movement. The metaphor of processional civility is but one way to suggest and remind that there is more than me; there is a third, an unseen and ever-present neighbor.

Professional civility is but one way to get at the postmodern rejection of unreflective confidence in two extremes, tradition or the self. Professional civility is a call to something beyond these polar positions, a call to the importance of the third. The notion of the third has many forms, from Bakhtin to Levinas to the communication work of Ken Anderson. In each case, the face of the unseated neighbor guides one's action. George Herbert Mead discussed the importance of the "generalized Other" (Mead, 1934). Benhabib took this notion to a clarity of face, suggesting the importance of the "particular Other" (Benhabib, 1992). In each case there is something bigger and more complex than me and the organization at stake.

Levinas uses the term "neighbor" to remind us of justice. The realm of the third is the realm of justice. It is concern for a standard beyond the organization and the self that calls for action. At its best the learning from the Nuremberg trials was a reminder of the third. Justice comes from concern for a neighbor, not situated within an organization alone or within the self, but in strands of a web of concern beyond the immediate preoccupation with the life that is before us.

References

Arendt, H. (1977). Eichmann in Jerusalem: A report on the banality of evil (Rev. and enlarged edition). New York: Penguin Books. (Original work published 1963)

Arendt, H. (1958). The human condition. Chicago: University of Chicago Press.

Arnett, R. C. (2001). Dialogic civility as pragmatic ethical praxis: An interpersonal metaphor for the public domain. *Communication Theory. 11*, 315-338.

Arnett, R. C., & Arneson, P. (1999). *Dialogic civility in a cynical age: Community, hope, and interpersonal relationships.* Albany, NY: SUNY Press.

Arnett, R. C., & Fritz, J. M. H. (2004). Sustaining institutional ethics and integrity: Management in a postmodern moment. In A. S. Iltis (Ed.), *Institutional integrity in healthcare* (pp. 41-71). Dordrecht: Kluwer Academic Publishers.

Arnett, R. C., & Fritz, J. M. H. (2001). Communication and professional civility as a basic service course: Dialogic praxis between departments and situated in an academic home. *Basic Communication Course Annual, 13*, 174-206.

Ashcraft, K. L. (2000). Empowering "professional" relationships: Organizational communication meets feminist practice. *Management Communication Quarterly, 13*, 347-392.

Bakhtin, M. (1981). *The dialogic imagination: Four essays by M. M. Bakhtin* (C. Emerson & M. Holquist, Trans.; M. Holquist, Ed.). Austin: University Of Texas Press.

Bakhtin, M. M. (1986). The problem of speech genres. In C. Emerson and M. Holquist (Eds.), V. W. McGee (Trans.), *Speech Genres and Other Late Essays* (pp. 60-102). Austin, TX: University of Texas Press.

Bellah, R., Madsen, H., Sullivan, W., Swidler, A., and Tipton, S. (1985). *Habits of the heart: Individualism and commitment in American life.* Berkeley: University of California Press.

Benhabib, S. (1992). *Situating the self. Gender, community and post-modernism in contemporary ethics.* Routledge: New York.

Friedman, M. (1975). *Touchstones of reality: Existential trust and the community of peace.* New York: E. P. Dutton.

Gadamer, H. G. (1975). *Truth and method.* New York: The Seabury Press.

Lasch, C. (1991). *The true and only heaven: Progress and its critics.* New York: W. W. Norton.

Levinas, E. (1998). *Ethics and infinity: Conversations with Philippe Nemo* (R. Cohen, Trans.). Pittsburgh, PA: Duquesne University Press.

Lyotard, J. F. (1984). *The postmodern condition: A report on knowledge* (G. Bennington and B. Massumi, Trans.). Minneapolis: University of Minnesota Press.

MacIntyre, A. (1981). *After virtue: A study in moral theory.* Notre Dame: University of Notre Dame Press.

Mead, G. H. (1934). *Mind, self, and society.* Chicago: University of Chicago Press.

Postman, N. (1985). *Amusing ourselves to death.* New York: Penguin.

Reiff, P. (1987). *The triumph of the therapeutic: Uses of faith after Freud.* Chicago: University of Chicago Press.

Sartre, J. P. (1953). Being and nothingness: An essay on phenomenological ontology (H. E. Barnes, Trans.). New York: Washington Square Press.

Sias, P. M. (1996). Constructing perceptions of differential treatment: An analysis of coworkers' discourse. *Communication Monographs, 63*, 171-187.

Simmel, G. (1955). *Conflict and the web of group affiliations.* London: The Free Press.

Travis, M. (1947). Sixteen tons. On *Folk Songs from the Hills* [LP]. Nashville: Capitol Records.

Weber, M. (1958). The protestant ethic and the spirit of capitalism. New York: Charles Scribner's Sons.

12 Forgiveness in the Workplace

Sandra Metts, William R. Cupach, & Lance Lippert

Although professional and interpersonal misconduct in its various forms and manifestations has no doubt been present in the workplace for many years, recognition of its importance for employee morale and organizational climate has emerged only recently in organizational literature. Once acknowledged, however, the phenomenon has become a catalyst for both scholars and practitioners who are interested in understanding, controlling, and managing a wide domain of disruptive actions in the workplace. These actions range from extreme forms of misconduct such as violence, physical threats, sexual harassment, and discriminatory pay practices that typically invoke litigation as a form of remediation, to the everyday acts of incivility such as rudeness, disrespect, vulgarity, and other transgressions that strain work relationships, damage trust, and otherwise diminish the workplace climate.

Although definitions and constitutive examples differ, consistent evidence indicates that workplace misconduct is personally and professionally costly. For example, survey responses from 775 people in North Carolina (Pearson, 1999, summarized in Peyton, 2003) reflect a pattern of reduced time, effort, and commitment invested in the workplace.

- ❑ 53% lost work time worrying about the incident or future interactions
- ❑ 46% contemplated changing jobs to avoid the instigator
- ❑ 37% believed that their commitment to the organization declined
- ❑ 28% lost work time avoiding the instigator
- ❑ 22% decreased their effort at work
- ❑ 12% actually did change jobs to avoid the instigator
- ❑ 10% decreased the amount of time they spend at work

We have learned much about the dynamics of organizational misconduct from the scholarship and professional wisdom of existing texts. However, there is still very limited knowledge regarding the links between organizational transgressions and the strategies victims employ to cope with transgressions and how coping strategies differ across a range of transgressions. Personal attacks, public humiliation, malicious rumors, insults, false accusations, being deceived, being ridiculed, and other transgressions that violate norms of mutual regard and respect threaten a recipient's self-esteem, professional reputation, and may evoke feelings of insecurity, fear, hurt, anger, and desire for retribution. It is not surprising that revenge for a perceived injustice or interpersonal transgression is common in organizations and prompts retaliatory theft and sabotage of co-workers' projects and organizational enterprise (Bies & Tripp, 1995; Crino, 1994). Surprising is the fact that organizational misconduct does not necessarily, or predictably, lead to the desire for retribution.

A method of coping with or responding to workplace transgressions that provides an alternative to retaliation and revenge is the emotional transformation known as forgiveness. Forgiveness transforms initial negative responses, particularly hurt, anger, and desire for retribution, into more positive orientations toward an offending person, although not necessarily the offense. Forgiveness does not mean forgetting or condoning the actions of another person that were hurtful. But it does mean that the psychic and emotional energy invested in "getting even" or "hurting back" is given over to acceptance that the event occurred, that it cannot be undone, and that feelings toward the offender can be separated from feelings about the event (Enright, 2001). An anonymous source quipped, "Forgiving someone who breaks a trust does not mean that we give him his job back" (Smedes, 1996, p. 178).

Although sometimes difficult to accomplish, forgiveness is a facilitative response; it serves to reduce the strain on mental and physical health, maintain or restore viability to the dyad involved, and serves to minimize discord or discomfort among various organizational members indirectly linked to the perpetrator and the victim (Aquino, Grover, Goldman, & Folger, 2003; Exline & Baumeister, 2000; Hebl & Enright, 1993; McCullough, Sandage, & Worthington, 1997). As Kurzynski (1998) argues, forgiveness is "a virtue that can result in better work relationships, motivating work environment, and higher morale," and the manager who forgives is not a pushover, but a "person of resolute strength and moral character" (p. 84). The bottom line, according to Stone (2002), is that forgiveness not only affects the personal lives of employees, but also increases retention rates, and ultimately, the profitability of the company.

In an interesting theoretical discussion of the evolutionary advantage of forgiveness, Newberg, d'Aquili, Newberg, and deMarici (2000) make the observation that although revenge may be enacted in order to restore equilibrium, aggressive behavior met with aggressive behavior eventually destabilizes a social system. If unchecked, reciprocal retaliation leads to chaos. Forgiveness as a response tends to defuse escalating tensions. In addition, when forgiveness, in the form of nonretaliation, is observed by others it may have the curious quality of generating empathy and warm regard for the victim, and these responses may motivate others to offer social support (Enright, 1996, p. 97).

The purpose of this chapter is to provide insight into the processes and factors that provide a link between organizational misconduct or transgressions and forgiveness. The chapter is divided into three general sections. First, we review the conceptual and definitional approaches to workplace misconduct currently found in scholarly journals and popular books. Second, we review the existing literature on forgiveness broadly construed and more specifically on forgiveness in the organization. Third, we present the findings from an empirical study that examines the nature of organizational transgressions as described by respondents who have recently experienced them, and the factors most likely to facilitate or inhibit forgiveness.

Conceptual and Definitional Approaches
to Workplace Misconduct

Incivility

Pearson, Andersson, and Wegner (2001) define workplace incivility as "low-intensity deviant behavior with ambiguous intent to harm the target, in violation of workplace norms for mutual respect. Uncivil behaviors are characteristically rude and discourteous, displaying a lack of regard for others" (p. 1397). A distinguishing characteristic of incivility is that the intent to harm is ambiguous rather than transparent, and open to some degree of interpretation on the part of the instigator, the target, or both (Pearson et al., 2001).

Workplace incivility can be manifested in such subtle forms as giving someone a "dirty look," asking for input and then ignoring it, "forgetting" to share credit for collaborative work, speaking with a condescending tone, interrupting others, not listening, and waiting impatiently over someone's desk to gain their attention (Andersson & Pearson, 1999; "Incivility," 2000). More overt forms of incivility might include emotional tirades and losing one's temper. Somewhere between these extremes are numerous everyday examples of workplace rudeness and impropriety that might include sending a nasty and demeaning note, making accusations about professional competence, undermining credibility in front of others, making condescending and demeaning comments, overruling decisions without expressing a reason, disrupting meetings, giving public reprimands, talking about someone behind his or her back, giving others the silent treatment, not giving credit where credit is due, giving dirty looks or other negative eye contact, and insulting others (Johnson & Indvik, 2001).

A somewhat different approach to incivility, or perhaps a more specific subset of incivility, is a focus on those actions that somehow impact the quality of interpersonal trust between organizational members (Lewicki & Bunker, 1996). For example, based on employee descriptions of workplace violations, Bies and Tripp (1995), identify two broad categories of events that affect trust: (1) A damaged sense of "civic order" including formal and informal rule violations and breach of contract, and (2) A damaged "identity" including public criticism, false or unfair accusations and insults to self or the collective.

Bullying

The term "workplace bullying" overlaps to some degree with incivility, but tends to encompass more intense and typically repeated acts of disregard and rudeness. Negative spirals of increasing incivility between organizational members can result in bullying (Beale, 2001), but isolated acts of incivility are not conceptually isomorphic with bullying despite the apparent similarity in their form and content. In cases of bullying, the intent of harm is less ambiguous, an unequal balance of power (both formal and informal) is more salient, and the target of bullying feels threatened, vulnerable, and unable to defend him or herself against recurring negative actions (Hoel & Cooper, 2001; Peyton, 2003).

Sexual harassment is one example of bullying that has received public, political, and legal attention. However, many other forms of bullying have also been identified. One of the most widely accepted typologies of bullying behaviors was initially proposed by Rayner and Hoel (1997), and subsequently refined in their own work and the work of others (e.g., Hoel & Cooper, 2001; Quine, 1999; Rayner, Hoel, & Cooper, 2002). This typology includes five types of bullying, each of which is manifested in a variety of ways (adapted from Peyton, 2003, p. 15).

❑ Threat to professional status (e.g., belittling opinions, public professional humiliation, accusations regarding lack of effort, intimidating use of discipline or competence procedures)

❑ Threat to personal standing (e.g., undermining personal integrity, destructive innuendo and sarcasm, making inappropriate jokes about target, persistent teasing, name calling, insults, intimidation)

❑ Isolation (e.g., preventing access to opportunities, physical or social isolation, withholding necessary information, keeping the target out of the loop, ignoring or excluding)

❑ Overwork (e.g., undue pressure, impossible deadlines, unnecessary disruptions)

❑ Destabilization (e.g., failure to acknowledge good work, allocation of meaningless tasks, removal of responsibility, repeated reminders of blunders, setting target up to fail)

Abuse

The term workplace abuse is very similar to workplace bullying in that it may appear innocuous when taken as an isolated event, but when embedded within a pattern of mistreatment it becomes debilitating to the recipient. However, abuse is distinguished as a particular form of bullying by its relational direction, i.e., managerial or supervisory misconduct directed to a subordinate. Bassman (1992) provides a commonly used list of abusive behaviors (pp. 7-24):

❑ Disrespect and devaluing the individual, often through disrespectful and devaluing language or verbal abuse

❑ Overwork and devaluation of personal life (particularly salaried workers who are not compensated)

❑ Harassment through micromanagement of tasks and time

❑ Overevaluation and manipulating information (e.g., concentration on negative characteristics and failures, setting up subordinate for failure)
❑ Managing by threat and intimidation
❑ Stealing credit and taking unfair advantage
❑ Preventing access to opportunities
❑ Downgrading an employee's capabilities to justify downsizing
❑ Impulsive destructive behavior

Responses to Incivility, Bullying, and Abuse

Most of the discussions concerned with ways to cope with misconduct, usually under the rubric of bullying and abuse, tend to focus on actions that victims might do to restore justice or prevent future episodes. For example, Rayner et al. (2002) suggest to readers that when they experience bullying they might use one of three responses: do nothing, confront the bully, or use silence to combat the bully. If bullying persists, Rayner et al. (2002) advises readers to try informal methods of control (e.g., go to the boss, go to personnel, go to the union or staff association, or make a group complaint). If these methods do not work, Rayner et al. (2002) recommends the use of formal methods of control or retribution (e.g., litigation), or to leave the organization. Finally, whatever option is chosen, readers are encouraged to recognize the need to "get back to normal" by reengaging with the workplace environment (at the same organization or at one's new organization).

While these are certainly reasonable actions to restore any sense of interpersonal justice and organizational order, and are presented with costs and benefits, there seems to be virtually no concern for the psychological "actions" that victims might perform as well. Forgiveness is rarely mentioned except as a possible way to cope with workplace anger (Allcorn, 1994) or as one step in the reconciliation process to restore trust. Ironically, however, the utility of forgiveness is sometimes referenced obliquely or implied as one possible option for dealing with workplace bullying. Typical of this approach is the description "getting back to normal" by Rayner et al. (2002):

> We are aware of several people who have become so tied up in getting retribution or court settlements that they seem to have spent a very large

number of years unable to free themselves of bullying at work, well after they left employment. If you are worried about this for yourself or anyone you know—do be concerned, as it is a real danger. Kiel, a Norwegian psychologist, asked his clients 'Is seeing justice done worth 20 years of your life?' (p. 156)

Clearly, the implication is that "letting go" (forgiving) is fundamental to "moving on."

Perhaps even more remarkable is the fact that empirical investigations of reactions to workplace bullying typically fail to include forgiveness as an option and yet find that respondents nevertheless report that they chose to forgive. For example, in a study of "revenge fantasies" elicited from MBA students who had experienced bullying on their job and "wanted to get even," Bies and Tripp (1995) were surprised to find that forgiveness emerged as a viable category of responses. The authors conclude with the comment,

> The forgiveness response was a surprise and clearly a phenomenon in need of further investigation. Why people forgive is an intriguing question, and also whether, when they forgive, they also forget... [F]orgiveness is interesting because the victim, not the perpetrator, restores trust. In other words, there is power in forgiveness. (pp. 259-260)

We turn now to a more detailed discussion of the phenomenon that so surprised Bies and Tripp (1995).

Forgiveness: Theory and Research

After a long tradition of discourse among religious scholars, interest in forgiveness has recently emerged among scholars in the social sciences (Gorsuch, 1988). As might be expected in any systematic investigation that crosses disciplines, conceptual issues have now been identified. Although most agree that achieving forgiveness involves an emotional transformation, the nature and consequence of this transformation is open to discussion.

We begin with the widely used definition of forgiveness first offered by McCullough, Worthington, and Rachal (1997). They define forgiveness as:

> a set of motivational changes whereby one becomes (a) decreasingly motivated to retaliate against an offending relationship partner, (b)

> decreasingly motivated to maintain estrangement from the offender, and
> (c) increasingly motivated by conciliation and goodwill for the offender,
> despite the offender's hurtful actions. (p. 323)

As indicated in McCullough et al.'s definition, forgiveness is often linked to the desire to achieve or willingness to work toward reconciliation. However, the question of whether forgiveness can be accomplished apart from reconciliation is a point of discussion in the forgiveness literature. Power (1994) maintains that forgiveness without reconciliation is not complete or true forgiveness. Similarly, Baumeister, Exline, and Sommer (1998) argue that "total forgiveness" includes both an intrapsychic dimension (an emotional attitude based on cognitive appraisals and interpretations) and an interpersonal action between people that returns them to conditions existing before the transgression. According to Baumeister et al., changing one's internal state without communicatively reconstructing the relationship is "silent forgiveness" and reconciling through interpersonal action without a corresponding change in emotional attitude is "hollow forgiveness."

However, other scholars argue that forgiveness and reconciliation should be treated as independent concepts (e.g., Fincham, 2000). At the heart of the independence position is the argument that linking the internal emotional response of forgiveness to reconciliation as a negotiated accomplishment between people distorts the complexity of both processes (e.g., Enright, Freedman, & Rique, 1998; Enright & Zell, 1989). For example, the injured party may fully relinquish negative emotions such as hate, anger, or resentment and even feel positive regard toward the other, but refuse to re-enter the relationship with the offender because trust cannot be restored (Freedman & Enright, 1996). People may also be unwilling or unable to forgive but re-enter the relationship because of perceived obligation (e.g., in order to raise children) or structural constraints (e.g., financial obligations or work assignments).

The issues characterizing these positions on definitions of forgiveness are not easily resolved. As Scobie and Scobie (1998) conclude, the differences would appear to have more to do with "a researcher's attitude toward forgiveness, i.e., which model they use, rather than forgiveness per se" (p. 376). For our purposes, we find utility in both positions. We agree that forgiveness is indeed a psychological transformation during which initial negative emotions are replaced by positive orientations toward the offender (if not the offense) and believe that it can occur independently of relational reconciliation. However, we believe that even when interaction between the offender and offended person does not lead to reconciliation, its content may nonetheless facilitate reconciliation. The efforts by an offender to explain his or her actions and ask for forgiveness create empathy and understanding that in turn facilitate the emotional transformation of forgiveness (Macaskill, Maltby, & Day, 2002). Andrews (2000) refers to this interactive accomplishment as "negotiated" forgiveness and distinguishes it from the more traditional individual level of forgiveness, "unilateral" forgiveness. This view of forgiveness as a psychological state that is influenced by interaction (which may or may not lead to reconciliation) underscores the emergent and dynamic properties of forgiveness and the meaning constructive power of communication.

A second issue apparent in forgiveness research is whether the transformation of negative emotions into more positive orientations toward the offender necessarily entails the complete elimination of all negative affect associated with the offense (McCullough, Hoyt, & Rachal, 2000). As Witvliet, Ludwig, and Vander Laan (2001) argue, "forgiveness still allows for holding the offender responsible for the transgression, and does not involve denying, ignoring, minimizing, tolerating, condoning, excusing or forgetting the offense" (p. 118). In a similar vein, Wade and Worthington (2003) suggest that forgiveness and unforgiveness are not reciprocally related and that "reduced unforgiveness does not imply forgiveness" (p. 344). Using a sample of college students attending a psychoeducational training program designed to induce forgiveness among persons who had been unable to forgive, Wade and Worthington (2003) compared the pattern of predictors for forgiveness and unforgiveness. Despite several similarities in these patterns, the differences were sufficient for the authors to conclude that forgiveness and unforgiveness are two distinguishable responses to interpersonal transgressions. Konstam, Holmes, and Levine (2003) reached a similar conclusion after finding that the correlates of forgiveness (e.g., emotion-focused coping, empathy) and unforgiveness (e.g., selfism) were distinctly different. The following section examines three different predictors of forgiveness (i.e., dispositional factors, offensive severity, and offender remediation attempts) in more detail.

Predictors of Forgiveness

Three domains of interest characterize investigations into factors that might influence the likelihood of forgiving or not forgiving an offense and/or the offender. These include dispositional factors or personality traits of the victim, the seriousness or severity of the offense, and features of the interaction between the offender and the victim following the offense.

Dispositional factors. A number of dispositional factors or personality traits have been found to make certain persons more or less likely to respond to transgressions with forgiveness rather than revenge or retaliation. For example, McCullough, Bellah, Kilpatrick, and Johnson (2001) examined the correlation among vengefulness (a dispositional factor), forgiveness, and the "Big Five" personality traits. They found that vengefulness was negatively correlated with forgiveness, conscientiousness, and agreeableness. In a similar vein, Konstam, Chernoff, and Deveney (2001) examined the relationship between forgiveness and an individual's proneness towards shame, guilt, anger, and empathetic responsiveness (dispositional factors). Results indicated that the guilt-prone style was positively correlated with forgiveness. People experiencing guilt are likely to engage in processes focused on conflict resolution and forgiveness. Furthermore, reduction of anger, ability for empathetic concern, and perspective taking, were all positively correlated with forgiveness, and rumination was negatively related to forgiveness (see also Davis, 1996).

Offensive severity. The seriousness or severity of the offense is a perceptual calculus constructed by the offended person. For example, if a person is late to one meeting, or is rude and demeaning on one occasion, these are hardly noticed. But if a pattern of such behavior emerges over time, any single "next instance" may be perceived to be very serious. Likewise, if a friend forgets a birthday or anniversary it is not likely to be as serious as if a spouse commits the same offense. In a summary of relevant research from psychology, Worthington (1998) lists degree of perceived hurt, degree of perceived intentionality, number of hurts, and objective or subjective nature of the hurt as criteria for offence severity. In a review of transgression research on personal relationships, Metts (1994) concludes that the severity of a transgression is a function of its reoccurrence, its public exposure to the social network, its violation of explicit (rather than implicit) relational rules, and its implication for the integrity and viability of the relationship. These dimensions have their corollaries in the workplace as evidenced by the repetition of offensive behaviors that constitute bullying, the inherent embarrassment in public humiliation in the workplace, the violation of explicit rules of work assignments and salary compensation as well as implicit rules of respect and cooperation, and diminished trust in workplace relationships.

Whatever the specifics of the event, if they combine in such as way as to constitute a severe or serious transgression, accomplishing forgiveness is more difficult. For example, Jones and Burdette (1994) found that across types of transgressions a positive correlation existed between perceived severity of the offense and likelihood that forgiveness is withheld. Subsequent research has supported this finding (e.g., Baumeister et al., 1998; Boon & Sulsky, 1997; Flanigan, 1998). One exception to this effect is reported by Wade and Worthington (2003), who found that severity of offense failed to predict both forgiveness and unforgiveness, at least in their sample of students attending a psychoeducational training program on forgiveness.

Offender remediation attempts. As indicated previously, forgiveness can be accomplished as a unilateral effort without communication between the victim and the offender. However, forgiveness is more easily and more fully accomplished when the offender uses some type of remedial strategy to address both the offense and the victim, usually by expressing regret or remorse and offering some explanation for the offense. By contrast, refusing to address the offense or the victim inhibits and even precludes the possibility of forgiveness.

Regret or remorse is typically found within the communicative action known as apology or concession. For example, as defined by Goffman (1967), a fully developed apology expresses remorse for untoward behavior, promises to avoid behavior of a similar nature in the future, separates the "bad" self from the "good" self as deserving of disdain, promises to make restitution, and makes a request for forgiveness from the victim. Not all apologies are so fully developed, but research indicates that some form of apology is a strong predictor of forgiveness in personal and professional relationships (Metts & Cupach, 1998; Takaku, 2001; Worthington & Wade, 1999). In one of the few studies using both forgiveness and unforgiveness as criterion variables, Wade and Worthington (2003) found that apologies (conceptualized as expressions of contrition) predicted less unforgiveness and more forgiveness. Of course, the effectiveness of apologies as remedial strategies depends on their sincerity, as perceived by the offended person (Darby & Schlenker, 1982; McCullough et al., 1998). An apology that is perceived as false or lacking in conviction loses its effectiveness.

Accounts provide some type of explanation for the offensive action and may be used in conjunction with an apology or in place of an apology. Accounts include justifications and excuses (Scott & Lyman, 1968). Justifications are attempts to reframe the victim's interpretation of the transgression and to reduce its negative connotation. Excuses are attempts to reduce the transgressor's responsibility for the act. Thus, when a transgressor uses justification he or she admits to committing the offense, but attempts to convince the offended partner that the action he or she committed was not really wrong, did not have serious consequences, was somehow justified by the actions of others, or was not as severe as it might appear to be. When a transgressor uses an excuse, he or she accepts the negative interpretation of the event, but denies responsibility by placing blame on others, on unfortunate circumstances, or on his or her inability to control certain behaviors (Scott & Lyman, 1968).

Accounts have been less fully studied in the forgiveness literature than apologies, but there is some evidence that justifications, which take responsibility for the transgression, and/or minimize its significance to the relationship's integrity (but do not minimize its significance to the feelings of the victim), facilitate forgiveness (Aune, Metts, & Ebesu, 1998; Couch, Jones, & Moore, 1999; Jones & Burdette, 1994; Metts, 1994). For minor offenses, excuses that deflect blame to extenuating circumstances also facilitate forgiveness (Couch et al., 1999).

Occasionally, however, persons refuse to provide an offering at all. They make no apology nor provide any account for the problematic event. Refusals, as explained by Schönbach (1980), involve denial by the transgressor that the transgression occurred or that the offended party has a right to challenge him or her. As might be expected, refusals are typically ineffective as a remedial strategy and, in fact, sometimes impede not only forgiveness but also reparation of the relationship (Metts, Morse, & Lamb, 2001; Mongeau, Hale, & Alles, 1994).

Forgiveness In the Workplace

Although books and essays on remediation attempts have proliferated in recent years, careful empirical research linking it to workplace misconduct is rare. One exception is that by Bradfield and Aquino (1999), who examined attributions of blame, offense severity, and offender likableness on forgiveness and revenge among 237 government workers who reported on a time during the past year when a co-worker had offended them. Path analyses indicated that revenge and forgiveness processes were distinct and that the most parsimonious model included the following: (1) cognitions about revenge or forgiveness are related to their behavioral manifestation, (2) blame attributions are influenced by offense severity, (3) blame attributions then influence revenge cognitions, but (4) offender likeableness influences forgiveness cognitions (pp. 624-625).

Summary

If we step back from the information presented to this point and distill the consistent themes, it becomes apparent that professional misconduct in its various forms and its varying degrees of seriousness threatens the quality of the workplace relationship. Forgiveness facilitates repair of relationships between transgressors and offended parties. The restoration of regard and cooperation in the working relationship then reengages the offended person within the work environment and reduces tension among co-workers. Thus, it would appear that forgiveness is uniquely situated between the transgression and the restoration of working relationships and thereby is also central to the restoration of a productive workplace environment.

A number of factors, both dispositional and circumstantial, influence the likelihood that the victim of a workplace transgression will forgive the transgressor. We propose a model focused on three factors that appear to be particularly influential. First, the seriousness of a transgression should be inversely associated with the likelihood of forgiveness. The extent of negative affect felt by offended persons (such as anger, hurt, and resentment) should index transgression severity and the likelihood of seeking revenge against transgressors rather than forgiving them. Second, some individuals are more easily offended by a particular transgression than other individuals. Those with a "thick skin" tend to diminish the perceived seriousness of a transgression, whereas those who are emotionally sensitive may inflate a transgression's severity. We propose, therefore, that the dispositional tendency to be guided by one's emotions will lead one to experience heightened negative affective reactions to an offense. Emotionally sensitive individuals will experience relatively greater degrees of anger and upset, thereby undermining their willingness to forgive a transgressor. Finally, the perceived severity of a transgression should be mitigated somewhat by the remedial actions of a transgressor. When a transgressor attempts to make amends for offensive behavior by providing an apology or account, the blow of the transgression is softened and the victim is more inclined to forgive. In order to test whether this profile is evident in the actual experiences of workplace members, we conducted a study as described below.

An Empirical Investigation of the Movement from Workplace Misconduct to Forgiveness

Respondents and Procedures

Using convenience and snowball sampling techniques, we distributed surveys to a diverse group of individuals with full-time work experience. We solicited participation from workers in various professions and industries, including health care (nursing staff and administration), education (faculty, staff and administration; K-12 and higher education), state government, telemarketing, print media, insurance, banking, transportation, and retail sales and service.

Respondents were given a survey on "transgressions in the workplace." The term transgression, rather than incivility, bullying, or abuse, was used to avoid limiting the types of events that might be recalled and to maintain consistency with the literature on forgiveness. The cover letter included the following description: "Transgressions occur when another person behaves in a way that negatively violates your expectations and personally offends you or hurts your feelings. Events that involve annoying, rude, unfair, malicious, or inappropriate behavior could be considered transgressions." Surveys were anonymous and in most cases returned to the researchers via a postage-paid return envelope included with the survey. In some cases the researchers collected sealed envelopes on site.

Respondents (N = 109) were predominantly female (73%), although the gender of the transgressor was fairly evenly split (53.3% female; 46.7% male). The average age of respondents was 35.6 and ranged from 17 to 64 years. The average age of the transgressor was 40.4 years. The sample largely consisted of White/Non-Hispanics (84.1%), with smaller numbers of Asian/Pacific Islanders (7.5%), American Indian/Alaskan Natives (1.9%), Hispanics (1.9%), Black/ Non-Hispanics (0.9%), and those who marked "Other" (3.7%).

Respondents were asked to provide a detailed open-ended description of a specific transgression committed against them in their workplace. We instructed them to think of an event when a co-worker, subordinate, or supervisor did something (or failed to do something) that offended or hurt them. On average, respondents reported on incidents that occurred 14 weeks prior to completing the questionnaire. When rating the seriousness of the transgression at the time it occurred, 70.4% indicated that it was moderately to extremely serious. The remainder rated the transgression they described as not at all serious or mildly serious. For 15.9% of the transgressions, respondents reported that they were in a position of greater workplace authority than the transgressor at the time of the transgression, whereas 57.9% reported that the transgressor was in a position of greater workplace authority. Respondents indicated that they and the transgressor had about the same amount of workplace authority for 26.2% of the transgressions.

Measures

Affective orientation. Respondents completed the Affective Orientation Scale developed by Booth-Butterfield and Booth-Butterfield (1990, 1994) to measure an individual's dispositional tendency to be aware of internal emotional cues and use them to guide interaction with others. The instrument consists of 20 seven-point Likert items (e.g., "I trust my feelings to guide my behavior," "I am very aware of my feelings," "Feelings only interfere with behavior" [reverse scored]). As in prior studies, the items exhibited good internal consistency (α = .88).

Feelings after the transgression. Respondents were asked to indicate the extent (1 = Not at all, 7 = Very much so) to which they experienced each of 15 emotions immediately after the transgression.

Factor analysis indicated that the emotion items clustered into three interpretable variables. Four items defined a factor representing *anger* (angry, outraged, resentful, and frustrated; α = .78) and five items defined a factor representing *hurt* (surprised, hurt, sad, betrayed, humiliated; α = .76). The third factor contained three items and was labeled *insecurity* (insecure, depressed, lonely; α = .83).

Transgressor's remedial behavior. Respondents indicated on 14 items the extent (1 = Not at all, 7 = Very much so) to which the transgressor engaged in behaviors subsequent to the transgression that did or did not attempt to repair the situation. Factor analysis yielded three factors. *Apology* consisted of behaviors by the transgressor that accepted responsibility and attempted to redress the respondent's loss of face ("apologized," "tried to repair the damage," "showed remorse," "accepted the blame for the transgression," "felt guilty," "promised that it would never happen again," "explained the extenuating circumstances;" α = .91). *Refusal* included items that depicted the transgressor denying the event or responsibility for it ("denied s/he committed a transgression," "tried to make the transgression seem less important than it was," "said that I was partially responsible for what happened," "denied responsibility for his/her actions," "downplayed how hurtful to me the transgression was;" α = .78. The third factor, *avoidance*, included two items ("just ignored me," "refused to talk about it;" α = .84).

Forgiveness. Forgiveness of the transgressor was assessed with 16 seven-point Likert-type items (e.g., "I wish this person well," "I seek revenge against this person" [reverse scored], "I forgive this person"). Some of the items were adapted from McCullough, Worthington, & Rachal (1997), and others were constructed for this investigation. Items were keyed so that higher scores represented greater degrees of forgiveness. The combined items demonstrated good internal consistency (α = .93).

Damage to the working relationship. Two items were designed to assess the extent to which the transgression caused damage to the working relationship between the transgressor and the respondent. Using a five-point scale (1 = No damage to 5 = Severe damage), respondents indicated the extent of damage at the time of the transgression, and the extent to which there is now lingering damage. Because these two items were substantially correlated, they were combined to create a single variable measuring damage (α = .79).

Results

The descriptions of the workplace transgressions provided by respondents were coded according to the content of the transgression. Initial coding was done by the first author and checked by the third author. There were very few disagreements and these were resolved through discussion. A description of the categories and examples is provided in the Appendix.

Overall, the nature of the transgressions reported by our respondents is comparable to the categories of incivility and bullying found in the literature. As indicated in Table 1, instances of profess-

Table 1
Transgression Frequencies and Percentages

Transgression	Frequency	Percent
Professional Misconduct	**36**	**39.9**
Poor Job Performance	20	22.2
Disconfirmation of Professional Competence	12	13.3
Inappropriate Response to Feedback	4	4.4
Interpersonal/Social Misconduct	**54**	**60.1**
Rude, Disrespectful, Unprofessional, or Belittling Communication	23	25.6
Chastised, Criticized, or Accused Unfairly, Excessively, or Publicly	13	14.4
Offensive Language/Sexual Harassment	4	4.4
Violations of Trust	14	15.6
Total	90	100.0
Missing/Uncodable	19	17.4

Note: Percentages are based on the 90 descriptions which were coded.

ional misconduct were relatively less frequent for this sample (approximately 40%) than instances of interpersonal or social misconduct (approximately 60%). However, it is interesting to note that almost half of all the transgressions can be accounted for by two specific categories: poor job performance (22.2%) and rude, disrespectful, belittling interpersonal communication (25.6%). The relative importance of these two categories no doubt reflects the systemic and interdependent nature of workplace relationships. That is, organizational goals are more efficiently accomplished when everyone meets his or her responsibility and coordinated responsibility is more likely when communication is constructive rather than destructive.

Table 2 presents the zero-order correlations of our predictor variables with the outcomes of forgiveness and damage to the working relationship. Virtually all variables correlate as expected, with the exception that affective orientation was not significantly associated with damage to the working relationship.

Table 2
Correlations of Affective Orientation, Emotions, Remedial Responses, and Seriousness with Forgiveness and Damage to the Working Relationship

	Forgiveness	Relational Damage
Affective Orientation	-.23*	.12
Angry	-.55**	.53**
Hurt	-.27**	.30**
Insecure	-.25**	.23*
Apology	.37**	-.25*
Refusal	-.39**	.34**
Seriousness of Transgression	-.44**	.47**

*p<.05, **p<.01 (two tailed)

Predicting forgiveness. To provide a formal test of our model of predictors of forgiveness, we performed hierarchical multiple regression analysis. Following a theoretical causal ordering, predictors were entered in the equation in three steps. In step 1 we entered the dispositional measure of affective orientation. Step 2 included variables assessing negative emotions felt at the time of the transgression, specifically angry, hurt, and insecure. Finally we entered the redressive action variables: apology, refusal and avoidance.

As shown in Table 3, each of the three blocks of variables demonstrated a significant increment in the variance of forgiveness explained, thus supporting our model. The final equation including all predictors accounted for approximately 48% of the variance in forgiveness ($F = 13.50$, $df = 7/101$, $p < .001$). Affective orientation and feelings of anger were associated with less forgiveness, and apology was associated with more forgiveness.

Table 3

Hierarchical Multiple Regression of Forgiveness on Affective Orientation, Emotions, and Remedial Responses

Predictors	β	R	$R^2\Delta$	$F\Delta$
Step 1		.228	.052	5.85*
Affective Orientation	-.228*			
Step 2		.564	.266	13.53***
Affective Orientation	-.098			
Angry	-.470***			
Hurt	-.035			
Insecure	-.136			
Step 3		.695	.165	10.77***
Affective Orientation	-.168			
Angry	-.319***			
Hurt	-.042			
Insecure	-.168			
Apology	.291***			
Refusal	-.101			
Avoidance	-.170			

*p<.05, ***p<.001

Predicting damage to the workplace relationship. To predict damage to the working relationship, we adopted a hierarchical regression model similar to the one used to predict forgiveness. Affective orientation, emotions at the time of the transgression, and the transgressor's remedial behavior were entered in successive blocks. In addition, we entered forgiveness into the equation in a fourth and final step. We anticipated that greater forgiveness would predict less relational damage, even after controlling for the other variables in the model.

Table 4
*Hierarchical Multiple Regression of Damage to the Working
Relationship on Affective Orientation, Emotions,
Remedial Responses, and Forgiveness*

Predictors	β	R	R²Δ	FΔ
Step I		.121	.015	1.60
Affective Orientation	.121			
Step 2		.543	.281	13.81***
Affective Orientation	-.008			
Angry	.482***			
Hurt	.076			
Insecure	.091			
Step 3		.600	.064	3.38*
Affective Orientation	-.009			
Angry	.414***			
Hurt	.090			
Insecure	.115			
Apology	-.188*			
Refusal	.191			
Avoidance	-.064			
Step 4		.735	.180	39.22***
Affective Orientation	-.108			
Angry	.225**			
Hurt	.065			
Insecure	.016			
Apology	-.015			
Refusal	.131			
Avoidance	-.164			
Forgiveness	-.591***			

*p<.05, **p<.01, ***p<.001

Table 4 shows the predictors of workplace relationship damage. Three of the four blocks of variables demonstrated a significant increment in the variance of forgiveness explained, thus largely supporting our model. The final equation including all predictors accounted for approximately 54% of the variance in damage to the workplace relationship (F = 14.67, df = 8/100, p < .001). Affective orientation was not significantly associated with relationship damage. However, the significant predictors of workplace damage paralleled the predictors of forgiveness. Respondent anger was associated with greater damage to the workplace relationship, and the transgressor's apology was associated with less damage to the relationship. In addition, forgiveness made a substantial unique contribution to predicting damage to the relationship, even when controlling for all the other variables in the equation. Forgiveness mitigated relationship damage, as expected.

Interestingly, the transgressor's apology becomes nonsignificant in the equation after including forgiveness as a predictor. This suggests that forgiveness mediates the association between apology and relationship damage. To test this further, we computed hierarchical regressions with apology and forgiveness only as predictors of relationship damage. When apology was entered first in the equation, forgiveness still made a substantial contribution in predicting damage ($R^2\Delta$ = .422, p < .001). However, when forgiveness was entered into the equation first, apology failed to make a significant contribution ($R^2\Delta$ = .000). Thus, forgiveness completely mediated the association between apology and damage to the workplace relationship.

We also found evidence that forgiveness mediates the association between perceived seriousness of the transgression and relationship damage. When seriousness was entered first in a hierarchical regression, forgiveness still made a substantial contribution in predicting relationship damage ($R^2\Delta$ = .288, p < .001). However, when forgiveness was entered first, seriousness made a small contribution in predicting relationship damage ($R^2\Delta$ = .020, p < .05). Thus, forgiveness mediates most of the association between seriousness of the transgression and damage to the workplace relationship.

Summary and Closing Comments

This chapter was motivated by what we see as a pressing need in the popular and scholarly literature to understand the role of forgiveness in the dynamics of workplace misconduct. At present, much attention in the popular press is given to strategies for coping with incivility and bullying behaviors, but seldom does forgiveness show up on these lists. Similarly, in the scholarly research, much attention is given to predictors and consequences of revenge and retaliation, but the option to forgive has to be provided by the more astute and experienced respondents. Based on the substantial evidence in the forgiveness literature that forgiveness heals—people, relationships, social networks, and the environment that surrounds them—its omission from the workplace misconduct dialogue is remarkable.

In order to understand more fully the link between workplace misconduct and forgiveness, we tested a model derived from both domains of interest. Our results were consistent with our expectations. Emotionally responsive individuals (measured as Affective Orientation) and those who experienced greater anger following the incident reported feeling less forgiveness. However, those who received an apology from the offender experienced greater forgiveness. And, as expected, forgiveness was associated with less damage to the workplace relationship. Perhaps more important, when examining effects on the workplace relationship, forgiveness emerged as a mediating variable. That is, an apology from the offender was associated with less relational damage, but its effect was indirect through its contribution to forgiveness. Likewise, the seriousness of the offense contributed to relational damage but only through its negative association with forgiveness.

In sum, our findings suggest that the organizational costs of workplace misconduct such as time lost from the job, employee turnover, low productivity and the like cannot be addressed without considering the restoration of workplace relationships. And the key to restoring cooperative and respectful work relationships is the willingness of an offended person to grant forgiveness, not with conditions and lingering resentment, but with sincerely felt positive regard.

References

Allcorn, S. (1994). *Anger in the workplace: Understanding the causes of aggression and violence.* Westport, CT: Quorum Books.

Andersson, L. M. & Pearson, C.M. (1999). Tit for tat? The spiraling effect of incivility in the workplace. *Academy of Management Review, 24,* 452-471.

Andrews, M. (2000). Forgiveness in context. *Journal of Moral Education, 29,* 75-86.

Aquino, K., Grover, S., Goldman, B., & Folger, R. (2003). When push doesn't come to shove Interpersonal forgiveness in workplace relationships. *Journal of Management Inquiry, 12,* 209-217.

Aune, R. K., Metts, S., & Ebesu, A. S. (1998). Managing the outcomes of discovered deception. *Journal of Social Psychology, 138,* 677-690.

Bassman, E. S. (1992). *Abuse in the workplace: Management remedies and bottom line impact.* Westport, CT: Quorum Books.

Baumeister, R. F., Exline, J. J., & Sommer K. L. (1998). The victim role, grudge theory, and two dimensions of forgiveness. In E. L. Worthington (Ed.), *Dimensions of forgiveness: Psychological research and theological perspectives* (pp. 79-104). Philadelphia: Templeton Foundation Press.

Beale, D. (2001). Monitoring bullying in the workplace. In N. Tehrani (Ed.), *Building a culture of respect: Managing bullying at work* (pp. 77-94). New York: Taylor & Francis.

Bies, R. J., & Tripp, T. M. (1995). Beyond distrust: "Getting even" and the need for revenge. In R. M. Kramer & T. R. Tyler (Eds.), *Trust in organizations* (pp. 246-260). Newbury Park, CA: Sage.

Boon, S. D., & Sulsky, L. M. (1997). Attributions of blame and forgiveness in romantic relationships: A policy capturing study. *Journal of Social Behavior and Personality, 12,* 19-44.

Booth-Butterfield, M., & Booth-Butterfield, S. (1990). Conceptualizing affect as information in communication production. *Human Communication Research, 16,* 451-476.

Booth-Butterfield, M., & Booth-Butterfield, S. (1994). The affective orientation to communication: Conceptual and empirical distinctions. *Communication Quarterly, 42,* 331-344.

Bradfield, M., & Aquino, K. (1999). The effects of blame attributions and offender likableness on forgiveness and revenge in the workplace. *Journal of Management, 25,* 607-631.

Crino, M. D. (1994). Employee sabotage: A random or preventable phenomenon? *Journal of Managerial Issues, 6,* 311-330.

Couch, L. L., Jones, W. H., & Moore, D. S. (1999). Buffering the effects of betrayal: The role of apology, forgiveness, and commitment. In J. M. Adams & W. H. Jones (Eds.), *Handbook of interpersonal commitment and relationship stability* (pp. 451-469). New York: Kluwer Academic/Plenum Publishers.

Darby, B. W., & Schlenker, B. R. (1982). Children's reactions to apologies. *Journal of Personality and social Psychology, 43,* 742-753.

Davis, M. H. (1996). *Empathy: A social psychological approach.* Boulder, CO: Westview Press.

Enright, R. D. (1996). Counseling within the forgiveness triad: On forgiving, receiving forgiveness, and self-forgiveness. *Counseling and Values, 40,* 107-127.

Enright, R. D. (2001). *Forgiveness is a choice: A step-by-step process for resolving anger and restoring hope.* Washington, DC: APA LifeTools.

Enright, R. D., Freedman, S., & Rique, J. (1998). The psychology of interpersonal forgiveness. In R. D. Enright & J. North (Eds.), *Exploring forgiveness* (pp. 46-62). Madison: University of Wisconsin Press.

Enright, R. D., & Zell, R. (1989). Problems encountered when we forgive one another. *Journal of Psychology and Christianity, 8,* 52-60.

Exline, J. J., & Baumeister, R. F. (2000). Expressing forgiveness and repentance: Benefits and barriers. In M. E. McCullough, K. I. Pargament, & C. E. Thoresen (Eds.), *Forgiveness: Theory, research, and practice* (pp. 133-155). New York: Guilford.

Fincham, F. D. (2000). The kiss of the porcupines: From attributing responsibility to forgiving. *Personal Relationships, 7,* 1-23.

Flanigan, B. (1998). Forgivers and the unforgivable. In R. D. Enright & J. North (Eds.), *Exploring forgiveness* (pp. 95-105). Madison: University of Wisconsin Press.

Freedman, S. R., & Enright, R. D. (1996). Forgiveness as an intervention with incest survivors. *Journal of Consulting and Clinical Psychology, 64,* 983-992.

Goffman, E. (1967). *Interaction ritual.* Garden City, NY: Doubleday Anchor Books.

Gorsuch, R. L., (1988). Psychology of religion. *Annual Review of Psychology, 39,* 201-221.

Hebl, J. H., & Enright, R. D. (1993). Forgiveness as a psychotherapeutic goal with elderly females. *Psychotherapy, 30,* 658-667.

Hoel, H. H., & Cooper, C. L. (2001). Origins of bullying: Theoretical frameworks for explaining workplace bullying. In N. Tehrani (Ed.), *Building a culture of respect: Managing bullying at work* (pp. 3-19). New York: Taylor & Francis.

Incivility in the workplace. (2000). *Worklife Report, 13,* 10.

Johnson, P. R., & Indvik, J. (2001). Rudeness at work: Impulse over restraint. *Public Personnel Management, 30,* 457-465.

Jones, W. H., & Burdette, M. P. (1994). Betrayal in close relationships. In A. L. Weber & J. Harvey (Eds.), *Perspectives on close relationships* (pp. 243-262). New York: Allyn & Bacon.

Konstam, V., Chernoff, M., & Deveney, S. (2001). Toward forgiveness: The role of shame, guilt, anger, and empathy. *Counseling and Values, 46,* 26-39.

Konstam, V., Holmes, W. & Levine, B. (2003). Empathy, selfism, and coping as elements of the psychology of forgiveness: a preliminary study. *Counseling and Values, 47,* 172-184.

Kurzynski, M. J. (1998). The virtue of forgiveness as a human resource management strategy. *Journal of Business Ethics, 17,* 77-85.

Lewicki, R. J., & Bunker, B. B. (1996). Developing and maintaining trust in work relationships. In R. M. Kramer & T. R. Tyler (Eds.), *Trust in organizations* (pp. 114-139). Newbury Park, CA: Sage.

Macaskill, A., Maltby, J., & Day, L. (2002). Forgiveness of self and others and emotional empathy. *Journal of Social Psychology, 142,* 663-665.

McCullough, M. E., Bellah, C. G., Kilpatrick, S. D., & Johnson, J. L. (2001). Vengefulness: Relationships with forgiveness, rumination, well-being, and the big five. *Personality and Social Psychology Bulletin, 27,* 601-610.

McCullough, M. E., Hoyt, W. T., & Rachal, K. C. (2000). What we know (and need to know) about assessing forgiveness constructs. In M. E. McCullough, K. I. Pargament, & C. E. Thoresen (Eds.), *Forgiveness: Theory, Research, and Practice* (pp. 65-88). New York: Guilford.

McCullough, M. E., Rachal, K. C., Sandage, S. J., Worthington, E. L, Jr., Brown, S. W., & Hight, T. L. (1998). Interpersonal forgiving in close relationships II: Theoretical elaboration and measurement. *Journal of Personality and Social Psychology, 75*, 1586-1603.

McCullough, M. E., Sandage, S. J., & Worthington, E. L. Jr. (1997). To forgive is human. Downers Grove, IL: InterVarsity Press.

McCullough, M. E., Worthington, E. L., Jr., & Rachal, K. C., (1997). Interpersonal forgiving in close relationships. *Journal of Personality and Social Psychology, 73*, 321-336.

Metts, S. (1994). Relational transgressions. In W. R. Cupach & B. Spitzberg (Eds.), *The dark side of interpersonal communication* (pp. 217-240). Hillsdale, NJ: Erlbaum.

Metts, S., & Cupach, W. R. (1998, June). *Predictors of forgiveness following a relational transgression.* Paper presented at the Ninth International Conference on Personal Relationships, Saratoga Springs, NY.

Metts, S., Morse, C., & Lamb, E. (2001, November). *The influence of relational history on the management and outcomes of relational transgressions.* Paper presented at the National Communication Association Convention, Atlanta, GA.

Mongeau, P. A., Hale, J. L., & Alles, M. (1994). An experimental investigation of accounts and attributions following sexual infidelity. *Communication Monographs, 61*, 326-344.

Newberg, A. B., d'Aquili, E.G., Newberg, S. K., & deMarici, V. (2000). The neuropsychological correlates of forgiveness. In M. E. McCullough, K. I. Pargament, & C. E. Thoresen (Eds.), *Forgiveness: Theory, research, and practice* (pp. 91-110). New York: Guilford.

Pearson, C. M. (1999). Tales of the uncivil workplace. *Training, 36* (7), 26-28.

Pearson, C.M., Andersson, L.M., & Wegner, J.W. (2001). When workers flout convention: A study of workplace incivility. *Human Relations, 54*, 1387-1419.

Peyton, P. R. (2003). *Dignity at work: Eliminate bullying and create a positive working environment.* New York: Brunner-Routledge.

Power, F. C. (1994). Commentary. *Human Development, 37*, 81-85.

Quine, L. (1999). Workplace bullying in an NHS trust. *British Medical Journal, 318*, 228-232.

Rayner, C. & Hoel, H. (1997). A summary review of literature relating to workplace bullying. *Journal of Community and Applied Social Psychology, 7*, 181-191.

Rayner, C., Hoel, H., & Cooper, C. L. (2002). *Workplace bullying: what we know, who is to blame, and what can we do?* New York: Taylor & Francis.

Schönbach, P. (1980). A category system for account phases. *European Journal of Social Psychology, 10*, 195-200.

Scobie, E. D., & Scobie, G. E. W. (1998). Damaging events: The perceived need for forgiveness. *Journal for the Theory of Social Behaviour, 28*, 373-403.

Scott, M. B., & Lyman, S. M. (1968). Accounts. *American Psychological Review, 33*, 46-62.

Smedes, L. B. (1996). *The art of forgiving: When you need to forgive and don't know how.* New York: Ballantine Books.

Stone, M. (2002). Forgiveness in the workplace. *Industrial & Commercial Training, 34,* 278-287.

Takaku, S. (2001). The effects of apology and perspective taking on interpersonal forgiveness: A dissonance-attribution model of interpersonal forgiveness. *Journal of Social Psychology, 141,* 494-509.

Wade, N. G., & Worthington, E. L. (2003). Overcoming interpersonal offenses: Is forgiveness the only way to deal with unforgiveness? *Journal of Counseling and Development, 81,* 343-353.

Witvliet, C. V. Ludwig, T. E., & Vander Laan, K. L. (2001). Granting forgiveness or harboring grudges: Implications for emotion, physiology, and health. *Psychological Science, 12,* 117-123.

Worthington, E. L. Jr. (1998). The Pyramid Model of forgiveness: Some interdisciplinary speculations about unforgiveness and the promotion of forgiveness. In E. L. Worthington (Ed.), *Dimensions of forgiveness: Psychological research and theological perspectives* (pp. 107-137). Philadelphia: Templeton Foundation Press.

Worthington, E. L., & Wade, N. G. (1999). The social psychology of unforgiveness and forgiveness and implications for clinical practice. *Journal of Social and Clinical Psychology, 18,* 385-418.

Appendix
Transgression Categories

Professional Misconduct

Behaviors, actions, and/or attitudes that reflect disregard for expectations related to job performance

1. Poor Job Performance

Supervisor, subordinate, or colleague is not performing tasks efficiently or appropriately. Includes dysfunctional management practices as well as other types of misconduct such as sharing duties and cooperating to get tasks or projects done.

> *An employee failed to complete a specifically assigned task. The employee was reprimanded numerous times of the task and even asked if it was completed or would there be a problem completing it. The employee stated, "no problem" –"I'll take care of it." Then at the time the task needed to be done—it wasn't! When the employee was asked again, they just stated; sorry I couldn't do it. By this time, it was too late for me to fix or complete the task myself. Frustrating.*

> *My boss would not address an issue that was happening to me. Every time it would happen I would let him know and he would do nothing or very little.*

2. Disconfirmation of Professional Competence/Performance or Authority

Lack of respect for or disconfirmation of professional skills, ability, knowledge, credibility, or authority.

> *I was the network technician on call. My supervisor told the help desk to call one of my co-workers instead of me if there was a problem.*

> *We were on a geo. sci. field trip. It's a driving trip, and I am a flagger to make sure everyone turns at the right place. I dance around, yell and wave my flags in an exaggerated manner because the kids in the cars think it's funny; they laugh and wave as they go by. During one of the stops, one of my fellow workers came up to me to say that one of the attendees complimented my flagging. I said thanks and jokingly asked the fellow worker to repeat that in front of <u>another</u> of our fellow workers who had voiced the opinion that I was making fool of myself by flagging the way I do. The person I was talking to at the moment then stated that he was in agreement with this other worker who said I was a fool. The person I was talking to is important to me so even though another worker had said the same thing, this hurt more.*

3. Inappropriate Response to Feedback

Excessive, belligerent, defensive, rude, unprofessional or otherwise inappropriate reactions to feedback regarding tasks, coordination, ideas, or suggestions for improvement. Inability to relinquish control when appropriate.

> Attempting to plan a discharge for a patient, I had plans in place; another nurse had some "better" ideas and therefore made efforts to implement those. As a result, the pt. and those who were involved in the plan became confused and upset. When I discover what had happened, I confronted the person to try and converge the ideas— however the nurse became upset with me—began yelling at me that I did not respect his judgment. I told him that I would not discuss it there. Later we resumed the conversation in a private location.

> My manager feels like she has supreme authority over the organization of the backroom. I feel she sometimes makes bad decisions. I tried to point out a more organized sensical choice for backroom management and she refuses to listen. I then told her she was not listening and she responded angrily.

Interpersonal/Social Misconduct

Not concerned explicitly with job performance, although because the context is the workplace, there are always implications for professional conduct. This category is similar to what most scholars mean by the term "workplace incivility" and places emphasis on interaction practices.

4. Rude, Disrespectful, Unprofessional, or Belittling Communication

Heart of the offense is not so much on criticizing job skills or performance, but attacking or criticizing personal character, competence, attitude, or behavior through rudeness, sarcasm, or confrontation. These messages are excessive and/or unnecessary. Often a typical style of the offender, but sometimes unique to the dyad or situation.

> My supervisor was concerned about meeting a deadline. She needed my work and my fellow officemates' work to meet that deadline. While informing us of the importance of our part in this, her tone was threatening and demanding. She cursed at us. This was the first in my 20+ years experience on my job where a supervisor has had this tone and used that kind of language. I have always performed professionally and been treated professionally so the whole experience was upsetting and shocking.

> I asked a co-worker a question and the response was not to answer since the co-worker said, "Why ask me something when my answer will probably be in contradiction to your response."

I was complaining about more new changes in the workplace, just kind of kidding around and she took it seriously and said, "Oh! Drop the attitude" in a very non-playful manner.

5. Chastised, Criticized, or Accused Unfairly, Excessively, or Publicly

These offenses seem to cluster around the circumstances of the criticism rather than its content. The reprimands are excessive, unfair, ungrounded, or done publicly in a way that has implications for one's professional reputation.

I was blamed for an incident that I had no control over in front of my co-workers by a supervisor.

My current boss tends to use condescending and unflattering remarks to prove himself right. This tends to happen more often corresponding to the "higher" level of audience that is present. During this particular instance I was reporting some controversial information that did not put my company in the most positive light. During my report, which I did not present as negative nor did it point fingers, my boss interrupted me and said that none of it was true and I had not done my research. Regardless of who is right and wrong about the business aspect, his approach to disagreeing with me was not one that I appreciated.

The assistant vice president reacted negatively to an email of mine. I had been asked to give feedback about a new structure change. Because I was on the road I sent the feedback as an email. Unfortunately all the comments from those on my team who gave me feedback were negative. The AVP saw it as my being negative despite a disclaimer. I was chastised in writing with all of management copied. I was then "counseled" by my new boss about the email and my negative attitude. The email has been circulated around the entire department of 300.

6. Offensive Language/Sexual Harassment

Profane or sexually suggestive language that is inappropriate to the workplace.

I recently went on vacation that included an opportunity to swim with a dolphin. Someone else asked how my vacation was. When I was answering the transgressor interrupted me with a "joke" in poor taste about sexually inappropriate behaviors with the dolphin. She repeated this "joke" several times over 2 days whenever she had a different audience.

This person, to whom I was a subordinate (and we are opposite sex from one another) on numerous occasions made sexual comments very inappropriate for the relationships such as: 'You can share my room" (when going to the same conference), "Why don't you become a mistress," "I've got extra room in my bed."

7. Violations of Trust Stemming From Manipulative or Deceptive Communication

These are instances where communication is used to deceive another person explicitly or by omission, is conducted "behind employees back," where employees are left out of the information loop, and where employees' privacy is somehow violated.

> *A co-worker lied to my boss about a shift at work. He told my boss I could work it when I told the co-worker twice that I could not work it.*

> *The transgressor had apparently talked about a certain encounter between he and I with another co-worker but had never said anything to me directly. I heard what he had said from our co-worker. When confronted, he flipped out, used a few choice phrases, and hung up the phone.*

> *I went to an internal web-site and found my name listed as the "back-up" for 3 co-workers whom I had no idea that I was backing them up on. This was a result of losing one employee in our unit, however I was not told I would be the back-up, nor was it explained to me what that responsibility entailed.*

13 | Towards Effective Work Relationships

Becky L. Omdahl

The preceding chapters present a challenging picture of problematic relationships in the workplace. The difficult images may be attributed to social discourse and complex roles (Duck, Foley & Kirkpatrick), types of problematic others (Fritz), gendered workplace processes (Liu & Buzzanell), deteriorating friendships (Sias), or events which are perceived as turning points in work relationships (Hess, Omdahl, & Fritz).

The costs of problematic work relationships are daunting. Stress, burnout, impaired mental health (Omdahl & Fritz), reduced job satisfaction, diminished organizational commitment, workplace cynicism (Fritz & Omdahl), emotional demands (Kramer & Tan), distress and jeopardized well being (Kinney) may await those working with difficult others.

Consistent with the admonitions of those addressing conflict over the centuries, the ultimate impact of challenging and even disturbing images may be less dependent on the pictures themselves than on the responses people have to them. The final chapters of this volume have explored distancing, professional civility, and forgiveness as ways to effectively manage problematic relationships in the workplace. In this concluding chapter, the focus is on how to work with difficult others in ways that maximize the potential for growth and well-being and minimize the chances of deleterious fallout.

These days, I spend considerable time reflecting on how people respond to problematic work relationships. My current roles as Faculty President, consultant for the Mayo Hospital and Clinic, and mediation trainer for the Minnesota State Bar Association provide a complex backdrop for pondering both the destructive and constructive ways people manage difficult relationships in the workplace.

While there are numerous lay books published on working with difficult people (e.g., Cava, 2004; Gill, 1999; Lilley, 2002; Lubit, 2003; Osbourne, 2002; Shepard, 2005; Solomon, 2002), there is virtually no systematic research behind the recommendations they offer. While some scholars advocate applying strategies derived from personal relationship research in business settings, scholars have pointed out clear differences among types of relationships. For example, Waldron (2003) points out that work relationships in contrast with personal relationships have different power structures, relationships forms, networks, task characteristics, and formal rules/procedural structure. If the goal is making recommendations based on organization research, the findings and assertions of the authors in this volume are an excellent foundation. Therefore, this chapter explores recommendations implicit in earlier chapters.

Principle #1: Cultivate Expectations for Professional Civility in the Public Sphere

As Arnett (this volume) pointed out, one of the best ways to minimize problematic relationships in the workplace is to hold reasonable expectations about what people owe one another in organizations. If one accepts that public sphere institutions exist to accomplish missions, and that roles of individuals within those institutions contribute to the mission, the rationale for professional civility becomes apparent. Professional civility facilitates momentum toward accomplishing the mission by minimizing non-mission focused demands.

Imagine a colleague arriving at work telling a long, emotionally-draining tale about a personal relationship. Contrast it with another colleague, who warmly greets colleagues, shares a short, uplifting story about an enjoyable experience, and gets on about the day's work. Needless to say, the second colleague has done a better job of moving self and others toward work. Later that day when support staff has failed to call the copier repair person, imagine that the first colleague throws a fit, publicly shaming the support staff. The second colleague stops by the desk of the support staff and offers a face-saving reminder. In doing so, it is highly likely that the second colleague has enabled resolution of the problem without compounding the problem with unnecessary emotional distress.

While the behaviors of the second colleague looks appealing, on a conceptual level, two concerns emerge in discussions about professional civility. The first is whether close relationships are discouraged in the workplace, and the second is whether professional civility is a tool of oppression.

Professional Civility and Relational Closeness

Emphasis on the "public sphere" seems to suggest that everyone should behave in impersonal roles. Research suggests that employees vary in their expectations of workplace relationships. People with a communal orientation often desire work relationships to be egalitarian friendships while those with agentic orientation focus on tasks accomplished through work relationships (Morfei, Hooker, Carpenter, Mix & Blakeley, 2004). Those with a communal orientation value often strive to exhibit more friendship behaviors (self disclosures, demonstrations of concern, etc.) than people holding an agentic orientation.

Do communal employees need to sacrifice friendships if the workspace is treated as a public sphere? No. However, professional civility in the workplace does require: 1) honoring the wishes of many people to have purely professional relationships at work; 2) respecting that people in work relationships should not be expected to expend energy engaging on friendship behaviors (e.g., listening to personal stories, asking questions about personal life); and 3) maintaining fair and impartial treatment of others in assigning work, and granting promotions, resources, attention, etc. While having friends at work can be a wonderful side benefit, professional civility presumes that people should be able to have task-focused relationships with the confidence of fair and respectful treatment.

Sias (this volume) pointed out additional considerations about friendship in the workplace. They often deteriorate and when they do, the deterioration poses four consequences: lessons about relationships; emotion and stress; impact on other organizational members; and learning how to better manage workplace relationships. In addition, Sias explained that people disengage from the deteriorating friendships using: 1) cost escalation in the form of increasingly negative behavior toward the other; 2) depersonalization using such behaviors as avoiding non-work topics of conversation and ending socialization after work; or 3) having a state of the relationship talk in which the relationship transformation is directly discussed. Sias and Perry (2004) found a clear preference for depersonalization, and they argued that it may be particularly effective for friendship deterioration at work because it removes "personalistic focus" while continuing the relationship at a functional level. Cost escalation is the least likely tactic for disengaging from a coworker relationship, perhaps because this strategy would pose the greatest challenge to politeness (see Brown and Levinson, 1987) and face concerns (see Goffman, 1967).

The research of Sias (this volume) and colleagues in conjunction with emphasis on professional civility leads to two recommendations: 1) before developing friendships at work, contemplate the potential costs of deterioration and commit to a professional transition (especially if self or potential friends are likely candidates for advancement); and 2) in the event a transition ensues, recognize that the strategy of depersonalization offers a path of professional civility in a public sphere. It pulls the relationship back to the professional and enables task effectiveness to continue. This is likely to maximally benefit self, others, and the organization.

Looking at work relationships more broadly than friendships, research by Hess (this volume) answers the question: how do we maintain an appropriate level of intimacy by employing distancing strategies? Research revealed that people reported using the following distancing strategies more in the workplace than in personal relationships: behaving according to social norms; seeing no association between self and other; opting for less immediate channels; describing other and self as separate; avoiding questioning the other; excluding the other; ignoring the other; impersonally treating the other; seeing the other as less than human; avoiding eye contact or touch; avoiding intimate conversation or jokes; ignoring thoughts or feelings of the other; and engaging in surface politeness. Only one distancing tactic (i.e., deceiving the partner about personal information) was reportedly used more often in personal than workplace relationships. In theorizing about when and how people employ distancing as a means of dealing with problematic coworkers, Hess (this volume) proposed a model explaining the role of distancing strategies in regulating the intimacy of relationships. Although Hess began his research by looking at the implementation of distancing strategies in relationships with disliked others, his new theorizing suggests that the use of distancing strategies may be the mechanism that regulates closeness in all workplace relationships. Consistent with earlier findings, given that work is a public sphere in which relationships are maintained to accomplish mission-linked tasks, people may implement more distancing strategies at work than in private relationships. It is clear that some distancing strategies (e.g., behaving according to social norms, avoiding intimate conversations or jokes) foster a greater level of professional civility than others (e.g., seeing the other as less than human), and that these would be better choices when distancing is needed.

Professional Civility and Emancipation

The second concern often voiced in discussions about professional civility in the workplace is whether the mission of the organization should be the highest order calling. Specifically, is emancipation or social justice a higher order calling? This issue often emerges as a subtext in discussions about the definition of professional civility. Is professional civility genuine respect or is it polite behavior? If it is genuine respect, then arguably it calls for inclusiveness and emancipation. If it is polite behavior, concerns are raised about whether "professional civility" is just another rhetorically wielded tool through which those with power command the respectful submission of the oppressed.

I regularly ask students in a large lecture what professional civility means. Invariably, students of color, disabled students, women, GLBT individuals, and the youngest and oldest students are the majority of those raising questions about "authentic respect." It is easy for those with power to say that those without power should politely discuss their concerns within the context of the mission. The question from those systematically denied power is, "What if we have diligently done that and continue to be denied opportunities to make real contributions to the mission?"

In a classroom discussion of bell hooks's book, *killing rage*, an African American student reported, "Just last week in a store, I'd gone up to the counter for help and the sales clerk was assisting someone else. She saw me, and I said, 'When you finish, could you help me find a certain size?' She nodded and said she'd be right over. When she stepped out from behind the counter, she saw some well-dressed, white woman walking into the department and helped her first. When she finally came up to me, I was seething but I forced myself to be polite. Looking back, I feel like my politeness just rewarded that clerk." We all understood that it was not that one clerk on that one day that made her seeth, it was the system whispering louder and louder at each dismissal "you're less than." Similar messages from colleagues and bosses who see hard work and fail to honor it as they would for others raise the volume of the taunt.

Advocates of professional civility who understand and oppose oppression emphasize genuine dialogue and inclusivity. Their definitions of professional civility go beyond lists of "polite behavior" to focus on authentic respect. They commit to routinely exploring new ways to involve and provide equal opportunities to all who are serious about contributing to mission. They also explain to others how organizational missions in a complex, global society are better served by true inclusiveness.

Arnett (this volume) focused on the role of the third as an agent promoting professional civility. He argues that if people commit to the unseen neighbor (noted in Levinas's words, remembering that "I am my brother's keeper" (1998, p. 98)) they guide their actions toward respect and tolerance.

Principle #2: Rather than Assuming the Other or Self is "Problematic," Consider More Constructive Attributions

Duck, Foley, and Kirkpatrick (this volume) challenge the more typical approaches of blaming "difficulty" to the behavior patterns and personality of another and argue that the concept of "difficulty" results from social interactions which create discursive realities. They assert that dyadic and social levels create social discourse about the nature of others, and that the ascribed "difficulty" often arises from the forces of roles and the creation of realities which are self serving.

Research conducted by Sillars (1980, 1981, 1994) revealed that when people in conflict generate person attributions, the conflict is more likely to be perceived as un-resolvable and less energy is expended in efforts to resolve the conflict. Thus, it may not be as productive in resolving conflicts for people to write off the other as "difficult." They would probably work harder to resolve the conflict if they looked for other causes such as role forces and/or a discursive reality created by others in the work environment.

With an eye toward broadening attributions for the behavior of others, it is important to consider whether organizations have expectations which support certain qualities and view others as problematic. Organizational expectations are often derived from experiences with the dominant, homogeneous type of employee. Are relational problems more likely for individuals who do not fit this profile? Liu and Buzzanell (this volume) argue the answer is yes. They presented the case study of a woman named Lucy who is representative of pink collar workers who are pregnant and in the work force. Lucy's experience reflected the findings of other researchers who point out that pregnancy, maternity leaves, and return to work outside the home often result in changes in workplace relationships. Some of the changes are positive in that colleagues may offer advice and stories about family life that increase rapport. However, others are negative and raise questions about the pregnant woman's ability to complete tasks, be promoted, and remain committed to the organization.

In facilitating effective relationships in the workplace, the question to ask is often: How can the workplace support diversity by honoring the needs of unique people and serve the long term mission of the organization? Flexibility leading to perceptions of respect and fairness, job satisfaction, and organizational commitment is one approach.

Consistent with working in the public sphere, employees also must assume responsibility for making constructive attributions about self as well as others. Accepting feedback as valuable information which improves work toward the mission rather than as a personal attack can be cultivated as a work attitude. Even in the face of situations in which the stakes are high (promotions are desired, praise for major projects is hoped for), examples abound in which people framed the situation in a manner pre-emptive of shame. When Jane Pauley (who had the greatest seniority) watched as Bryant Gumbel was promoted to lead anchor on the Today show, she concluded that NBC was trying to get it right on the race issue. Instead of interpreting it as a personal slam, she interpreted the promotion of her black, male colleague as a sign of valued, long over-due, social change. Jane Pauley chose the non-shaming route.

Research on hopelessness and depression demonstrates mental health disadvantages for attributions to causes which are global and stable rather than those which change with time and context (Abramson, Seligman, & Teasdale, 1978; Satterfield, Folkman, & Acree, 2002). For example, assume three coworkers often go for lunch together. If two go off for lunch without inviting or explaining their behavior to a third, the third could interpret it from the vantage point of "they must have needed to talk about the project they're both working on" rather than "they must not really like me." While all options are not equally likely choices for all people (for example, depression is associated with attributions that are internal, global, and stable), people can learn to foster attributions that promote good working relationships as well as self esteem.

Principle #3: Minimize Shame

The taunts of being "less than," "unvalued," and "flawed" are the voice of shame, and while shame speaks loudly through discrimination (Ray, Smith, & Wastell, 2004), it knows no demographic boundaries. Shame is described as the most powerful emotion (Retzinger, 1991), and is associated with perceiving self as inadequate. Many employees feel it lurking at performance evaluations and major project reviews, but most fail to see it hiding in the shadows of the water cooler and sitting atop computers as they fire off emails. Supervisors, managers, and administrators are often unaware of the role it plays and the degree to which they engender it in subordinates. Problematic relationships in the workplace would be markedly reduced if shame were better managed. To fully comprehend shame is to capture the key principle behind face giving, face saving, and the need for self protection. Those who navigate shame can prevent most problematic interactions and bring to constructive resolution most that emerge.

In working on marital violence, Retzinger (1991, 1995) proposed a theory of shame. Retzinger claims that shame is tripped when the behaviors of another are interpreted as threatening the bond between self and other. Two categories of action are commonly perceived as threatening relational bonds: 1) behaviors which overtake or engulf self (as may occur when another dominates or asks overly invasive questions), and 2) behaviors which abandon (as may occur when another leaves unexpectedly or chooses to spend time with another person or group). Given the profound pain associated with shame, the natural tendency is to substitute anger rather than feel the shame. Retzinger argues that because shame is seldom overtly discussed, the spiral that unfolds is anger (expressed as a substitute for the shame) followed by anger (the response of the other person who is covering his/her shame). So shame begets shame is observed as anger/rage elicits anger/rage.

Perceptions of discrepancy between self as observed by another and desirable self (i.e. shame as conceptualized above) has serious fallout. Kinney (this volume) argues that when self discrepancy is experienced due to negative messages from another, self protection becomes an important psychological response linking the message to distress and well-being. Messages perceived as negative are significantly correlated with: intrusive thinking; thoughts of revenge and of escaping the situation; negative affect; avoiding or punishing social strategies; relational maintenance strategies; hostility; and psychosomatic symptoms. Furthermore, negative affect is related to distress and decreased well being. Social response strategies which are confrontational, defiant, or avoidant are positively correlated with distress and decreased well-being. In contrast, using a strategy of passive aggressiveness (e.g., criticizing the powerholder to others) was negatively correlated with decreased well-being and psychosomatic symptoms. This led Kinney to conclude that self-protection may be experienced through passive-aggressiveness and that it may function as a "psychological and emotional energizer that alleviates distress." Criticism may function to reassert a level of control and allow individuals to justify themselves. Relational maintenance strategies such as trying to make the relationship better and apologizing were related to decreased well-being and psychosomatic symptoms. It is apparent that once the shame cycle is tripped, there is a lower internal payoff for implementing constructive, relationship-repair strategies than protecting self through passive aggression.

How can shame in the workplace be minimized? Many employees carry sensitivity to engulfment (fear of the other finding flaws) or abandonment by others (rejection due to discrepancy between desired and observed self) to work. Much of this sensitivity emerges when performance is on the line. The likelihood of eliciting shame can be reduced by wording feedback in ways that focus attention on constructive remedies rather than personal flaws. Consider the following possibilities for offering feedback to an employee. Which is better at preventing presumptions that self is flawed?

Option 1: "It is very important that everyone in the unit be highly proficient at transcribing with few errors. I noticed that over this past week, your transcription work has many errors. You need to reduce those errors."

Option 2:   "It is very important that everyone in the unit be highly proficient at transcribing with few errors. You've been transcribing for only one week now, and like everyone else who is new, certain kinds of errors are occurring in your work. We need to reduce those errors. Now that you have a sense of what the work is like, it's a good time to try some strategies to target the types of errors you're making. I can suggest some strategies that others have found effective, but you're the one who will know which approaches might be a good fit for you. Most people find that by devoting strategic effort, they can get the error rate down significantly."

Feedback which emphasizes stages of development and places the emphasis on effort and strategies reduce the likelihood of shame. Such feedback normalizes the problem (self is like similar others rather than "bad" or "flawed"), and they infer a high likelihood of improvement (we grow, we implement wise approaches and the outcomes change rather than we are lacking some aptitude or ability). Perceptions that self is valued rather than flawed decreases the likelihood that the relational bond will be broken.

If shame arises from relationship disconfirmation, then the antidote should be steady, appropriate relationship confirmation. Consistent and appropriate messages about closeness/distance, dependence/ independence, availability/unavailability, and valuable contributions/non-valuable contributions will reduce the likelihood of eliciting needless shame. A boss who consistently maintains availability to all employees at commonly understood times, who clearly communicates which behaviors are valued and values them in all employees, and who affirms the importance of the working relationships with all employees is far more likely to build pride and confidence than trip shame and insecurity. A boss who meets only with favorite employees, notices and praises their accomplishments, and affirms only the relationships with them, is likely to find others feeling undervalued and some expressing overt anger or passive aggression as a result of shame.

Principle 4: Manage Stress with Effective Coping Strategies

People often find problematic relationships in the workplace to elicit considerable negative fallout and contribute to a progression through stages of burnout. Omdahl and Fritz (this volume) found the higher the proportion of problematic bosses and co-workers (but not subordinates), the higher the levels of all three stages of burnout and three stress symptoms (i.e., anxiety, depression, and negative thoughts). In addition, their research revealed that stages of burnout unfold in the order proposed by Maslach and Jackson (1982) (i.e., emotional exhaustion followed by depersonalization and then reduced personal accomplishment). Fritz and Omdahl (this volume) also found deleterious consequences for working in a network characterized by a high proportion of problematic relationships. The proportion of problematic bosses and co-workers (but not subordinates) correlates highly with reduced job satisfaction and organizational commitment and increased cynicism. Other researchers have found that chronic stressors (like problematic work relationships) influence how well people deal with stressful events in the workplace (Elfering et al., 2005).

Over the years, numerous scholars have studied stress and burnout (e.g., Lazarus & Folkman, 1984; Snyder, 1999) and developed measures for coping strategies (Brough, O'Driscoll, & Michael, 2005; Eyles & Bates, 2005; Folkman & Lazarus, 1985). As a result of decades of research, there are clear recommendations on how to cope with workplace (and other) stressors. Two coping strategies which are consistently identified as maximally effective are problem solving and cognitive reappraisal (Lazarus & Folkman, 1984; Elfering et. al., 2005). In problem solving, the person explores the sources of stress and designs a plan or strategies to overcome the stressors. In cognitive reappraisal, the person reframes the experience in such a way that benefits or growth points are identified (e.g., through this conflict, I am learning more about myself and the other person; this is an important lesson for me).

Both of the strategies identified above fall under the umbrella of problem solving approaches to stress. Specifically, the strategy of problem solving is focused on the problem and involves some combination of the following: seeking or using information/advice, thinking through the factors contributing to the stress, analyzing different options, and designing a plan. Reappraisal is also focused on the problem, but rather than working toward eliminating it, the goal is to see the problem as a constructive force. In contrast to problem-solving approaches are emotion-focused coping strategies. Emotion-focused efforts attempt to reduce psychological discomfort by withdrawing, denying, or avoiding the stressor without trying to remedy the situation (Dumont & Provost, 1999). Another way coping strategies have been categorized is in terms of approach and avoidance (Herman-Stahl, Stemmler, & Petersen, 1995; Phelps & Jarvis, 1994). The effective strategies both fall within the category of approach. Discussions of types of approaches also reveal why social support is found to be effective in some studies and ineffective in others. Specifically, if a person is problem focused during socially supportive interactions, effectiveness would be expected, but if a person is emotionally focused in this pursuit, the result is likely to be ineffective.

Included in the list of emotion-focused efforts which are arguably ineffective is avoiding or masking. The pitfalls of this coping strategy were evident in the research of Kramer and Tan (this volume). They found that with disliked others, respondents usually began negative spirals with negative episodes characterized by negative emotion (predominantly anger and frustration or disappointment) which they attempted to mask. Due to emotion management, the relationships characteristically remained negative or deteriorated further and efforts to minimize the relationships through physical or psychological distance increased. Not surprisingly, these relationships became increasingly costly compared to other relationships (Kramer and Tan, this volume). Problem solving and reappraisal offer clear advantages over the more emotionally focused approaches like masking.

Principle #5: Facilitate Forgiveness

Metts, Cupach, and Lippert (this volume) note that professional misconduct threatens quality of workplace relationships, and they point to forgiveness as the approach with the power to repair relationships. They proposed a three factor model to explain how forgiveness is used in organizational relationships. First, they proposed a negative relationship between the seriousness of the transgression (with a parallel degree of negative affect) and the likelihood of forgiveness. Second, they argue that people who are more emotionally sensitive (i.e., more easily offended with a tendency to inflate the severity of the transgression) will be less likely to forgive the transgressor. Finally, they propose that the remedial actions of the transgressor (e.g., attempts to make amends by offering an apology or account) will soften the blow of the transgression, serving to mitigate the perceived severity and increasing the likelihood of forgiveness.

The research support for their models suggests that forgiveness is facilitated when people minimize the severity of the offence, work on overcoming sensitivity, and apologize for transgressions. While acknowledging that there are personality differences in sensitivity, to a large extent these are strategies under volitional control.

Principle #6: Involve Third Parties for Assistance

When the parties involved in problematic workplace relationships are not able to restore their relationships on their own or through direct interaction, external third parties or colleagues or managers may offer assistance. Research on ombudsdspersons reveals that they may choose an advising strategy through which they speak to a single party, act as a go-between the two parties, or facilitate discussions among involved parties (Kolb, 1986). Third parties can play roles ranging from little to high levels of intervention: moderation involves low levels of intervention; conciliation is characterized by moderate levels of intervention; and consultation refers to high levels of intervention in the forms of advice and even directives (Fisher and Keashly, 1991).

Mediation may also be used as a way to work through problematic disputes. While mediators facilitate and manage the process of reaching terms of agreement, the actual terms are between the participants. It is often appealing to disputants to have a neutral third party guide the process while they retain control over the agreements reached (Sheppard, 1984). Research suggests that the involvement of third parties is beneficial when un-resolvable problems arise (Grieg, 2005).

Summary

Hess, Omdahl, and Fritz (this volume) examined turning points in work relationships. Seventy-nine percept of the relationships chosen by participants as "problematic" started out as positive relationships. This suggests that constructive action may have precluded the descent into the problematic realm. Facilitating expectations consistent with professional civility, considering a wide array of attributions, choosing non-shaming language, effectively coping, forgiving, and using third parties are practices promoting wellness for both individuals and organizations. Given the deleterious fallout from extremely problematic relationships (see Omdahl and Fritz, Fritz and Omdahl, and Kinney, all in this volume), there are situations in which seeking a new position or new employer may be a wise decision.

Considerable future research is needed to determine best practice strategies in working with different types of problematic others at work (e.g., a micro-manager compared to a drama king/queen or a hustler), and to evaluate the long term impact of strategy implementation. While this volume presents the ongoing research in several programs of study which offer rich description and theoretical explanations, research on "what works" is a work in progress. Over the next decade, the research on this area is expected to multiply to answer new theoretical and applied questions. Given the amount of time and energy people invest in organizations, research on these topics has the potential to make valued contribution to scholars and workers alike.

References

Abramson, L.Y., Seligman, M.,E. P. & Teasdale, J.D. (1978). Learned helplessness in humans: Critique and reformulation. *Journal of Abnormal Psychology, 87,* 49-74.

Brough, P., O'Driscoll, M., & Michael, T. (2005) *Journal of Occupational and Organizational Psychology, 78,* 53-61.

Brown, P., & Levinson, S. (1987). *Politeness: Some universals in language use.* Cambridge, England: Cambridge University Press.

Cava, R. (2004). *Dealing with difficult people: How to deal with nasty customers, demanding bosses, and annoying co-workers.* Firefly Books, Limited.

Dumont, M., & Provost, M.A. (1999). Resilience in adolescents: protective role of social support, coping strategies, self-esteem, and social activities on the experience of stress and depression. *Journal of Youth and Adolescence, 28,* 343-363.

Elfering, A., Grebner, S., Semmer, N., Kaiser-Freiburghaus, D., Ponte, S, & Witschi, I. (2005). Chronic job stressors and job control: Effects on event-related coping success and well-being. *Journal of Occupational & Organizational Psychology, , Vol. 78,* 237-252.

Eyles, D. & Bates, G. W. (2005). Development of a shortened form of the Coping Responses Inventory-Youth with an Australian Sample. *North American Journal of Pscyhology, 7,* 161-170.

Fisher, R. J., & Keashly, L. (1991). The potential complementarity of mediation and consultation within a contingency model of third party intervention. *Journal of Peace Research, 28,* 29-42.

Folkman, S. & Lazarus, R. S. (1985). If it changes it must be a process: A study of emotion and coping during three stages f a college examination. *Journal of Personality and Social Psychology, 48,* 150-170.

Gill, L. (1999). *How to work with just about anyone: A 3 step solution for getting difficult people to change.* Simon and Schuster.

Goffman, E. (1967). *Interaction ritual.* Garden City, NY: Doubleday.

Greig, J. M. (2005). Stepping into the fray: When do mediators mediate? *American Journal of Political Science, 49,* 249-266.

Herman-Stahl, M.A., Stemmler, M., & Petersen, A.C. (1995). Approach and avoidant coping: implications for adolescent mental health. *Journal of Youth and Adolescence, 24,* 649-665.

hooks, b. (1995). killing rage: Ending racism. New York: Henry Holt and Company Owl Books.

Kolb, D. M. (1986). Who are organizational third parties and what do they do? In R. J. Lewicki, B. H. Sheppard, & M. H. Bazerman (Eds), *Research on negotiations in organizations, Volume 1* (pp. 207-278). Greenwich, CT: JAI.

Lazarus, R. S., & Folkman, S. (1984). *Stress, appraisal and coping.* New York: Springer.

Levinas, E. (1998). *Ethics and infinity: Conversations with Philippe Nemo* (R. Cohen, Trans.), Pittsburgh, PA: Duquesne University Press.

Lilley, R. (2002). *Dealing with difficult people.* Kogan Page, Limited.

Lubit, G. (2003). *Coping with toxic managers, subordinates, and other difficult people: Using emotional intelligence to survive and prosper.* Financial Times/Prentice Hall Press.

Maslach & Jackson (l982). Burnout in health professions: A social psychological analysis. In G. Sanders and J. Suls (Eds.), *Social psychology of health and illness* (pp. 227-251). Hillsdale, NJ: Lawrence Erlbaum.

Morfei, M. Z., Hooker, K., Carpenter, J., Mix, C., & Blakeley, E. (2004). Agentic and communal generative behavior in four areas of adult life: Implications for psychological well-being. *Journal of Adult Development ,11*, 55-58.

Osbourne, C. (2002). *Essential manager: Dealing with difficult people.* Dorling Kindersley Publishing.

Phelps, S.B., & Jarvis, P.A. (1994). Coping in adolescence: Empirical evidence for a theoretically based approach to assessing coping. *Journal of Youth and Adolescence, 23*, 359-372.

Ray, L., Smith, D., & Wastell, L. (2004). Shame, rage, and racist violence. *British Journal of Criminology, 44*, 350-368.

Retzinger, S. (1991). *Violent emotions: Shame and rage in marital quarrels.* Newbury Park, CA: Sage.

Retzinger, S. (1995). Identifying shame and anger in discourse. *American Behavioral Scientist, 38*, 1104-1113.

Satterfield, J. M., Folkman, S., Acree, M. (2002). Explanatory style predicts depressive symptoms following AIDS-related bereavement. *Cognitive Theory and Research, 26*, 393-401.

Shepard, G. (2005). *How to manage problem employees: A step-by-step guide for turning difficult employees into high performers.* John Wiley & Sons.

Sheppard, B. H. (1984). Third party conflict intervention: A procedural framework. In B. M. Staw & L. L. Cummings (Eds.), *Research in organizational behavior, 6*, 141-190.

Sias, P. M. & Perry, T. (2004). Disengaging from workplace relationships: A research note. *Human Communication Research, 30*, 589-602.

Sillars, A. (1980). Attributions and communication in roommate conflicts. *Communication Monographs, 47*, 180-200.

Sillars, A. (1981). Attributions and interpersonal conflict resolution. In J. H. Harvey, W. Ickes, & R. Kidd (Eds.), *New directions in attribution research* (Vol. 3, pp. 281-306). Hillsdale, NJ: Lawrence Erlbaum.

Sillars, A., & Wilmot, W. W. (l994). Communication strategies in conflict mediation. In J. A. Daly and J. M. Weimann (Eds.), *Strategic interpersonal communication* (pp. 163-190). Hillsdale, NJ: Lawrence Erlbaum.

Snyder, C. R. (1999). Coping: The psychology of what works.

Solomon, M. (2002). *Working with difficult people.* Prentice Hall Press.

Waldron, V. R. (2003). Relationship maintenance in organizational settings. In D. Canary & M. Dainton (Eds.), Maintaining relationships through communication: Relational, contextual, and cultural variations (pp. 163-184). Mahwah, NJ: Lawrence Erlbaum Associates.

Contributors

Ronald C. Arnett (Ph.D, Ohio University) is Chair and Professor in the Department of Communication & Rhetorical Studies, Duquesne University, specializing philosophy of communication and communication. Dr. Arnett is the author of over sixty articles, four books and two edited books. Among his publications are: *Dialogic Civility in a Cynical Age: Community, Hope, and Interpersonal Relationships* (1999, co-authored with Pat Arneson); *Dialogic Education: Conversations about Ideas and Between Persons* (1992); *Communication and Community: Implications of Martin Buber's Dialogue* (1986); and *Dwell in Peace: Applying Nonviolence to Everyday Relationships* (1980); *Communication Ethics in an Age of Diversity* (1996, co-edited with Josina Makao); and *The Reach of Dialogue: Confirmation, Voice and Community* (1994, co-edited with Ken Cissna and John Anderson). Email: arnett@duq.edu

Patrice M. Buzzanell (Ph.D., Purdue University) is Professor in the Department of Communication at Purdue University where she specializes in feminist organizational communication theorizing and the analyses of gendered workplace processes, particularly as they relate to career communication. She has published over 45 journal articles and chapters in outlets such as Human Communication Research, Communication Monographs, Communication Theory, and Management Communication Quarterly. In addition to editing Management Communication Quarterly, she has edited two collections, Rethinking Organizational and Managerial Communication from Feminist Perspectives (2000) and Gender in Applied Communication Contexts (2004, co-edited with Lynn Turner and Helen Sterk) and has published numerous essays, reviews, and instructional materials. Email: pbuzzanell@cla.purdue.edu

William R. Cupach (Ph.D., University of Southern California) is Professor of Communication at Illinois State University where he conducts research on problematic interactions in interpersonal relationships, including such contexts as embarrassing predicaments, relational transgressions, interpersonal conflict, and obsessive relational pursuit. In addition to numerous monographs and journal articles, he has co-authored or co-edited eight books. His most recent book, with Brian Spitzberg, is *The Dark Side of Relationship Pursuit:*

From Attraction to Obsession and Stalking (2004). He previously served as Associate Editor for the *Journal of Social and Personal Relationships* and is the current President of the International Association for Relationship Research. Email: wrcupac@ilstu.edu

Steve Duck (Ph.D., University of Sheffield) is Professor in the, Department of Communication Studies at the University of Iowa. He co-founded the International Conferences on Personal Relationships (1982 onwards), founded and then edited the Journal of Social and Personal Relationships (from 1984-1998); founded the International Network on Personal Relationships (1987) and served as its President in 1996; founded and edited the Handbook of Personal Relationships (first edition 1988, second edition 1997). He has published 35 books on such issues as personal relationship growth and breakdown, television production techniques, the development of social psychology, and social support. Email: steve-duck@uiowa.edu

Megan K. Foley (M. A., University of North Carolina) is currently a Ph.D. student in the Department of Communication at the University of Iowa.

Janie M. Harden Fritz (Ph.D., University of Wisconsin-Madison) is Associate Professor of Communication & Rhetorical Studies at Duquesne University. Dr. Harden Fritz conducts research on communication processes that connect, sever, and restore the ties that bind individuals to the institutions of which they are a part. Current projects include an investigation of responses to communication about ethical standards of conduct in organizations; professional civility and cynicism in organizations; a longitudinal study of employee reactions to unpleasant work relationships; and issues of public and private communication and relationships in organizations. Her work has been published in *Management Communication Quarterly*, *Journal of Business Ethics*, *Journal of Public Management and Social Policy*, and elsewhere. Email: harden@duq.edu

Jon Hess (Ph.D., University of Minnesota) is Associate Professor in the Department of Communication at the University of Missouri-Columbia. His research has examined how people constructively handle relational challenges (such as maintaining nonvoluntary relationships with disliked partners) and how people manage closeness and distance in relationships. His research has been published in *Human Communication Research, Personal Relationships, Journal of Social and Personal Relationships, Management Communication Quarterly,* and elsewhere. His dissertation won the International Network on Personal Relationships (now IARR) Dissertation Award.

Terry A. Kinney (Ph.D., University of Wisconsin) is Associate Professor in the Department of Communication at Wayne State University. His research interests include examining how message characteristics activate emotions and how message strategies affect well-being. His research has been published in *Human Communication Research, Communication Monographs, Communication Studies, Journal of Social Psychology, Motivation & Emotion,* and *Academic Emergency Medicine.* Email: terrykinney@wayne.edu

D. Charles Kirkpatrick (M.A., University of Iowa) is a doctoral candidate and interpersonal/group scholar at The University of Iowa. His teaching and research interests involve conflict management, identity construction, communication theory, and both quantitative and qualitative methods. He is currently working on a case study of ineffective group decision-making utilizing the constraints model. He has over twenty years of experience in public and private organizations. Email: dan-kirkpatrick@uiowa.edu

Michael W. Kramer (Ph.D., University of Texas), is Professor at the University of Missouri. His research centers on three main areas: employee transitions in organizational settings, emotion management in organizations, and group communication process, particularly in non-profit organizations such as community theater. His research has been published in journals such as *Communication Monographs, Human Communication Research, Journal of Applied Communication Research, Management Communication Quarterly, Academy of Management Journal, Small Group Research.* His dissertation won the ICA W. Charles Redding Dissertation Award in 1991. Email: kramerm@missouri.edu

Lance Lippert (Ph.D., Southern Illinois University at Carbondale) is Associate Professor in the Department of Communication at Illinois State University. His research interests include culture and relational communication in organizations, health care communication, organizational change, humor use, mediated communication, and communication pedagogy. Email: llipper@ilstu.edu

Meina Liu (M.A., Tsinghua University) is lecturer in the Department of Communication at the University of Maryland where she specializes in analyzing and theorizing the influence of emotion on negotiation in multicultural, organizational contexts. She has published in the *Journal of Applied Communication Research, Journal of Business Communication, Communication Research,* and *Intercultural and International Communication Annual.* She conducted her doctoral studies at Purdue University and currently is completing her dissertation. Email: liu@umd.edu

Sandra Metts (Ph.D., University of Iowa) is Professor in the Department of Communication at Illinois State University. Her research interests include applications of politeness theory to personal relationships, sexual communication in developing relationships, and forgiveness following a relational transgression. She has served as associate editor for the *Journal of Social and Personal Relationships* and *Personal Relationships* and is a former president of the Central States Communication Association. Email: smmetts@ilstu.edu

Becky L. Omdahl (Ph.D., University of Wisconsin-Madison) is Professor in the Department of Communication, Writing, and the Arts at Metropolitan State University. Her research interests include the reception, management, and communication of emotion in interpersonal and organizational contexts; empathy; stress and burnout; fear appeals messages; and the deleterious consequences of negative relationships in the workplace. Her articles appear in such journals as *Communication Monographs* and *Journal of Advanced Nursing,* and she has a book entitled, *Cognitive Appraisal, Emotion, and Empathy* (1995). Her dissertation won the National Communication Association Outstanding Dissertation Award in 1991. Email: becky.omdahl@metrostate.edu

Marshall Scott Poole (Ph.D., University of Wisconsin-Madison) is Professor in the Departments of Information and Operations Management and Speech Communication at Texas A&M University. Dr. Poole's research interests include group communication, group and organizational decision-making, computer-mediated communication systems, conflict management, and organizational innovation. He has authored over 100 articles, book chapters, and proceedings papers. He is coauthor of *Working Through Conflict* (4th edition, 2000) and *Strategic Organizational Communication* (4ᵗʰ edition, 2001) and coeditor of *Communication and Group Decision Making* (1996) and *Research on the Management of Innovation* (2000). He received the Academy of Management's award for best published article in 1995, the National Communication Association's award for best book on Group Communication in 2000, and for best book in Organizational Communication in 2001. In 2002 he received the College of Liberal Arts Research Award. Email: mspoole@tamu

Patricia M. Sias (Ph.D. 1993 - University of Texas-Austin) is Associate Professor in the Edward R. Murrow School of Communication at Washington State University, where she studies workplace relationships, employee information experiences, and collaboration. Her work has been published in a variety of journals, including *Communication Monographs, Human Communication Research, Western Journal of Communication, Journal of Applied Communication Research,* and *Communication Research.* In addition, she has authored several book chapters and is co-editor (with Michael Salvador) of *The Public Voice in a Democracy at Risk.* Email: psias@wsu.edu

Claire L. Tan (M.A. Applied Linguistics, Macquarie University, Australia) is a Ph.D. student at University of Missouri-Columbia. Her research interests include organizational communication, and intergenerational interactions at the workplace. Email: clt882@mizzou.edu

Author Index

Subject Index

Maternity leave
  and return to work, issues, 48
  effects of, on workplace
    experience and interaction, 47–48
  laws and policies, 48, 56
Mental health. *See* Burnout
Mentor-protégé relations,
  dysfunctional, 50
Mentoring, as outcome of positive
  work relationships, 89
Metaphor
  of relationship between
    organizations and
    communication, 9
  professional civility as, 233, 239
Microdeviance, 6
Microdeviant(s), 6
Micropractices, of gender and
  supervisory relations, 48, 60, 62
Misbehavior in the workplace, xv,
  249, 250. *See also* Workplace
  misbehavior; Workplace
  misconduct
Misconduct. *See* Workplace
  misconduct
Mission, of organization, 234
Modernity
  and worker, 240
  as metaphor of amalgamation, 241
  as pulling public and private life
    together, 241, 242
  disdain for traditional life, 240
  displacement of persons, 240
Moderation, as third party strategy
  for managing problematic work
  relationships, 291
Mutual accommodation, 7–8
Mutual interdependency, 7–8

Narrative(s), 51
  humble, 239
  meta-, 239
  petite, 239
Negative affect, 181
  results of/states related to, 181, 193
  transfer of, 212
  See also Negative emotions
Negative communication spirals, 12
  See also Negative messages

Negative emotions, relinquishing,
  and forgiveness, 256. *See also*
  Negative affect
Negative interactions, 195
  Nonproductive responses to, 195–
    196
  See also Interactions; Negative
    messages; Disliked others
Negative messages
  from supervisor, outcomes of, 182,
    193
  responses to, 182–183
  result of labeling as negative, 193
  See also Interactions
Negative sense of self, 7
Negative spiral of relational
  deterioration, as part of emotion
  episodes with disliked others, 171
Negative work relationships, xiv, 90,
  141
  as stressors, 110
  boss/coworker interactions, 50, 51,
    53–56
  outcomes of, 112–113
  relative status as factor affecting
    influence of, 141
  See also Troublesome work
    relationships
Negativism, ix
Negativity, 14
Negotiation of leave arrangements
  when pregnant, 48
Nonvoluntary relationships, 7, 89, 90,
  54, 205
  and social exchange, 206–207
  defined, 206
  with disliked partners, 206, 214
Norms
  as influencing affiliative strategy
    choice, 224
  for workplace behavior as
    influence on distancing, 216–217

Obnoxiousness, xiv, 5, 6
Ombudsperson, as external third
  party for managing problematic
  work relationships, 291
Organizational citizenship, lack of, as
  potential cause of workplace
  cynicism, 136